A Concise History of Finland

Few countries in Europe have undergone such rapid social, political, and economic changes as Finland has during the last fifty years. David Kirby here sets out the fascinating history of this northern country, for centuries on the east–west divide of Europe, a country not blessed by nature, most of whose inhabitants still earned a living from farming fifty years ago, but which today is one of the most prosperous members of the European Union. He shows how this small country was able not only to survive in peace and war, but also to preserve and develop its own highly distinctive identity, neither Scandinavian nor eastern European. He traces the evolution of the idea of a Finnish national state, from the long centuries as part of the Swedish realm, through self-government within the Russian Empire, and into the stormy and tragic birth of the independent state in the twentieth century.

DAVID KIRBY is Professor of Modern History at the School of Slavonic and East European Studies of University College London. His previous publications include *The Baltic World 1772–1993: Europe's Northern Periphery in an Age of Change* (1995) and *The Baltic and North Seas* (with Merja-Liisa Hinkkanen, 2000).

D1225403

CAMBRIDGE CONCISE HISTORIES

This is a series of illustrated 'concise histories' of selected individual countries, intended both as university and college textbooks and as general historical introductions for general readers, travellers, and members of the business community.

For a list of titles in the series, see end of book.

A Concise History
of Finland

DAVID KIRBY

CAMBRIDGE
UNIVERSITY PRESS

CAMBRIDGE UNIVERSITY PRESS
Cambridge, New York, Melbourne, Madrid, Cape Town, Singapore, São Paulo, Delhi

Cambridge University Press
The Edinburgh Building, Cambridge CB2 8RU, UK

Published in the United States of America by Cambridge University Press, New York

www.cambridge.org
Information on this title: www.cambridge.org/9780521539890

First published 2006
Third printing 2008

Printed in the United Kingdom at the University Press, Cambridge

A catalogue record for this publication is available from the British Library

ISBN 978-0-521-83225-0 hardback
ISBN 978-0-521-53989-0 paperback

For the two Ls in my life –

Laurie and Louis

CONTENTS

ILLUSTRATIONS

MAPS

FIGURES

PREFACE

Finland can fairly lay claim to have been one of the big success stories of the modern age. The transformation of what less than a century ago was a poor agrarian land on the northern periphery of Europe into one of the most prosperous states of the European Union today is a remarkable story, but is by no means an uneventful one. The gaining of independence from Russia in 1918 was accompanied by a bitter civil war which left its scars upon the body politic of Finland for decades. Finland fought three wars between 1939 and 1945, twice against the Soviet Union and once against Germany, and suffered grievous loss of life in addition to almost a tenth of its territory. The political history of the independent republic was for much of the twentieth century conflict-ridden and far removed from the image of consensual stability and good European membership that is projected today. The reinvention of Finland over the past two decades as a confident and assertive Eurostate, no longer in the shadow of the Soviet Union, has also been paralleled by a re-evaluation of the nation's history and identity. In particular, Finland's recent past has come under severe scrutiny, as part of what may be seen as a purging process not dissimilar to the examination in eastern European countries of 'blank spots' in the recent past.

This reassessment of the nation's past constitutes one of the starting-points for this book. It is primarily a political history, though due consideration is given to the social, cultural, and economic forces which have shaped that history, both in the short term and over the centuries.

Whilst adopting a conventional chronological structure, I have attempted to highlight those features which have made Finland what it is today. In particular, I have highlighted the spatial, temporal, and political dimensions that have helped determine how language and culture have evolved. The ways in which the inhabitants of a cold and rather infertile northern land have sought to adapt and innovate, how the land has been a means of sustenance and a symbol of nationhood, are at the heart of being Finnish. The struggle to wrest a living from the soil is an epic and abiding theme, running from the earliest days of human settlement as the massive ice-cap began to retreat, right up to the huge efforts in the late 1940s to resettle thousands of refugees. In this sense, Finland has been very much a frontier country, and this may well account for the two contradictory and conflicting forces that have made their mark in Finnish life over the centuries. The first seems to be strongly driven by a desire to harness and utilise all possible resources. It has created a strong tradition of obedience to authority, reinforced by the Lutheran church, strong bureaucratic institutions, and a rigid respect for the law, but it has also preferred co-operation and consensus to coercion. The second is a far less formally defined tradition, of wildness, lawlessness, a kind of frontiersman mentality that ignores or disobeys the law. The seven brothers of Aleksis Kivi's eponymous nineteenth-century novel, who flee the constraints of civilisation to live a wild, free life; the *puukkojunkkarit* or roaring boys of Ostrobothnia, with their big knives and boastful swagger; the bootleggers of the inter-war prohibition era, purveying lethal alcohol for thirsty customers around the land; even the lost, pathetic characters of Aki Kaurismäki's films: all stand within this loose tradition of truculent defiance, with its deep distrust of the *herrat*, or gentlefolk. This is a tradition that is easily lost in the glossy presentation of the success story, but it has also played a part in shaping the Finland of today.

The history of modern Finland seems to alternate between long periods of relative tranquillity and little visible change and short, intense bursts in which everything is transformed, and it appears to be going through one of these periods at the present time. I have attempted to understand and make sense of these changes against the background of a recent past that I myself experienced at first hand, and which shaped my own perceptions of and ideas about Finland, and I freely admit that many of my conclusions may be coloured by this experience. Over the years, I have benefited greatly from discussions with colleagues in Finland and the UK; without this, I would not have been able to write this book, and I would like to thank them all for their kindness and support. I must also thank the personnel of the National Board of Antiquities and of the Labour Archives in Helsinki for their help in the selection of the plates. I also wish to thank the trustees of the Presidential Archive for allowing me to reproduce the photograph of President Kekkonen being welcomed by President Kennedy in 1961.

Finland is officially a two-language state, and much of the historical terminology is of Swedish origin. Where I have deemed it appropriate, I have given the Swedish term with a Finnish equivalent. The names of provinces, counties, and towns are given only in Finnish, except in cases where historically the Swedish term is better known, for example, in the Treaty of Nystad of 1721. I have also given in parentheses, and in some cases used, the Finnish term for major institutions, such as the parliament.

I

A medieval marchland

The physical contours of northern Europe, including the 338,145 sq.km. of land and water that constitute the present-day republic of Finland, were essentially shaped in the aftermath of the great Ice Age. The retreating mass of ice scoured the crystalline bedrock of the Fenno-Scandian shield, leaving in its wake thousands of shallow lakes, eskers and drumlins, and a deeply indented coastline that is still emerging from the sea as the land recovers from the tremendous compression of the glaciers. Only in the far north of Finland does the land rise above a thousand metres. To the east, the Maanselkä ridge is a watershed for the rivers that run westwards into the Gulf of Bothnia and eastwards into the White Sea. The great lake systems of central and eastern Finland are separated from the coastal regions by a further series of ridges running in a south-eastward direction towards the south coast. Almost a quarter of the surface area of this inland region is covered by water, and a further 20 per cent is classified as wetland, mostly bogs and morasses. With all but a tiny tip of land lying north of the sixtieth parallel (Oslo and the Shetland Islands lie on this latitude, Stockholm slightly further south), Finland can claim to be the most northerly of all the countries of mainland Europe, stretching over a thousand kilometres from the northern shores of the Baltic towards the Arctic Sea. Summers are warm, but brief; winters long, dark, and cold, though there is a considerable difference between the south-west, with snow cover on average between 70 and 110 days a year, the eastern regions, averaging 160–90 days, and the north, averaging 200–20 days. The inhabitants of this northern land have had to learn to live with winter, the floods of spring, and the vagaries of the summer months, when frosts in May or August can wreak havoc with crops, and this has helped shape a culture in which stubborn resilience, patient endurance, and hard work are held in esteem.

Finland is above all a land of trees, mostly pine and spruce, vast forests stretching as far as the eye can see; even today, over half the land surface of the country is still woodland. It was in all likelihood the forest, rich in game, that attracted settlers from the south and east some nine thousand years ago. Artefacts and bone remains from the Mesolithic period reveal an extensive hunting and fishing culture, essentially confined to the coastline and main watercourses. Elk were an important source of meat, bones, sinew, and hide, and were also an inspiration to Neolithic artists in wood and stone; seals provided blubber, meat, and skins for consumption and trade; fish, pike in particular, birds, nuts, and berries all supplemented the diet of these early settlers.

From around 3300 BC, the area of present-day Finland was on the westernmost limits of a new culture, producing pottery with a characteristic comb pattern. It is thought that the bearers of this new culture from the Volga region also spoke a Finnic language, which, in turn influenced and modified by other languages with which it came into contact, developed into what philologists term Proto-Finnish. These people appear to have settled largely south of the Gulf of Finland, though one group from which the Sami are linguistically descended seems to have broken away at an early stage and migrated to the lands north of the great lakes of Ladoga and Onega. Contacts with Ancient Baltic and East Germanic peoples significantly altered the Proto-Finnic language, and the culture of the peoples who spoke it. From the southern shores of the Gulf of Finland, the peoples who were to constitute the four main dialect groups of the Finnish language, South-West Finnish, Häme, Savo, and Karelian, moved northwards by land and sea over the next centuries.

By the beginning of the Bronze Age in northern Europe, around 1500 BC, two sharply differentiated main cultural zones had emerged. The inhabitants of the western and southern shores were strongly influenced by contacts with Scandinavia and Central Europe, those of the hinterland continued to receive their cultural impulses from the east. In the more fertile soils of the river valleys and coastal plains, farming became the cultural norm; in the forests and moors of the north and east, the hunting and fishing culture continued to flourish. The origins of the Finnish people, and in particular, the 'eastern' and 'western' aspects of settlement and culture, remain a subject of much debate and occasional controversy, and this debate has influenced and continues to shape the way Finns perceive themselves and others. How the Finns themselves have been perceived by outsiders is quite another matter. The 'Finns' (*phinnoi, fenni, screrefenni*) mentioned by the earliest authors (Tacitus in the first century AD, Jordanes in the sixth) who attempted to identify the inhabitants of this hyperborean region were in fact hunter-gatherers of the far north – the sort of people who might indeed have had trade dealings with a traveller such as the ninth-century Norwegian Ottar, whose account of his travels in the north was preserved for posterity by King Alfred of Wessex.

The dwellers in these far northern lands were described in a twelfth-century history of Norway as 'people who regrettably worship false gods, namely, the Karelians and Kweni, the Hornfinns and the Biarmi'. The Kweni and Biarmi are known from other sources as traders in furs, and seem to have operated in an area between the White Sea and the northernmost part of the Gulf of Bothnia: as a distinctive group, they have long vanished into the mists of time. The Hornfinns were probably Sami, 'Finns' to the Norwegians (the northernmost region of Norway is known as Finnmark). The Karelians began to spread out from their heartland around lakes Ladoga and Onega during the twelfth and thirteenth centuries – eastwards to the mouth of the northern Dvina, northwards to the shores of the Arctic, where they clashed with the Norwegians, whilst in the west they came into conflict with the Häme tribe. At the same time, they also began to come under the influence and control of the Orthodox church and the principality of Novgorod.

The medieval European image of the 'Finns' as primitive hunters, practitioners of magic, and sellers of wind to stranded seafarers thus owed much to the tales of North Atlantic adventurers. Of the peoples who lived along the Baltic coastline and gradually settled the hinterland, we have remarkably little written evidence, although a thirteenth-century description of the sea route from Denmark to the eastern Baltic shows that this was a well-used sea route in Viking times, and archaeological finds also indicate that the shipbuilding technology of the Vikings was known and practised in western Finland.

The word 'Finland' came into common usage during the middle ages, though the area it was meant to embrace remained vague and ill defined. Significantly, the term was used as a means of indicating the consolidation of central authority: by Pope Gregory IX in 1229, announcing that *Finlandia* had passed under his protection, and by King Magnus Ladulås of Sweden in 1284 when he named his brother Bengt duke of Finland. Sources from the period before the consolidation of Catholic and Swedish authority, such as runic inscriptions and Orthodox monastic chronicles, refer more commonly to tribes, such as the Häme. These tribes possessed the organisational ability to make war and engage in trade, and were sufficiently powerful to cause trouble to their neighbours when the occasion demanded; but in common with the other peoples within what Robert Bartlett has termed the arc of 'non-literate polytheism' stretching from the Elbe to the Arctic circle, they were eventually drawn into the institutional framework of Latin Christendom. As a political entity, Finland owes its existence to the realm which gradually established itself between the eleventh and thirteenth centuries on the central plains of present-day Sweden. The expansion and consolidation of the kingdom of the Svea and Göta embraced Norrland and Dalarna to the north and west, the island of Gotland, and what came to be known as Finland Proper (*Varsinais-Suomi, Egentliga Finland*). For the seafaring peoples of northern Europe, the shallow waters of the Baltic were a ready means of communication during the sailing season rather than an obstacle (though the icing up of the sea in winter did effectively cut off communities otherwise linked by seaways and waterways), and there is plentiful evidence of intermingling and mixed settlement of the peoples around the north-eastern Baltic rim before the so-called 'crusades' which have conventionally marked the beginning of the period during which Finland became a part of the Swedish kingdom.

Plate 1 Map of northern Europe, printed in Sebastian Münster's
Cosmographia of 1552. The first detailed map of northern Europe to be
printed was the *Carta Gothica*, later renamed *Carta Marina*, of Olaus
Magnus, published in Venice in 1539. The wilderness dominates much of
the map, as well as Olaus Magnus's description of the northern peoples
published sixteen years later. Signs of human habitation and cultivation
are confined to the south-western corner, Finland Proper. To the north
and east are the beasts of the forest, fish, and fowl, with the occasional
crew steering a boat over the waters of a lake or sleds drawn by horses
or reindeers over the frozen sea. This simplified version of the *Carta
Marina* was reproduced in Sebastian Münster's *Cosmographia*, first
published in Basel in 1544, and running to numerous editions thereafter.
Münster's account of the languages spoken in Finland is a fair indication
of the general state of ignorance and confusion about such distant places.
In the words of his English translator, George North, 'the inhabitantes
of Fynland do speake two sundry languages. From Wiburg to Berga or
Sibbona (Viipuri to Porvoo or Sipoo), they do for the most part speake
the Sclavon tong, but nere the Sea coastes they use at thys present the
Swecian language, and in the myddest of the Country, theyr proper
speeche.'

The early eighteenth-century historian Algot Scarin believed the
absence of pre-Christian monuments or fortified sites indicated that
the sacred rites of the Finnish people must have been different from

those of the other Nordic nations, and that Sweden was already possessed of a proper supreme authority whilst the Finns were still nomads. Historians of a more intensely nationalistic era tended to see in the crusades the establishment of Swedish rule over the Finnish people – a 'Swedish conquest' as M. G. Schybergson described it in his *Finlands historia* of 1903 - and the implantation of western Christian values. More recent scholarship has drawn attention to the fact that the Swedish state itself was in the very early stages of construction, and that much of what happened in the Finnish half of the realm was also taking place in the western half. The crusades themselves, although inspired by the general enthusiasm for taking the Cross and its message to the infidel and the heathen, were less significant than the slower process of establishing an institutional presence. There is much uncertainty over the date and nature of the first crusade, which was first described over a hundred years later in the 1270s. It is supposed to have occurred during the brief reign of King Erik (1155/56–60), and the work of conversion was in the hands of an Englishman, Henry. As both men were murdered shortly thereafter and elevated to popular sainthood, there is reason to be wary of the accretion of legend. The story of Henry's murder by Lalli, and the miraculous events that followed, is of comparatively late provenance, whilst Erik's saintly qualities were promoted by his son in order to reflect honour and prestige upon his family. The brief incursion was probably not unconnected with the increasing conflict between the Swedish realm and the princes of Novgorod, who were also seeking to augment their position west of lakes Onega and Ladoga. Raids and counter-raids, rather than planned and sustained campaigns, were the norm, and it is highly unlikely that Erik had the resources or inclination to support a crusade to convert the heathen Finns.

That some kind of missionary activity was taking place is, however, indicated in the bull *Gravis admodum*, sent to the archbishop of Uppsala and his subordinate bishops by Pope Alexander III in 1171 or 1172, though the main thrust of this missive indicates that such work was having only limited success. The bull may have been intended to stir the Swedes into action, or it may also have been part of a campaign by the exiled archbishop of Lund, in the Danish kingdom, to reassert his authority over the newly created Swedish

Plate 2 Bishop Henry trampling his murderer Lalli underfoot. From the *Missale Aboense* of 1448. According to the earliest versions of the legend, dating from the thirteenth century, Henry was an Englishman, elected bishop of Uppsala, who accompanied King Erik of Sweden on crusade to Finland in the 1150s. Here, he was murdered on a frozen lake by a peasant, Lalli, egged on to do the deed by a spiteful wife. A thirteenth-century poem, fragments of which remain, has Henry decreeing before his death that his body shall be borne on a wagon drawn by two oxen, and be buried at the spot where the oxen came to rest. This happened to be Nousiainen, the first seat of the bishop of Finland, and although the see was finally transferred to Turku in the thirteenth century, Nousiainen remained a centre of pilgrimage throughout the middle ages. Lalli was justly punished for his impiety, losing his scalp when he tried to pull off the bishop's cap he had stolen. It is tempting to see in this fateful encounter between the first Finn recorded in history, a 'wild' man, and the 'civilised' westerner a paradigm for the later development of Finnish identity.

archbishopric. The expansion of trade into the eastern Baltic, which brought German merchants to Gotland and Novgorod, the consolidation of Danish power in northern Europe, and the creeping eastward progress of forcible conversion along the southern shores of the Baltic, may also have prompted renewed papal interest in northern Europe. Danish forces raided the Finnish and Estonian coastline several times between 1191 and 1202. The military Order of the Sword-Brothers, established in 1200 by Albert of Buxtehude, bishop of Riga, were busily engaged further south with the forcible conversion of the Livs around the mouth of the river Daugava. Papal correspondence indicates that the Swedes also carried out crusading raids, though they appear not to have attempted to build a more permanent presence in Finland until Danish forces had finally shifted their attention to the southern shores of the Gulf of Finland, conquering the Estonian stronghold of Lindenisse in 1219 and laying the foundations of the castle that still dominates the skyline of the modern city of Tallinn.

By the middle of the thirteenth century, there existed a recognisably Christian community in the relatively fertile plains of Finland Proper and on the scattered islands of the Åland archipelago. The see of the bishop was finally established on the banks of the river Aura, and work had begun on the cathedral in what was to be for almost six hundred years the capital of Finland: in Swedish, Åbo, or 'settlement by the river', in Finnish, Turku, or 'trading place'. Under the energetic leadership of Bishop Thomas, missionary work to the heathen Häme of the hinterland had begun. The work of conversion was not, however, a monopoly of the Catholic church. Russian Orthodoxy, having extended its influence into the region around lakes Ladoga and Onega was also active amongst the Häme. The crusade called by Pope Gregory IX in 1237 against the Häme became in fact a full-blown clash between the forces mustered by the church and the king of Sweden and the prince of Novgorod, Alexander Nevsky. The Russian chronicler records that the Swedish forces were heavily defeated in 1240 in a battle at the confluence of the rivers Neva and Izhora. However, according to the *Erikskrönikan*, a rhyme-chronicle written in the 1330s, the Swedes were revenged some nine years later, when, led by the powerful nobleman Birger Jarl, the Häme were finally subjugated. In the words of the chronicle, 'They settled the land with Christian men / and there I trust they still remain, / And the land was turned to our belief / which gave the Russian king much grief' (trans. Eric Christiansen). The fact that Sweden and Norway were locked in a serious conflict in 1249–50 makes the dating of this second crusade unlikely, and it has been argued that it actually took place a decade earlier, *before* the disastrous campaign against Alexander Nevsky, at a time when Novgorod was being hard pressed by the Mongols. Whatever the truth of the matter, the building of strong fortresses in Turku and Häme was a highly visible symbol of the presence of Swedish royal authority on the eastern shores of the Gulf of Bothnia. The foundations of a third castle were laid at the end of the century, at Viipuri on the eastern frontier, and a lengthy period of warfare between Sweden and Novgorod was formally ended in 1323 with the signing of a peace treaty. The precise terms of the peace of Oreshek (Pähkinäsaari, Nöteborg) have caused much dispute amongst historians. It would appear that the two parties ensured a fairly careful delineation of the frontier in the Karelian isthmus, which was divided in two, but thereafter the line of the frontier is open to interpretation. It is likely that the two parties were less interested in securing territory than in defining spheres of influence for taxation purposes over the peoples who dwelt in the vast tracts of forest and moor that stretched northwards from the great lakes to the Arctic. Novgorod was subsequently seriously weakened by internal convulsions and threatened by Mongols, Lithuanians, and the knights of the Teutonic Order, and was therefore in no position to assert its rights. The claim to authority, and the rights of taxation, were, however, remembered and renewed by the first Russian settlers on the Arctic coast in the sixteenth century.

The institution of a Swedish royal council, the emergence of a regular administrative structure and a fiscal apparatus, and the codification of law codes during the reigns of Magnus Ladulås (1275–90) and Magnus Eriksson (1319–64) are the most evident signs of the consolidation of a realm that was also heavily involved in ambitious territorial and dynastic ventures in northern Europe. The Finnish lands were to all intents and purposes integrated into this realm, overseen by the king's representative, the *capitaneus Finlandiae*. In recognition of the expansion of territory beyond the limits of Finland Proper, Dan Niklisson was named in 1340 as *particum orienticum prefectus* (governor of the eastern parts), and his successor, Gerhard Skytte, was also named as governor of the Eastland, a term that continued in use until the sixteenth century. The governor was also castellan of Turku castle and had authority over the two other castle fiefdoms, although the castellans of Viipuri on the eastern frontier were usually able to maintain a fairly independent position as marcher lords. At the end of the fourteenth century, new bailiwicks were created for the 'New Land' (Uusimaa, Nyland) on the southern coast, whose skerries and inlets had attracted settlers from Sweden in the previous two centuries, and for the region of Satakunta in the southwest. This administrative reorganisation was largely the work of the powerful magnate Bo Jonsson Grip, who had secured the Finnish fiefs as a reward for assisting Albrecht of Mecklenburg to the throne of Sweden. Bo Jonsson also pushed the frontier northwards into Ostrobothnia, laying the foundations of Korsholm castle and successfully resisting the attempts of Novgorod to eject his forces.

The administration of the Finnish lands was entrusted to members of the nobility; and although formidable figures such as Bo Jonsson Grip and Karl Knutsson in the early fifteenth century were able effectively to create their own power bases there, this did not loosen the ties with the rest of the realm. In the words of Eric Christiansen, 'the effect of this ungovernability was not to separate the province from Sweden, but, rather, to encourage the growth of Swedish institutions as a means whereby local interests could be protected'. Justice was dispensed, disputes settled, and fishing and hunting rights sorted out by a variety of law meetings held in the hundred. The jurymen of these courts were drawn from the local peasantry, though the man in charge of the hundred was invariably a member of the local squirearchy. From 1435, when the land was divided into two circuits, Norrfinne and Söderfinne, an annual high court was to meet in Turku in the week before St Henry's feast day (18 July). There were several variants of King Magnus Eriksson's Land Law in circulation, together with the revised codification of the laws issued under the name of King Kristoffer in 1442, and it was not until 1608 that a definitive printed version of the Land Law was available in Finland.

Magnus Eriksson's long reign ended in chaos. His nephew Albrecht of Mecklenburg eventually succeeded in establishing his claim to the throne, but at the cost of major concessions to the magnates, led by Bo Jonsson Grip. Albrecht in turn was outmanoeuvred by Margareta, daughter of the great Danish king Valdemar Atterdag (1340–75), and wife of Magnus Eriksson's son

Håkon, king of Norway (1339–80). Having persuaded the Danish nobility to accept her infant son Olav as the successor of Valdemar Atterdag in 1375, Margareta succeeded in having Olav proclaimed king of Norway some ten years later, and was seeking in 1387 to persuade the Swedes to support his claim to the Swedish crown when the seventeen-year-old Olav died. Fearful of the return to power of the Mecklenburgers, the Danish and Norwegian nobility elected to choose Margareta as their regent. The Swedes followed suit a year later, also granting Margareta the right to nominate the future king. It took a further decade to smoke out the last of the freebooters and pirates who had managed to establish themselves on Gotland during Albrecht's misrule, but, in 1397, Margareta's appointed heir, Erik of Pomerania, was crowned in the Swedish town of Kalmar as ruler of the three kingdoms. The letter of union which was also drawn up has been the subject of much controversy ever since, in terms both of the form of the document – it was written on paper and signed by seventeen high-ranking councillors from the three kingdoms, none of whom subsequently attached their seals to the document as they promised to do – and the meaning of its contents. It recognised Erik as elected king for his lifetime, and that in the event of the king having legitimate male issue, representatives of the three kingdoms would elect one of his sons as his successor. The union document decreed that each country was to be governed by its own laws and by native-born men of noble rank, but it sought to close loopholes which would allow lawbreakers sanctuary in one of the other countries of the union. It was also a mutual defence and assistance agreement, and the king was to conduct negotiations with foreign powers in concert with his councillors from the three kingdoms.

To a great extent prompted by the shared unfortunate experiences of the previous decades of misrule and unrest, the Union of Kalmar was a project ambitious in scale, and one that soon began to run into difficulties. Margareta effectively ruled the three kingdoms until her death in 1412, and had sufficient authority and power to be able to impose her will. In Finland, for example, she was able to bring fiefs directly under crown control instead of leasing them out to the nobility, and she also sought to claw back tax land which had passed into the hands of the *frälse*, the upper stratum of society that enjoyed tax-free status in return for providing military services to the sovereign. Erik XIII (1397–1439) endeavoured to follow Margareta's rather autocratic policies, but soon alienated the nobility of Sweden by appointing foreigners to the principal fiefdoms. Erik's costly wars increased the burden of taxation, which led to unrest and peasant uprisings. The most serious of all occurred in 1434, when the peasants of the mountainous region of Dalarna on the Swedish–Norwegian border rose up under the leadership of a minor local nobleman, Englebrekt Englebrektsson. Although Englebrekt himself was murdered in 1436, Erik was never able to regain control in Sweden, and was to lose the confidence of the Danish nobility as well. Not one of the union kings was able effectively to establish control over all three kingdoms. Sweden proved the most difficult. The intrigues and machinations of a small, closely knit group of magnates made the union unworkable here, and might well have plunged Sweden into an aristocratic anarchy; the consensual principle not only survived, but was significantly strengthened – in the council of the realm (*riksråd*), and through the evolution of the estates, meeting in local and, from the mid-fifteenth century, national meetings (*riksdag*).[1]

How did these long and wearisome tussles between the union kings and the Swedish magnates affect Finland? The 'Eastlanders' played little active part in the great Englebrekt revolt, with the exception of the aged bishop of Turku, Magnus Olovsson Tavast, who was one of the high personages selected to mediate between the king and his Swedish subjects in November 1434. The 'Eastland' had been accorded the same right to participate in the election of the king as the other seven law districts of the realm in 1362, when the law-man (*lagman*) was invited to come with a jury of priests and twelve peasants to the traditional ceremony of electing the king at the Mora stone near Uppsala. Recognising the problems of travel from Finland, especially in winter, the letter decreed that the ceremony should proceed if the Eastlanders' delegation did not arrive in time, and stipulated that the law-man should 'do immediately what he would have done, had he arrived at the right time, the next time he came before the king'. In the late winter of 1457, the council of the realm tried to compel Christian of Oldenburg to make terms concerning the regency before he was officially hailed as king, on the grounds that the Finnish delegation would not arrive in time for the ceremony. Christian countered this by ordering the election to take place in Turku. On 24 June 1457, the election of Christian as king of Sweden was duly performed there by members of the council of the realm, the law-men, the chapter of Turku cathedral, the lesser nobility and representatives of the peasants of Finland Proper, and the burghers of Turku.

The election in Turku of the king and the formal restoration of the union was above all a political act dictated by a complex struggle for power. In like manner, possession of the Finnish fiefs also bolstered the political position and income of the contenders – invariably members of the magnate class, such as Karl Knutsson Bonde and, under King Christian I (1457–81), the Axelsson Tott clan. The rapid extension in the final decades of the fifteenth century of the state of Muscovy, which swallowed up the principality of Novgorod in the 1470s, and the convoluted politics of the Kalmar union, once more brought conflict to the eastern frontier. As long as the Axelsson clan controlled the key Finnish fiefs and castles, they were prepared to invest in measures to defend their holdings from the incursions of Karelian raiders. But the clan was weakened by death, and by 1483, the man elected regent of Sweden, Sten Sture, had taken over most of their Finnish fiefs. Preoccupied with the threat from Denmark and from his internal enemies in Sweden, Sten was inclined to strip resources away from Finland. The devastation brought about by Karelian and Russian raiding parties deep into Häme and Ostrobothnia from 1495 onwards and the heavy cost of maintaining the army nevertheless severely reduced Sten Sture's income from his Finnish fiefs. His unwillingness to send reinforcements to relieve the hard-pressed forces defending Finland from Russian attacks brought the army to the verge of mutiny, and helped push the council of the realm into dismissing him as regent. The union was renewed once more with the election of Hans as king, though Sten Sture still retained considerable possessions, including the Finnish fiefs. The newly elected king's efforts to regain control of some of these fiefs resulted only in his defeat and the return of Herr Sten as regent in 1501.

Control of these territorially huge fiefs was an important aspect of the political struggles of the fourteenth and fifteenth centuries.

The magnates sought to extract as much revenue as possible from them, yet the yoke of feudal servitude never descended upon the necks of the Swedish or Finnish peasantry, as happened to their counterparts to the south and east. For one thing, the crown never abandoned its rights. Although the fiefs were frequently leased out for long periods of time, this was for a stated period, often the lifetime of the holder. Furthermore, the holder was usually obliged to make due provision for the interests of the realm as a whole. In receiving the fief of Kastelholm on the Åland islands in 1485, Nils Eriksson Gyllenstjerna was, for example, 'faithfully to build and improve the walls and buildings of the said castle of Kastelholm, which are needful for the said castle, to the benefit and use of the crown of Sweden, as he has promised us willingly to do' in return for enjoying the revenue from the taxes, fees, and fines. In practice, the holding of fiefs was confined to the small circle of powerful nobles who also dominated the king's council; it did not spread to the lesser nobility.

Access to and participation in the processes of royal justice was never supplanted by the law and customs of the manorial court in the kingdom of Sweden. The manorial system was weakly developed in Finland as a whole, compared with the rest of the kingdom, although it was rather more evident in the fertile south-west. Those who advised or assisted the king by providing men and horses for his wars were known as *frälse* (*rälssi* in Finnish), and were exempt from royal taxes on their land. Entitlement to this claim could be challenged – Margareta and her son, for example, reviewed the entitlements given during the reign of King Albrecht – and the composition of the *frälse* changed considerably over time. It is likely that the number of parcels of land in Finland that could be considered tax exempt (*frälsejord, rälssimaa*) was greater than that calculated by the Swedish economic historian Eli Hecksher, but what is beyond dispute is the overwhelming dominance of the peasant farm in Finland, where the tax-paying peasant (*skatte-bonde, verotalonpoika*) owned some 95 per cent of all cultivated land at the end of the middle ages. Of the 250 or so noble manors that were recorded in the early sixteenth century, mostly to be found in Finland Proper and in the more recently settled river valleys along the southern coast, only seven produced an annual income of more than one hundred marks.

Plate 3 The Castle of Viipuri on the eastern frontier. The tower of St Olaf, seen here in a photograph from the 1930s, was begun at the end of the thirteenth century, and substantially rebuilt in the sixteenth century. Around the tower a substantial fortress grew, protecting the town of Viipuri (now Vyborg), which acquired its charter in 1403. The town and castle endured several sieges. In 1495, as winter approached, the Russians abruptly abandoned the siege when they seemed on the verge of capturing the stronghold. Their withdrawal prompted Bishop Magnus Stiernkors to claim that the cross of St Andrew had appeared in the sky to frighten off the attackers (the decisive assault occurred on 30 November, St Andrew's day). Another legend attributed magical powers to the commander of the fortress, Knut Posse, who is supposed to have blown up a cauldron stuffed with explosives and an assortment of toads and snakes, causing the besiegers to flee in panic. The town and castle fell to the Russians in 1710, and passed under Russian control thereafter until Alexander I restored the conquered territories of Russian, or 'Old' Finland to his newly acquired Grand Duchy in 1812. During the early decades of Finnish independence, Viipuri castle had a symbolic value as the fortress against the east, as this photograph is intended to show. Viipuri and the Karelian isthmus were lost to the Soviet Union in 1940. Now, they are rather sad and poignant reminders of the past to Finnish visitors.

Unable to live off their estates, the lesser nobility had to secure office, as bailiffs, stewards and in particular, as sheriffs and district judges. Thus was established the tradition of service to the crown that was the characteristic hallmark of the Finnish nobility until the twentieth century.

The policy of alliance with Muscovy contemplated by the Danish kings in their efforts to dislodge the powerful Sture clan and regain control of Sweden certainly did little to win over those with estates and revenues in Finland. The bishop of Turku was an enthusiastic supporter of the idea of a crusade against the Orthodox Russians, favouring a more aggressive policy towards Muscovy than the regent Sten Sture, and engaging in active diplomacy to try and forge a joint front with the master of the Teutonic Order in Livonia. In this, he was ably supported by the archbishop of Uppsala, and lobbying in Rome persuaded Pope Alexander VI to issue a crusading bull in June 1496 against the enemies of Christianity who, sixty thousand strong, had 'most grievously destroyed a great part of the diocese of Turku belonging to the realm of Sweden, burning churches, desecrating the name of Christ and his saints, killing, robbing, insulting, violating and raping the wives and maidens of these parts, murdering the menfolk and placing the yoke of slavery upon many thousand Christians'.[2] There was the threat of a renewed Russian onslaught once the truce of 1497 ran out in 1503, though a twenty-year truce was eventually negotiated with Ivan III's governor of Novgorod by the castellan of Viipuri, Erik Turesson Bielke. In 1510, this was transformed into a sixty-year peace, though the Muscovite side managed to insist on a conference to mark out the frontier according to the terms of the 1323 treaty. Setbacks in his war against Lithuania obliged Vasili III (1505–33) to agree in 1513 to postpone this meeting for a further five years. The Russian insistence on revisiting the boundaries delineated in the treaty concluded between Sweden and Novgorod in 1323 was in response to what they considered Swedish encroachments in Savo and along the Ostrobothnian coast, but it was also part of a new assertiveness, with Vasili for example ordering taxes to be collected and justice to be dispensed amongst the Sami of the far north. Tensions between the colonisers and the Karelians flared up frequently; there were complaints of Karelians stealing church property at Tornio at the head of the Gulf of Bothnia, and of frequent raids in the Karelian isthmus. Vasili promised to hang those found guilty of such malfeasance, but complained for his part of the continuous raiding of his lands by the 'men of Sweden', whilst the governor of Novgorod provided evidence of villages built by settlers from the other side of the frontier.

In addition to having to cope with the threat of renewed incursions by the Russians, the eastern half of the realm was also vulnerable to attack from the sea. A strong Danish fleet commanded by Sören Norby occupied the Åland islands in 1507, and there were further raids on Porvoo and Turku in the following two years. The newly elected regent, Sten Sture, known as the younger, was quick to ensure possession of the Finnish fiefs, securing the loyalty of the peasantry and nobility of western Finland and managing to outflank his rival, Nils Bosson Grip, by doing a deal with the widow of the powerful castellan of Viipuri to win that vital fortress to his interest. The castellans of the Finnish strongholds and the local nobility remained loyal to the Sture cause even after its leader had been killed in battle against the force of King Christian II of Denmark in 1520, but the threat of attack from Christian's Muscovite allies meant that they were unable to offer much assistance to the beleaguered widow of the dead regent. Stockholm finally surrendered to the Danish king in September 1520. After initially offering generous amnesty terms to the leading adherents of the Sture party, perhaps to ensure the peaceful handing over of the Finnish strongholds to his own appointees, Christian compelled the Swedish council and estates to acknowledge him as their lawful and hereditary king and had most of the leading members of the Sture party executed in the infamous 'Stockholm bloodbath'. Executions were also carried out in Finland by the king's agent, Rolef Madsen.

Christian's triumph was short-lived. In 1521, the young Gustav Eriksson Vasa, a relative of the Sture clan, raised the flag of revolt in Dalarna, and advanced upon the capital, taking Västerås in April, and Uppsala in the summer. Gustav Vasa was acclaimed regent of Sweden by the council in August 1521, but his cause suffered a severe setback when the Danish admiral Sören Norby was able to destroy much of his fleet, thereby hindering the rebels' attempts to blockade Stockholm into submission. Christian was able to use his close connections with the Habsburg dynasty to persuade the emperor Charles V to institute an Imperial ban on trade with Sweden. For Gustav Vasa, the financial and material backing of the north German ports, above all Denmark's old rival Lübeck, was vital. Although he was able to secure the backing of individual merchants, the councillors of Lübeck did not finally commit themselves to the rebel cause until 1522, sending a fleet to Gustav Vasa's assistance in the autumn. This fleet, with its Swedish allies, inflicted a sharp defeat over Sören Norby off Vaxholm in the autumn of 1522, thus severely weakening the maritime link between the Finnish provinces and the beleaguered garrison in Stockholm.

Stockholm finally surrendered to Gustav Vasa in the summer of 1523, shortly after the *riksdag* had acclaimed him king of Sweden. Christian had already been deposed by a noble revolt in Denmark, and had fled to Holland, leaving his commander Sören Norby to carry on the struggle in the north. Norby rejected Gustav Vasa's offer of clemency, but a short autumn campaign compelled his forces in Finland to abandon their strongholds and retire. From his base on the island of Gotland, Norby continued to pose a threat to the new order, and the exiled Christian II strove tirelessly to find backers for his cause: but Norby was driven off in 1526, and Christian himself was imprisoned by his uncle and successor as king of Denmark, Fredrik I (1523–33).

The end of the union brought out the strategic importance of the Eastland, but also showed clearly that the centre of power lay across the water, in Sweden. In spite of the gradual integration into the realm of the lands along the shoreline of the gulfs of Bothnia and Finland, much of the hinterland remained very much on the periphery, in much the same manner as the regions north of Uppland. Beyond the plains of south-western Finland, where one-third of the total number of Finnish farms recorded in sixteenth-century tax records were located, the forests and the lakes dominated the landscape almost completely. The density of settlement in a farming parish such as Masku, just to the north of Turku, was a hundred times greater than in the remote hinterland settlement of Tavinsalmi in the east. Most of the eighty-odd stone-built churches were located in Finland Proper, Satakunta, and Häme. Four of the six medieval towns, including Turku, and four of the six religious settlements, including the Franciscans on the island of Kökar, were

Map 1 The kingdom of Sweden in the late middle ages.

here.[3] South-western Finland was in fact on the eastern edge of a belt of long-established permanent settlement that stretched across the central Swedish plains from Västergötland to Uppland and it had much stronger cultural and economic links with that heartland than with the hinterland stretching away to the northern and eastern horizons.

There was nevertheless a steady expansion of the frontiers of permanent settlement throughout the middle ages. New hamlets and villages were created in the core areas of settlement. Colonisers from Sweden settled on the skerries and inlets of the southern coast, establishing a Swedish-speaking presence there that has lasted to the present day. The shores of the eastern Baltic attracted settlers from further afield, in particular, from the German lands. Many entered the service of the crown, but there was also a considerable influx of traders and merchants. The major trading towns of the realm all had a significant minority of burghers of German origin. Nine of the fourteen burghermasters of Turku between 1400 and 1471, and twenty of the thirty-six town councillors, were of German origin; the proportion of Germans recorded on the town's lists of burghers in the fourteenth century was even greater.

Colonisation was actively encouraged by the crown, eager to augment its tax revenues. The costs of defending newly settled areas, such as the lake region of Savo on the eastern frontier, where the castle of Olavinlinna was built at great expense in the 1470s, had the effect, however, of driving settlers further into the forests in search of lands beyond the reach of the tax-collector. The settlement of Savo was particularly vigorous, expanding far beyond the region – to the Ostrobothnian coast and into the wilderness on the northern limits of Satakunta in the sixteenth century, and even across the Gulf of Bothnia to the forests of Värmland in the seventeenth century. The colonisation of Savo encroached upon the lands of the Karelians, and a long period of bitter frontier skirmishing followed.

By the end of the middle ages, there were four major economic zones of settlement and land usage in the eastern half of the Swedish kingdom. On the hundreds of rocky islands of the south coast, stretching from the shores of the Karelian isthmus to the Åland islands, fishing was the main occupation, supplemented by summer grazing, bird-catching, and egg-collecting. In the wildernesses of northern Ostrobothnia, the settlers reared cattle, fished, and hunted; fields were small and here, too, the cultivation of grain was of negligible significance. Stretching in a great arc from the Karelian isthmus through the region of Savo as far as lake Oulujärvi, and across to the northern wildernesses of the Häme region was a zone in which burn-beat cultivation predominated. There were three principal sub-zones of field cultivation, of which the oldest was to be found in Finland Proper, the southern parishes of Satakunta, and the larger parishes of the Åland islands. In the area of later cultivation, which extended eastwards into the Karelian isthmus and into Häme and the northern parishes of Satakunta, and the third zone in southern and central Ostrobothnia, hunting, fishing, and cattle-rearing (especially in Ostrobothnia) played a central role in the household economy. A further zone, beyond the frontiers of settlement and stretching from the Atlantic to the White Sea, was inhabited by nomadic peoples, descendants of the earliest waves of migrants after the Ice Age, who fished, hunted, and herded reindeer. The evidence of place-names indicates that this zone had once been much larger, and it was a useful source of income for the neighbouring peoples, who mounted regular tax-gathering expeditions into the lands of 'the people who live apart' (a probable explanation of the term 'Lapp'). The furs and skins thus procured remained a vital element in the economy of the northern frontier well into the sixteenth century. For families who farmed within the zone of permanent settlement to the south, spring and summer fishing expeditions into the wilderness were also an important means of supplementing food supplies and income. The pike in particular was a much-prized fish, which, in the words of the sixteenth-century cleric and historian Olaus Magnus, 'not only provide sufficient sustenance for people throughout four large northern kingdoms, but when salted and dried in the sun are exported even farther by ship, stacked like great piles of logs, to be sold across the whole of Germany'.

The wilderness, known in Finnish as *erämaa*, was never very far away from any place of human habitation. Even in the oldest areas of land cultivation, it could be found on the hilly margins. It was a valuable resource in a poor land, freely accessible to all who were able to mark out and claim a defined area as their hunting and fishing grounds. These *erämaat* were often at a considerable distance from inhabited areas; in Ostrobothnia, for instance, some two or even three hundred kilometres from the coast. Hunting expeditions into the wilderness began to decline from the sixteenth century

Plate 4 Burn-beat cultivation. The cutting down and burning of selected areas of woodland for the purposes of cultivation was practised for centuries in Finland. The technique varies according to the type of woodland, either mostly deciduous (*kaskenpoltto*) or coniferous (*huuhta*). The *huuhta* technique was highly destructive of the forest, since it allowed for only one crop. Seventeenth-century eastern Finnish settlers in the upland Swedish region of Värmland who took with them their time-honoured practices of land clearance soon ran foul of the authorities, anxious to preserve precious supplies of timber for the iron industry, and many were subsequently bundled off to the banks of the Delaware to try their skills in the forests of the new world. The big advantage of burn-beat cultivation over more conventional methods of land clearance – which in Finland might involve laborious uprooting of stumps, removal of stones, and draining of bogs – was that it produced a crop with relatively little effort. Overall yields on *kaski* land were probably less than on ploughed land, but land cleared by the *huuhta* technique – and it took four years from cutting to cultivation – often produced enormous returns in their one season of fruitfulness. As such, it proved attractive to the new settlers of eastern Finland, who were also able to supplement their food stocks by fishing and hunting. Burn-beating was still practised in parts of eastern Finland until the twentieth century, as shown in this photograph, taken in the parish of Eno in 1893 by the ethnographer J. K. Inha.

onwards, as the crown laid claim to the wilderness in order to encourage settlement, and there is evidence of noblemen claiming ownership of tracts of wilderness for possible future colonisation; but hunting and fishing never became exclusive royal or noble privileges, and free access to the wilderness has remained a valued right to the present day.

In the course of time, the *erämaa* might be settled and cultivated, with huts put up by hunters and fishermen to store their gear and provide rudimentary accommodation enlarged into a house and farm. The usual method of clearance was to cut and burn the trees and undergrowth; it was also possible to grow crops on the cleared site, fertilised by the ash. This form of cultivation, known as swidden or burn-beat, has in northern Europe long been regarded as peculiarly Finnish. It is highly likely that some form of burn-beat technique was used to clear land in western Finland in the early middle ages, and was certainly still used to prepare woods for new cultivation in later times, but this was only a transitory step. It did not become the norm for cultivation, as did burn-beating in much of eastern Finland. The wilderness was able to absorb and support the vigorous colonisation of the sixteenth and seventeenth century. By the middle of the eighteenth century, however, as rural Finland experienced a strong population growth, the supply of land suitable for burn-beat cultivation was shrinking rapidly. At the best of times, yields from the land wrested from nature were meagre. As the pressure on land mounted, harvest failures could and did spell disaster for many thousands.

Wresting a livelihood from the wilderness, whether fishing, hunting, or the planting and harvesting of grain, necessitated co-operation and teamwork. As a rule, men hunted, ploughed, sowed, and reaped with the scythe, but there are instances of women doing this work. Indoor work and the dairy were usually the preserve of women, though in eastern Finland, men did the brewing and also prepared meat for the pot. Both sexes participated in land clearance, and in field work. Groups of peasants came together to hunt seals, build boats, fish the lakes, and clear the land. In Häme and western Finland, communally owned mills were not uncommon, with the peasant shareholders each grinding their own corn until millers, paid in housing, meadowland, hay, fuel, and a share of the grain, began to be employed in the eighteenth century. Many of the seasonal tasks of the farming community, such as harvesting, were shared efforts. These strong traditions of working together for the common good under-pinned the producers' co-operatives that took form at the beginning of the twentieth century, and provided a readily understood basis for the great upsurge of the associational activity – religious revivalism, the temperance movement, glee clubs, voluntary fire brigades, the youth movement – of the nineteenth century.

Such communal activity was more common in the more popu-lous regions of western Finland, where the village also functioned as an organisational unit (though far less so than in Sweden). Further east, where labour was at a premium, the family tended to form the basis of communal activity, and it was here that the extended, or so-called 'big family' was most commonly found, especially amongst the Karelians around lake Ladoga. These units were amalgams of two or more core families, with their servants and lodgers, living and working together. Big families were most commonly formed by brothers, and were patriarchal in structure. Whereas the Swedish custom of the heir, usually the eldest son, agreeing to provide housing, fuel, and benefits in kind to the head of the family and his wife as a precondition for entering into full possession of the farm had come into widespread use in western Finland by the end of the middle ages, no such provision existed in eastern Finland. Inheritance practices also differed: in the burn-beat lands of the east, the land usually passed to the males in the house-hold on the basis of their contribution to the work. This meant, for example, that brothers-in-law or adopted children could and did inherit. Women in general did not inherit land, but received a dowry in kind upon marriage. In western Finland, on the other hand, all children had the right to inherit land – according to the medieval land laws, brothers were to inherit two parts to their sisters' one. Furthermore, the law permitted members of the family to challenge the transfer of an inherited holding outside their own ranks.

In general, medieval Finland seems to have been less affected by the great demographic and agricultural crises of much of the rest of Europe. It was largely spared from the Black Death, and there is relatively little evidence of deserted farmsteads, certainly in comparison with neighbouring Norway. A huge, heavily forested land mass, sparsely populated even in the fixed-field regions of the south-west, it remained on the outer limits of the continental European world vision, even after the publications of the Magnus brothers, the *Historia de omnibus Gothorum Sveonumque regibus* (*The history of all the kings of the Goths and Svea*) of Johannes, published in 1554, and the widely read *Historia de gentibus septentrionalibus* (*The history of the northern peoples*) of Olaus, published a year later. But the Finns were by no means totally isolated or cut off from the rest of Europe. There is ample evidence of active involvement in trade throughout the southern and eastern Baltic, and trade often acted as the principal filter and disseminator of mainland ideas and innovations to the northern lands. Finns also studied abroad. Two students from the bishopric of Turku were registered at the university of Paris as early as 1313, and a further forty-four are known to have studied there, including three who became rectors of the faculty of philosophy. In the fifteenth century, German universities attracted Finnish students, though some ventured even further afield to Italy. In common with the other peoples of Europe, Finns went on pilgrimage. Saint Birgitta's encounter in Rome with a man from the diocese of Turku, ignorant of the Swedish language and unable to find in the Holy City a confessor who could understand his language, suggests that even humble peasants might find their way abroad. The church was able to recruit amongst the native population, and to provide an education in the cathedral school of Turku; there were also schools in Viipuri, Rauma, and Porvoo. But with little or no possibility of princely or noble patronage, the Finnish periphery could not compete with richer areas of Europe in the output of verse or chronicles, not even with the Swedish heartland, where a vernacular literature was being created. 'Where Sweden was poor, Finland was poorer,' concludes Eric Christiansen, 'in educated men, in books, in churches, in towns, in arts, in schools'; and this disparity was to endure, colouring the relationship of the two halves of the kingdom and leaving a complex legacy of snobbish superiority on the one side, and resentful feelings of inferiority on the other.

The church was the great torchbearer of education and the arts in Finland, and its head, the bishop of Turku, was a figure of considerable authority. Almost all the last Catholic bishops were members of the leading families of Finland. Magnus Olovsson Tavast (bishop 1412–50) enjoyed an extremely long and varied career, studying at the university of Prague, making a pilgrimage to Jerusalem, serving for a time as chancellor to King Erik XIII, playing an active role in the politics of the Kalmar union, and as bishop, doing much to adorn and beautify the cathedral and churches in his diocese. His protégé and successor, Olaus Magnus (1450–60), enjoyed a glittering career at the university of Paris before returning to Finland in 1437. Konrad Bidz (1460–89) was an active ecclesiastical administrator, and instigated the printing in Lübeck of a missal for the use of the Finnish clergy. Magnus Stiernkors (1489–1500) and Arvid Kurck (1510–22) were heavily involved in the political manoeuvrings and diplomatic intrigues of the last phase of the union conflict.

Administering to the spiritual needs of the inhabitants of a vast and empty marchland on the outer limits of fixed settlement posed many problems for the church. The settlers of the hinterland were virtually unprovided for; as Bishop Laurentius Suurpää (1500–6) complained, the peasants in Savo lived fifteen or more Finnish miles (one mile was the equivalent of six kilometres) from the nearest church, which meant they seldom or never attended church services and lived in consequence 'like Lapps or pagans'. 'Many false gods here / were worshipped far and near', noted the reformer and bishop of Turku (1554–57), Mikael Agricola, in the preface to his Finnish translation of the psalter, and he went on to list in detail these gods of the Karelians and the peoples of Häme. Agricola and his fellow-reformers undertook the task of bringing the people closer to God with much earnestness and zeal, and with the support of the state; but the old beliefs proved difficult to eradicate. Well into modern times, the parish priest continued to struggle against the vestiges of paganism; as late as the 1920s, one of the questions asked of the clergy during church visitations enquired about recent occurrences of pagan practices in the parish.

As the new king of Sweden strove to establish his authority, what was the position of that part of his realm that Gustav Vasa in his voluminous correspondence frequently referred to as 'thetta landsände'? In 'this end of the country' there were in the 1550s some 34,000 farms, a couple of hundred manorial estates, and a handful of towns whose combined population probably did not exceed 7,000, or the population of late-medieval Stockholm. The population and resources of the land had undoubtedly been increased by vigorous colonisation and settlement during the middle ages, and there were probably slightly over a quarter of a million inhabitants in Finland, or roughly a quarter of the population of the kingdom as a whole. The supposed fecundity of Finnish women aroused comment from contemporaries. Olaus Magnus attributed this to the qualities of Finnish beer, and he noted disapprovingly that a surplus of strong young women left the shores of Finland annually for Germany to work as servants, when they might be used with profit by the king of Sweden to establish new provinces.

This was a land of free peasants, rude and unlettered, but by no means unenterprising. Farmers along the coast built and sailed boats laden with butter, skins, dried fish, and livestock to trade with the merchants of Stockholm, Tallinn, and even further afield; and even though the hunting and trapping economy was beginning to diminish in importance, there was still a flourishing fur trade from northern Russia to the Ostrobothnian coast. The forests provided the materials for buildings, domestic utensils, and farming implements. The only buildings of stone were the steeply roofed parish churches, the handful of castles and monasteries, and the occasional manor-house. A few, such as the dean of Turku cathedral, Påvel Scheel, may have amassed a modest fortune from their economic activities; but there was virtually no conspicuous consumption, no commissioning of works of art, no acquisition of precious jewels, no charitable bequests. The late-medieval paintings that still adorn the walls of many of Finland's oldest churches reflect a world of simple, humble piety, as do the verses of the *Piae cantiones*, a collection first published in 1582. It has been suggested that a deep-seated suspicion of wealth and a belief in the honest goodness of poverty, which is revealed in much folk poetry dating back to the middle ages and which was still very much in evidence well into the nineteenth century, was in all likelihood implanted by the mendicant Dominican friars. If so, it reflected no more than the everyday reality of a hard life on the margins of cultivable land.

These poems occasionally reveal a perception of Sweden as a distinctly separate entity. Poems from western and central Finland, such as *The Widow*, see Sweden as a wealthier land. There are bitter hints of Swedish oppression in the poem *Magdalene*, collected in Häme – the Finnish slave lives on fish-bones left by the Swedes – but this is an isolated example, and there is little evidence of the kind of ethnic hatred expressed towards the Baltic German overlords in Estonian folk poems, for instance. Religious differences and a long tradition of border raids divided the Finns of Savo and Häme from the Karelians, for whom all within the Swedish realm were enemies of the true faith.

The final breaking of the Union of Kalmar and the establishment of the Vasas as rulers of the Swedish kingdom in the sixteenth century inaugurated an era of significant religious, social, and economic change. In the course of his long reign, the first Vasa king, Gustav I, set in train a number of administrative and fiscal reforms which would make better use of the resources of his vast but sparsely populated lands. He also succeeded in breaking the power of the church, which had used its economic strength and spiritual authority to cow and coerce his predecessors of the Sture clan. The removal of Christian II by the Danish nobility enabled Gustav Vasa to establish a bond of mutual interest with Fredrik I, the new king of Denmark, and his successor, Christian III (1534–59), and he was also able to maintain peace on the eastern frontier until the final years of his reign.

Notwithstanding several rebellions, one of which threatened for a time to bring down the dynasty, Gustav Vasa bequeathed to his ambitious sons an independent kingdom where the principle of hereditary succession had been acknowledged by the estates in 1544. In spite of the political and religious upheavals of the next fifty years – Erik XIV (1560–69) was deposed, Johan III (1569–92) provoked religious controversy, and his Catholic son Sigismund was rejected in favour of his uncle, Karl IX (regent from 1594, king 1604–11) – the Vasa dynasty remained in the saddle. In spite of serious challenges to the authority of the crown which had imposed heavy tax burdens on the peasantry to pay for seemingly unending military campaigns, had angered the clergy with its interference in church affairs, and had alienated the nobility, the accession of the seventeen-year-old Gustav II Adolf (1611–32) marked the beginning of a remarkable partnership between ruler and estates which was to help sustain the immense war effort that propelled Sweden to the front ranks of the European powers during the first half of the seventeenth century. Sweden's rise to the status of a great power on the European stage, however, was to have far-reaching consequences for the eastern half of the kingdom. The frontiers of Finland were also pushed eastward, but the overall effect of this expansion was to push the old core of Finland Proper away from the centre of royal power, Stockholm, and ultimately to expose a periphery poor in resources and manpower to attack from the rising power of imperial Russia.

2

The Swedish legacy

Between the accession of Erik XIV in 1560 and the death of Karl X (1654–60), hardly a year passed when Sweden was not at war. Five major wars were fought against Denmark during this hundred-year period, with Sweden gradually gaining the upper hand and acquiring territory to the south and west that has remained Swedish to the present day. In the east, Sweden succeeded in expanding a bridgehead in northern Estonia acquired in 1561 to embrace most of Estonia and Livonia by 1629. The virtual collapse of the Muscovite state following the death of Boris Godunov in 1605 enabled Sweden to push back the Finnish frontier to the shores of lake Ladoga and to establish a land bridge to the Estonian territories through the acquisition of Ingria. The entry of Sweden into the Thirty Years War in 1629 and the astonishing victories that carried Gustav II Adolf and his forces deep into the Catholic heartland of Germany marked an entirely new phase. Sweden was now able to command lavish French subsidies and make war 'pay for itself' by a variety of methods from forced contributions to outright extortion. Its battles were fought by polyglot armies; the men conscripted back home constituted only a small minority of the Swedish forces fighting in Germany. More territory, this time on the north German coast, was acquired in the final peace settlement in 1648. Within seven years, Sweden was once more enmeshed in war, its armies drawn deep into Poland in a bewildering series of marches and battles, and twice flung against the old enemy, Denmark. The subsequent period of peace after 1660 revealed how overstretched

Sweden had become. Careful management of the crown's resources and a series of military reforms during the reign of Karl XI (1660–97) enabled Sweden to sustain two more decades of war against a wide coalition of forces before the sudden death of Karl XII in 1718 and national exhaustion brought an end to the age of military greatness.

The faded banners and trophies of war that adorn the museums and great houses of Sweden are reminders of the glory and renown of Swedish arms across the European continent. Sweden's expansion was, however, achieved at great cost. The creation of an armed force capable of winning victory on the battlefield and of defending conquered territory imposed heavy burdens on a poor kingdom whose total population barely exceeded a million at the beginning of the seventeenth century. Finland's share of that burden seems to have been disproportionately high. In the five-year period 1626–30, for example, of the 51,367 men who were conscripted into the Swedish army through a rote system, almost a third (15,281) were from Finland. Few of those who saw active service in the field returned home (although most died of disease in camp rather than wounds on the battlefield). There was provision for maintaining the conscripts from crown resources, which was placed on a more systematic footing in the 1680s. This proved to be a more flexible and stable system than the costly and often unreliable payment of wages to hired troops, and it established deep and enduring roots in the countryside of Sweden and Finland, where the farms and cottages allotted to the officers and soldiers remained distinctly identifiable as such well into modern times. Wealthier peasants could avoid the rote by agreeing to furnish a horse and rider for the cavalry. The regulation of this method of recruitment at the end of the seventeenth century confirmed the emergence of a peasant elite, the *rusthollari*, who in return for equipping a horseman and providing him with a cottage and patch of land, were allowed significant tax reliefs. Like the soldiers' dwellings, the *rustholli* farms scattered across the provinces of south-western and central Finland were a consequence of the military state created by Sweden's rulers in the sixteenth and seventeenth centuries.

The readiness of the wealthier peasantry to provide horsemen for the cavalry was undoubtedly welcome to the crown, for the obligation of the nobility to do so had been seriously undermined during the course of the sixteenth century. But, as Robert Frost has

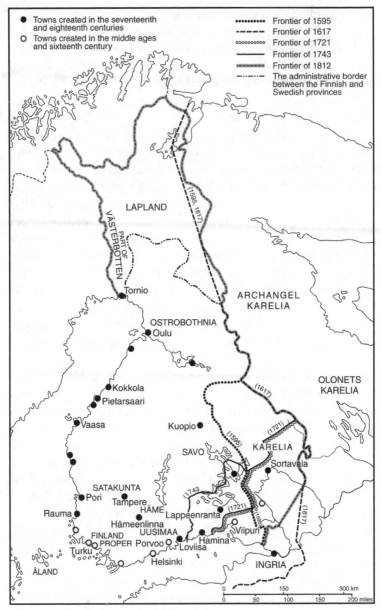

Map 2 The frontiers of Finland, 1595–1812.

Plate 5 A sergeant's dwelling, Juva. The system of recruiting men into the armed forces that evolved during Sweden's age of greatness rewarded those who served with land and a dwelling, according to their rank. The rank-and-file soldier might expect a modest cottage; officers, who also took on administrative tasks, were often given sizeable two-storey houses with land. The dwelling-house pictured here probably dates from the late eighteenth century, and would have furnished a non-commissioned officer with a large room heated by an oven, in which the family ate, worked, and slept, and one or two small chambers for more private use.

noted, if the nobility were reluctant to serve out of obligation, they were more than happy to serve for reward. Most were poor. In return for their services as officers, the crown was able to reward them with an income from the land, much of which had passed under royal control as a result of the Reformation. The Finnish nobility in particular took full advantage of this during the long wars on the eastern frontier in the latter half of the sixteenth and early decades of the seventeenth century. Whereas the crown sought to reduce the number of fiefs in Sweden proper, it was willing to increase their number in Finland as a means of paying those members of the aristocracy who had distinguished themselves in the king's service, though it was unwilling to accede to the demands of these fief-holders for further privileges.

By 1600, the number of farms in noble hands had risen sharply from a modest few hundred to over two thousand in Finland. At the same time, there had been a steady decline in the overall number of farms, which meant that the growing burden of taxation fell on ever fewer shoulders. The nobility zealously guarded their right of tax exemption, and their tenants were also not obliged to quarter men-at-arms or provide horses for the army. Others who performed useful military service, such as defending the frontier, were also granted tax exemption on their land. The brutal and arrogant behaviour of the officials who sought to extract taxes and services from those crown or freehold peasants who were unable to obtain such exemptions provoked anger and resentment. In 1589, a delegation of three hundred Finnish peasants betook themselves to Stockholm with a petition for the king, in which they listed at length their grievances. They complained that they were mocked by rich farmers who had taken their farms by deception or bribery, denied justice, and cheated by officials, who lived in luxury whilst the crown's demesnes were stripped bare. These haughty bailiffs and scriveners created their own retinues, who also robbed, raped, and pillaged the peasantry. In the eyes of the petitioners, official-dom was one big, corrupt conspiracy that sought to cheat the king and milk the poor:

They all band together against the poor peasants, and are further aided by the rich peasants, whom they help with gifts and bribes. Some bailiff's servants marry the daughters of rich farmers and relieve their father-in-law of the obligation to provide transport and other services, wherefore an even greater burden falls upon the neck of the poor. In such manner do Finland's officials torment the poor peasant and frighten him with their great pomp, for they travel between their farms with fifty or sixty men, so that simple folk are more afraid of their arrogance than they are of the king himself.

In spite of royal efforts to relieve the situation, complaints about the exactions of the king's officials continued, and there were occasional clashes between troops and peasants. At the end of November 1596, a serious revolt broke out in southern Ostrobothnia. The homes of hated local officials were looted and burned, and troops quartered in the district were attacked and driven out. This uprising was bloodily suppressed on New Year's Eve, and peasants who rose up in Häme and Savo were likewise scattered by a show of force. There was a second uprising in February 1597, this time in northern Ostrobothnia. Although better armed than their predecessors, these rebels were also routed in battle at Santavuori on 24 February 1597.

These uprisings, known in Finnish history as the 'Club War', took place against a tense political situation. Elected king of Poland in 1587, Sigismund was slow to arrive in Sweden to claim his crown on the death of his father Johan III in 1592; and when he did, at the end of September 1593, he found it impossible to break the alliance of his uncle, Duke Karl, and the council of the realm. A committed Catholic, Sigismund was obliged to accept the affirmation of the Lutheran faith made at the church council hastily convened by Duke Karl in Uppsala, and to hand over the government of the realm in his absence to the duke and council. Karl, a ruthless and ambitious man, managed to browbeat the council into accepting him as regent in 1594, and although the subsequent *riksdag* at Söderköping insisted that he govern with the advice and consent of the council, the duke was more than a match for the aristocratic constitutionalists who sought to bind him.

The one notable figure who refused to bend to his will was Sigismund's commander in Finland, marshal of the realm and admiral of the fleet, Klas Fleming. In order to get rid of Fleming, Duke Karl resorted to all the tricks of which he was eminently capable. He lent a sympathetic ear to the complaints of the Finnish peasantry, issuing letters of protection and promising to do away with the hated practice of quartering troops on their farms. The peasant uprisings in Finland during the winter of 1596–97 kept Fleming fully occupied there, at a time when the struggle for power between the duke, the council, and King Sigismund was very much in the balance. Fleming's death in April 1597 did not greatly alter the situation. His successor as royal commander, Arvid Stålarm, was obliged to abandon Turku to Duke Karl's invading forces in September, but easily regained control of the castle after the duke returned to Stockholm. Stålarm's invasion of Sweden in the following summer had to be aborted when the main invasion from the south failed to materialise, and the defeat of the king's delayed invasion in September 1598 proved to be a fatal blow to Sigismund's cause. The main Finnish strongholds capitulated to Duke Karl after a brief summer campaign in 1599. Karl, soon to be hailed as king by the estates of the realm, imposed stiff fines on the clergy, allowed his troops to plunder the farms of those he had not expressly included in his letters of protection, and had those whom he most hated and feared executed in the market place in Turku, after a trial at which the duke overrode all legal niceties.

The brutal suppression of the peasant revolt in Finland left a deep impression. The Finnish historian Yrjö Koskinen, who grew up in Ostrobothnia, made frequent references to still vivid folk memories of the gruesome aftermath of the revolt in his pioneering study of the 'Club War', published in 1857–59. There were to be no further major uprisings here or elsewhere in the Swedish realm during the next hundred years, even though the fiscal and other pressures on the peasantry in no way diminished. In this respect, the absence of peasant tumults in the northern kingdom was in marked contrast to the revolts that afflicted France, that other great wager of war in seventeenth-century Europe. Why was this so? One obvious difference is that it is more difficult in a thinly populated land to bring together a sufficient number of discontented people to form the core of an uprising. Those who felt themselves oppressed also had a number of other options open to them. They could and did use the courts, and, as we have seen, readily turned to the king with their petitions. There is evidence to suggest that the king or regent did take heed of these complaints, though how effective their letters of protection or commands were is open to question. In the worst case, the poor farmer and his family might abandon the land, move elsewhere in search of better luck, or simply be swallowed up into the ranks of the landless. The crown showed a willingness to recruit Finns as settlers of the deserted farmsteads of the conquered territories in Estonia, and there was continued vigorous internal colonisation, which was beginning to push into the territory of the Sami and deep into the forests on the Swedish–Norwegian frontier. And one must also remember that, although for the great majority the demands of incessant warfare bore heavily upon their subsistence economy, there were those who profited or were able to take advantage of chance and good fortune.

The intensely religious and nationalistic Yrjö Koskinen did not shrink from claiming that 'the bloody surge that tossed the Papacy back to the shores of the Rhine and Danube began as an insignificant rippling of the water in the marshes of Ostrobothnia', or that the foundations of Finland's civilisation were laid at this epochal moment 'when its sons under Sweden's banners shed their blood on the battlefields of Europe'. This image of an identity forged in warfare is a powerful and recurring one in modern Finnish historiography. Even before Finland became an independent state, the exploits of fictive heroes in the wars had become an integral part of the national treasury of myths. But Yrjö Koskinen also argued that the conflict between Karl and Sigismund reduced Finland to greater dependence upon Sweden, and that during the subsequent era of Swedish greatness the Finnish language and nationality were further subjugated. Nationalist historians of a later generation also took up Yrjö Koskinen's suggestion that a sense of national identity existed, albeit rather weakly, amongst the land's leading people, and they argued that the Finnish nobility developed a distinct and separate set of 'national' interests during the long wars against the Russians. The creation of a Grand Duchy of Finland for Gustav Vasa's second son, Johan, and of a princely court in Turku during the early 1560s to accommodate the ambitions of Duke Johan before he was imprisoned by his morbidly jealous brother Erik XIV, the rapid increase in the number of Finnish military companies, and of distinctive heraldic devices and escutcheons such as the Finnish lion, gave added substance to these claims. But, whilst it is true that decades of warfare on the eastern frontiers afforded members of the leading noble clans in Finland the opportunity to secure high rank in the army, and considerable rewards for their services, the interests they pursued so vigorously during the reign of Johan III pertained rather more to their rank than to a notion of a separate and distinct *patria*.

The cohesiveness of the Finnish nobility undoubtedly suffered a severe setback as a result of Duke Karl's vengeful and divisive policies; but the nobility of Sweden also suffered at the hands of the duke, and members of noble families from both halves of the kingdom went into exile in the lands ruled by Sigismund. Between the accession of Gustav II Adolf in 1611 and the peace of Nystad (Uusikaupunki) in 1721, the composition and character of the nobility of the kingdom of Sweden underwent considerable change.

Incessant warfare and the crown's willingness to reward those who could provide useful services opened up the ranks of the aristocracy to newcomers, many of foreign extraction. The number of noble families more than tripled during the reign of Queen Christina (1632–54). There was also a massive increase in the transfer of taxable land to the nobility, with the most powerful families in the realm amassing huge land holdings. The restoration of these alienated revenues, the so-called *reduktion* of the late seventeenth century, enabled the crown to regain a degree of fiscal independence, and it caused some grief to the more recently ennobled who had benefited most from the crown's generosity, but the nobility remained in possession of their own estates. Few of these estates in Finland were large enough to provide an income sufficient to maintain the standard of living expected of a nobleman. Service to the crown was essential, and in the competition for prestigious posts and high rank, the landed gentry in Finland tended over the years to fare less well than their Swedish counterparts.

As part of Gustav Adolf's general restructuring of the administration of the realm, the office of governor-general for Finland was instituted in 1623. This proved not to be a permanent post, and the office-holders were of variable quality. The one whose memory endures in Finnish history is Per Brahe, who held the post twice, in 1637–40 and again between 1648 and 1654. Sweden's incessant wars had drained and exhausted the eastern half of the realm, and the energetic Brahe found much to occupy him. He devoted much time and effort to improving the administrative and judicial infrastructure, but he also sought to promote economic development, founding new towns and trying to prevent circumvention of the regulations which were meant to ensure trade remained in the hands of the urban burghers. The extension of the postal network to Finland during Brahe's first period of office was an important and symbolic link, though the abominable quality of the roads meant that direct sea links to the capital were swifter and more reliable routes of communication for the trading communities along the Ostrobothnian coast.

Per Brahe was also one of the moving forces behind the creation of a university, or academy, in Turku in 1640. This, and the establishment in the same town of a high court for Finland in 1623 undoubtedly strengthened the distinctive identity of Finland Proper. But in other respects, however, Finland Proper ceased to be part of the heartland of the realm, as it had been in medieval times. Turku remained a small provincial town; Stockholm, founded around the same time, grew and became the centre of patronage and influence. In addition to the acquisition of new territories on the southern shores of the Baltic, the Swedish kingdom proper also expanded, to embrace the island of Gotland, the provinces of Jämtland and Härjedalen on the Norwegian frontier and Halland on the west coast after 1645, the west-coast province of Bohus and the rich southern farmlands of Scania and Blekinge after 1660. All this meant that Finland Proper, a region that had been a crucial strategic and fiscal asset in the politics of the Kalmar union period, became not only more marginal to the heartland of the realm, but also now had its own outer periphery to the east. The sons of the nobility and clergy of Finland Proper were in general less than enthusiastic about starting their career in the eastern wilderness, preferring to hang about nearer the centre of the realm in hopes of preferment. The growth of a centralised administrative system inevitably reinforced the importance of Swedish as the language of communication (although Latin long remained the chief language of education and of culture). An anonymous survey of the kingdom of Sweden, published in London in 1632, is clearly speaking about Finnish speakers when it cites the poor pronunciation of Latin words like *gratus* (*ratus*), *Dominus* (*tominus*) and *spes* (*pes*) as sufficient reason 'why the Nobles, Merchants, and others of ability, send their youth to be instructed in the Swedish tongue, by which meanes they are afterwards fitted for the learning of any other', a revealing indication that the swedification of the higher social orders was already under way in Finland. The government for its part was aware of the need to appoint appropriately qualified men to offices requiring a knowledge of Finnish, but the petitions of peasants complaining that bailiffs or judges were unable to understand them and had little or no knowledge of local customs or circumstances – and over half of the district judges appointed in Finland between 1653 and 1680 were of Swedish or foreign origin – tell a different story.

The priesthood constituted a second intermediary layer between the common people and royal authority, and was recruited mostly from native-born men. Many clergymen were sons of well-established clerical families in south-western Finland, though the church here also attracted bright boys from the ranks of the peasantry. In eastern Finland, the clergy was largely recruited from the clerical and burgher families of Viipuri, which had become Finland's second bishopric in 1554. Some parishes, especially in the vicinity of Turku, offered a comfortable living, but most offered at best a meagre livelihood, which the vicar often had to supplement. A new incumbent might find himself obliged to maintain the family of his predecessor as a condition of entry into the living; marriage to the widow or an eligible daughter was a not uncommon outcome. Many priests sought to ensure security by having their son trained up for the priesthood in order to succeed the father, and a number of livings in western Finland and Ostrobothnia were occupied by several generations of the same family.

The leaders of the Reformed church set high standards of worship and discipline, and frequently expressed their frustration and disappointment that their flock fell far short of these standards. Isak Rothovius, bishop of Turku between 1627 and 1652, strove mightily to enforce church discipline and strict adherence to the true Evangelical faith, and did much to improve the quality and training of the priesthood. The ability of the congregation to understand the fundamentals of the Lutheran faith was to be strengthened by constant repetition and learning by heart, and if necessary, physical chastisement. In his primer (*ABC-kiria*, 1543), the reformer Mikael Agricola urged readers young and old who could speak the Finnish language to learn the commands of God and reminded them in good Lutheran fashion that the Law might frighten the soul, but Christ gave it solace. The publication a good hundred years later under the auspices of Bishop Johan Gezelius the Elder (1664–90) of Finnish and Swedish editions of a combined reader and catechism, together with the measures laid down by Gezelius for teaching children to read and write, were slow, however, to bear fruit. Visitation records show disappointingly low levels of literacy, even in southwest Finland, and priests in charge of confirmation classes continued to rely on learning by heart rather than from the book. Slow, dogged persistence, aided by the stipulation of the 1686 Church Law that confirmation classes be held regularly at suitable locations around the parish, began to yield results, as parishes gradually got rid of their illiterate clerks and even began building special school rooms in which the clerk could teach the basics of reading and writing to the local children. The church was also in the forefront of the expansion of settlement northwards, into the terrain of the Sami people. In the uplands of the far north, as the consistory of Härnösand observed in 1686, the reformation had only recently begun to make inroads 'and the old worshippers of Satan in that place live on and hobble on both legs, serving Baal and God'. A report submitted to the frontier commissioner in 1748, however, suggests that not only had the Sami in the southern parish of Kuusamo embraced Christianity, but also the Finnish language. Four decades later, the local clergyman Elias Lagus noted that Sami was only spoken in the far north of the parish, alongside Finnish. The church made some effort to inculcate Christianity through the medium of Sami, but it was less than tolerant of Sami culture. The burn-beat cultivation methods employed by the Finnish settlers threatened the fragile ecosystem which sustained the local hunting economy; the Sami had either to adapt to the newcomers' own economy, or move away. By the time the tourists curious to know more about such an exotic people began to make their way northwards in the eighteenth century, much of Sami culture had been lost or destroyed.[1]

The Lutheran church had more mixed fortunes in its attempts to win over the Orthodox population of the new territories of Käkisalmi and Ingria acquired (but not incorporated into the realm) after the final peace with Muscovy was signed in 1617. In spite of a steady influx of settlers from Savo into the region and the flight of many of the local population, there remained a significant minority of Orthodox believers. Government policy towards these congregations wavered between the permissive and intolerant. When Johan Gezelius the Younger as superintendent of Narva attempted to pursue a more vigorous policy of conversion by targeting the Votes and Ingrians, who for reasons of linguistic affinity to Finnish were deemed easier to win over, he was ordered to curb his activities, which threatened to lead to uproar and possible Russian intervention. The government also refused to countenance the demands of the bishop of Viipuri, Petrus Laurbecchius (1696–1705) for a total prohibition of the Orthodox faith, on the grounds that this would contravene the peace treaties concluded with Muscovy.

Sweden emerged from the great wars that raged in central Europe in the first half of the seventeenth century in desperate need of recuperation and consolidation. The assertion of royal power and authority by Karl XI in the final decades of the century allowed the crown to recover some of its squandered resources and permitted an overhaul of the system of conscription, before Sweden was once again plunged into war. The Great Northern War was initiated by an anti-Swedish coalition led by the ambitious ruler of Muscovy, Peter I (1689–1725). The young and inexperienced king of Sweden, Karl XII (1697–1718) succeeded in scattering his enemies in a brilliant series of campaigns in 1700–01, but failed to end the war. Instead, his armies were drawn deep into Poland and the Ukraine, where defeat at the hands of the Russians at the battle of Poltava (1709) marked the turning-point in Sweden's fortunes. Karl XII retreated across the Turkish frontier and spent the next years trying to escape the clutches of Ottoman hospitality, as his remaining armies were driven back across the Baltic. Finland, which was afflicted by famine in the years 1695–97, with the estimated loss of over 100,000 lives, now found itself once more in the front line, having enjoyed over a century of virtual freedom from the incursions of Russian troops. Viipuri fell to the Russians in 1710, the whole of southern Finland was conquered three years later, and Ostrobothnia was evacuated by the Swedes in 1714. Losses in the war were heavy: an estimated 50,000 men perished of disease or wounds, many thousands more were taken away into captivity, or fled to Sweden.

The peace signed in 1721 brought to an abrupt end the century of Swedish dominance of the eastern Baltic, and exposed Finland to the threat of renewed attacks and occupation from a powerful eastern neighbour. Now styling himself emperor of all the Russias, Peter had made arrangements for the administration of the territories of Viipuri, in addition to Käkisalmi, Ingria, and the Baltic provinces, even before Sweden ceded them. The great loss of life and the trauma of occupation (even though it is generally acknowledged that the folk memory of the 'great wrath' has exaggerated the misdeeds of the Russians) placed a question mark against some of the illusions of greatness, and against the ability or even willingness of the government in Stockholm to protect Finland. In 1709, the Swedish-born Israel Nesselius, professor of rhetoric at the university in Turku, had cast doubts upon the loyalty of the Finns, who, in his opinion, should have long since been forced to learn Swedish. Within two years of the restoration of peace, Finnish peasant representatives were calling for an impartial commission of enquiry into the after-effects of the war, and were not afraid to drop the heavy hint that, crippled with taxation and other impositions, the people might well be tempted to go over to the enemy. Aware of the necessity of winning back the loyalty and confidence of the local population, the two commissions appointed, for western and eastern Finland, proceeded with caution and many assurances of goodwill. Assessing the scale of damage and granting relief from taxation occupied most of their time, though they also made recommendations for improving the economy, such as the construction of canals and manufactories.

Finland had to endure Russian occupation once more in 1742–43, this time as a consequence of the ill-prepared attack launched by the war party, known as the Hats, which dominated the Swedish government. The war enabled Peter the Great's daughter, Elizabeth, to seize power in St Petersburg and have herself proclaimed empress. The successful Russian counter-attack against Finland in the summer of 1742 was preceded by a manifesto, printed in Finnish and Swedish versions, offering protection to all inhabitants of Finland who did nothing to assist the Swedish forces but sought to live 'in neighbourly amity and peace with us'. The manifesto also intimated that the Duchy of Finland might wish to separate from Sweden and become an independent state, which Russia would be willing to assist militarily. Although rumours of Finnish discontent with Swedish rule had been picked up and conveyed to St Petersburg by the Russian ambassador to Stockholm, there is no conclusive evidence to suggest that the idea of Finnish independence was anything more than a ploy designed to further the Russian policy of interfering in the affairs of its neighbour. The occupation of Finland, for the second time within a generation, did however expose signs of dissatisfaction with the government in Stockholm. A letter from a group of local landowners in the Häme parish of Sysmä, addressed to the commander of the Russian forces in southern Finland, welcomed the protection extended by Elizabeth in a war that the writers claimed had not been sought by a single inhabitant of Finland. The meeting of the estates of southern Finland which convened in Turku at the request of the Russians in autumn 1742 voted unanimously for the duke of Holstein, Karl Peter Ulrik, to be declared king but were frustrated in their attempts to persuade the empress to agree to this.[2]

The lamentable performance of the army, for which the Hats were roundly blamed, the subsequent occupation of Finland and the loss to Russia of further territory on the eastern frontier at the peace concluded in Turku in 1743 added weight to demands for improved defences and better treatment for the inhabitants of Finland. The *riksdag* of 1746–47 approved the construction of new fortifications in Finland. The fortress of Sveaborg, built on a series of islands guarding the harbour of Helsinki, was a costly if impressive monument to its chief architect, Augustin Ehrensvärd. Reputedly impregnable, it was ignominiously surrendered to the Russians in 1808, bombarded by the Anglo-French fleet in 1855, was briefly held by revolutionary Russian mutineers in 1906, and is now a pleasant tourist attraction. Arguably the more effective defence measure was the building of an oared flotilla which was able to mount a vigorous challenge to Russian dominance of the shallow waters of the skerries along the southern coast of Finland. Pressure from Finnish representatives in the *riksdag* of 1746–47 also led to the setting up of a deputation for Finland, on which Finnish-born members were in the majority. The report submitted by the deputation, which was highly critical of the policies of the government and of past neglect, proposed measures to assure the inhabitants of Finland that they would in future be better protected and their concerns heard. It endorsed earlier demands that officials having dealings with the common people in Finland should be able to do so without having to resort to an interpreter, and it also wanted the majority of higher offices to be held by Finnish-born men. Although individual Finnish-born men did rise to pre-eminence at court, in government, and in the church, they were in comparison with their Swedish-born counterparts far less in evidence amongst the top post-holders in Sweden. Often lacking clout or connection to secure such jobs, they also faced competition on their home turf from Swedes or foreigners eager to make their mark. Just over half of the county governors appointed in Finland between 1721 and 1808 were of Finnish origin. Those hailing from Sweden predominated in the more favoured postings, whilst the less popular governorships in the north and east tended to be occupied by men from Finland. Three-quarters of the bishops and professors of the university in Turku were of Finnish origin, but Swedes dominated the top jobs in the high court in Turku and the Finnish army. Many of those from outside who took up employment in Finland stayed and entered the ranks of the Finnish social elite, further adding to the pool of aspirants for a career in the courts, army, or administration.

The estates had seized the opportunity of a contested succession to the childless Karl XII to push through a new constitution in 1719, with additional amendments in 1720. This ensured that the king could rule only with the council's consent and advice, and gave the *riksdag* powers to draft legislation, raise taxes, and propose members for the council. The *riksdag* was to meet regularly, and its hundred-strong secret committee, drawn from the estates of nobility, clergy, and burghers, was given powers to scrutinise all important affairs of the realm. Although the *riksdag* ordinance of 1723 sought to lay down the procedures for nomination of representatives, there was little clear definition of who had the right to vote. It has been estimated, however, that roughly a third of all households in Finland by the middle of the eighteenth century had some right to representation in the *riksdag*. Although numerically the peasants made up the largest part of this electorate, it was the nobility, and particularly the office-holders, who dominated the affairs of the realm. The constitutional settlement, in defining the composition and functions of each estate and of the administration, strengthened the corporatist and bureaucratic foundations of the Swedish state, a legacy which accompanied the Finnish provinces ultimately transferred to Russian overlordship in 1809.

This efflorescence of parliamentarianism during the so-called 'Age of Liberty' (1720–72) was in many ways blighted by factional intrigue and squabbling, but it did open up an arena for public debate, on a scale hitherto unknown. Distance and the costs of staying in the capital were a cause of worry for the Finnish delegates, and the Finnish nobility did attempt without success to persuade the 1726–27 *riksdag* to allow them to meet separately, in the presence of a royal representative. Finland, with far fewer bishoprics, towns, and electoral districts for the peasantry, was also seriously under-represented in comparison with the Swedish mainland; revealingly, fewer than 15 per cent of the non-noble members of the secret committee were from Finland. Nevertheless, issues of concern to the inhabitants of what was now known as *rikets förmur*, the outer bailey of the realm, were regularly raised, and special attention was paid to the economic development of Finland. But on the whole, it was particularist concerns, rather than anything that might be deemed a 'national' interest, that determined the attitudes and shaped the demands of the representatives sent to the *riksdag*. Thus, the strongly protectionist trade policies and commitment to defence spending of the ruling Hat party won the support of the burghers of Helsinki, which was developed as a military base, and the merchants of Turku, who enjoyed trading privileges, whilst the lesser traders and artisans, and the towns of Ostrobothnia which were denied direct access to international trade, were inclined to support the Caps, with their policy of retrenchment and reform.

The *riksdag* of 1765–66 was dominated by the Caps, who swept to victory in the three non-noble estates after another lacklustre performance by the Swedish army, this time against Prussia, had left the country in a state of financial crisis. The turmoil and party strife of this parliamentary session, which threatened once more to erupt in 1771, was skilfully used by the new ruler Gustav III (1771–92) to proclaim the realm in danger and to stage a bloodless coup in 1772. The restoration of royal power was initially welcomed on all sides by a populace weary of corruption that had weakened the integrity of the realm, of ineffective foreign policies that had undermined the glories of Sweden's past greatness, and of governments that seemed incapable of resolving the serious financial and economic problems of the country. By the 1780s, however, discontent was beginning to simmer in the ranks of the nobility, including many of the Finnish army officers who had given their backing to the coup.

In a brief essay attempting to summarise the balance-sheet of the Finnish contribution to the realm during the early modern period,

the economic historian Sven-Erik Åström concluded that economically, and to some extent politically as well, Finland's relationship to
the kingdom as a whole resembled that of a colony. Although it did
derive some benefit after 1720 from investment in fortifications and
institutions and was able to retain taxes levied for the administration and defence of the land, Finland paid a high price in terms of
human and material resources in the drive for greatness in the
seventeenth century. It is interesting to note that it was during the
eighteenth century, when Finland occupied the attention of government far more than it had done in the previous century, that doubts
about the effectiveness and value of Swedish rule began to surface,
though this can also be seen as part of an intense national re-evaluation of Sweden's status and of the relationship of state and subject
that had serious political as well as social repercussions in Sweden
proper. As we shall see, there was certainly a heightened awareness
of Finland as something distinct and separate, which could trans-
cend local or particularist concerns; whether the disparate regions or
administrative divisions that remained under Swedish rule after
1743 (when for the first time, a serious effort was made to delineate
and guard the frontier with Russia) could cohere into something
resembling a national entity is quite another matter.

As the long centuries of Swedish rule neared an end, the great
majority of the population of this eastern half of the kingdom
existed much as had their ancestors, finding their sustenance from
the land, the forests, and waters. Judging from scattered written
references, Finland was also badly affected by the 'little Ice Age'
that set in during the seventeenth century. Long, cold winters,
spring floods, and sudden night frosts in August meant poor harvests and the threat of famine. The worst of all these natural
disasters occurred at the end of the seventeenth century. The population of Finland was reduced by a quarter during the hunger years
of 1696–97. As usually happens in such natural disasters, death
visited more frequently those least able to fend for themselves –
infants and children, the elderly, and sick. In purely economic
terms, recovery was surprisingly swift. Within two years, records
show that a mere 8 per cent of the farmsteads remained abandoned;
many had been taken over by a relative following the death of
the principal occupant. But farming on the margins, with poor

equipment and inadequate enrichment of the soil, in addition to the vagaries of the climate, remained at the best of times a hazardous venture. A normal harvest would yield enough grain to provide basic nourishment, with fish and the produce of the forest supplementing the monotonous diet of gruel and bread; but, as the economic historian Eino Jutikkala drily notes, the Finnish farmer would have to stint on his bread if he fancied ale or even small beer, and storing grain against the bad times was on most farms simply out of the question.

The meagreness of the Finnish diet was frequently commented on by travellers. The French dramatist Jean Regnard, who travelled through northern Finland in the 1690s, observed that the further inland one went, the more extreme the poverty; grain was virtually unknown, and bread was made from ground fish bones and bark. His compatriot Bernardin de St-Pierre also noted that bread was commonly made from the inner bark of the silver birch mixed with the roots of marshland vegetation, 'un aliment détestable qui empoissonne beaucoup de ces malheureux'. Another French visitor was amazed at how the Finns could sustain their strenuous labour on a few dried fish and a bowl of sour milk, and his party surprised a group of peasants in northern Finland by drinking wine, which the locals mistook for lamb's blood.

Much of the work was back-breaking and yielded little reward. The taking into cultivation of new land to cope with the pressures of a rising population in the eighteenth century involved clearing brushwood, cutting down trees and grubbing up the stumps, raising and moving countless rocks and boulders, digging drainage ditches, and preparing the land, all for yields that were at best barely sufficient to feed the family and pay the tax man. Seasonal occupations, such as seal hunting, were often as arduous and ill-rewarded. Reporting to the Swedish Royal Academy in 1757, for example, Johan David Cneiff calculated that the Ostrobothnian seal hunter's average earnings from his three months of dangerous work might add up to no more than sixty-six copper riksdollars, which was probably less than the costs of outfitting his expedition. In other words, unless the catch was good, there was no profit to be had from the trip. All the eight men took with them on their three-month trip on the ice were six enormous sourdough rye loaves,

Plate 6 Preparing birch-bark bread. Bread made partially, or in the worst times wholly, of the inner bark of the silver birch was regularly eaten in large areas of eastern and northern Finland into modern times. So common was its consumption that it was even suggested that a sample be sent to the Great Exhibition of 1851 as a typical product of Finland. Collecting the bark was, however, a complicated and a seasonal process, which meant that it could not easily be produced as an emergency substitute in times of famine. Medical opinion tended to regard the bread, known in Finnish as *pettuleipä*, as unwholesome and lacking in nutritional value. There were attempts in the famine years of the 1830s and 1867–68 to persuade the rural population to make bread from lichen, which country folk for their part deemed poisonous. Research conducted on behalf of the Finnish defence forces in the 1970s confirmed the peasants' suspicions, concluding that it was difficult to extract toxic substances from lichen, whereas birch-bark was both non-toxic and nutritious. The elderly couple photographed in the north-eastern parish of Taivalkoski would probably have been accustomed to grinding the bark for bread. This picture was taken in 1917, when acute grain shortages necessitated resorting to this survival technique in large areas of the country.

Plate 7 Tar-boats on the Oulu river. Tar was Finland's main export commodity from the mid-seventeenth century until it was overtaken by sawn timber in the nineteenth century. Preparing and cutting the trees, boiling off the tar in specially made pits, putting it into barrels, and transporting it down the rivers to the nearest port provided much-needed work, and was a useful source of income. By the eighteenth century, most of the tar trade was handled by the Ostrobothnian ports, though they were forbidden by law to trade directly with foreign merchants. This ban on trade was finally overturned in 1766, after much vigorous campaigning in the *Riksdag* and elsewhere by the merchants of the Ostrobothnian towns and their supporters. The Oulu river, where this picture of tar-boats and their rowers resting on their long and arduous journey was taken, was one of the principal routes from the hinterland.

baked iron-hard and wrapped in straw to stop them going mouldy. They drank brackish sea water and supplemented their diet with what they could catch.

The harsh meagreness of a subsistence economy was the constant reality for the great majority of the population; yet a contemporary survey of the Finnish economy in 1738–41 claimed that there was no part of the country in which grain was not sold in normal times. In most districts, however, the amounts were very small; the only substantial trade in grain was the surplus from the burn-beat lands of Savo, carted each autumn to the west coast by the farmers and their small, hardy horses. In times of bad harvest, Finland depended on imports of grain, mostly from Estonia and Livonia. A poor harvest often stimulated trade in fish, hides, skins, and other animal products, for the simple reason that the peasant had to pay his taxes. It has been calculated that three-quarters of the income earned by the farmers of Ostrobothnia in the 1690s from the sale of tar, timber, butter, train oil, and fish went to satisfy the tax-collector, and most of the rest was spent on buying salt. These calculations are however based on officially recorded sales, and it is highly likely that as much again was earned through illegal trade.

The crown's efforts to restrict trading rights to the towns were easy to circumvent. In spite of the protests of town burghers, peasant traders continued to ply their wares in their own boats and to do good business with Karelian and Russian merchants who bought up their furs, dried fish, and wooden utensils. Most of this trade was local or regional; but during the course of the seventeenth century, Finland's forests became a valuable resource whose products – tar and timber – were vital commodities in the expansion of global maritime trade. Most of the Swedish tar sold on the Dutch and English markets came from the hinterland of Ostrobothnia and the Saimaa-Päijänne lake system, where peasants prepared and cut the pines and extracted the tar, which was sent in barrels down the rivers and watercourses to the coast. Falling prices for pitch and tar during the first half of the eighteenth century effectively ended the export of these commodities from the southern Finnish towns, with their poor communications with the hinterland. They turned instead to the export of sawn timber, aided by the introduction of the new multiple-bladed saws that were installed in the water-driven sawmills built on or near the rapids and falls of watercourses on both sides of the post-1721 frontier. Although the commercial policy of the Russian government was as restrictive as that of Sweden, it was significantly easier to set up and operate a sawmill across the new frontier. There were no restrictions on the use of the new Dutch multi-bladed saws, for example, whereas their use was officially prohibited in Sweden until 1739. The Swedish navigation acts, which sought to confine exports to native bottoms, hampered the development of trade in sawn timber from the southern Finnish ports, and there was significant movement of timber across the frontier to the ports of Viipuri and (after 1743) Hamina. There was also a flourishing illicit trade in salt and tobacco, obtained more cheaply on the Russian side. So widespread was the evasion of the regulations that the exasperated burghers of Loviisa, founded in compensation for the loss of Hamina at the peace of 1743, complained frequently of widespread collusion between the peasantry, crown officials, and the new subjects of the Russian tsar.

Although the number of Finnish towns had grown since the middle ages, they were few in number compared to the total for the realm as a whole, and were for the most part tiny coastal settlements, little more than villages. The largest town in Finland, Turku, had barely more than six thousand inhabitants in the mid-eighteenth century, and the urban population as a whole totalled no more than twenty thousand, of which a mere 2,774 were merchants, and 4,031 artisans. The burghers of these towns struggled in vain to combat the violation of the restrictions that were meant to channel trade into their hands, and indeed, many of the town merchants connived at evading these regulations. There were pitifully few successful manufactures in the towns – most of the industry established in Finland was in the form of rural forges and mills – and the small garrisons established in the eighteenth century in towns such as Helsinki and Loviisa contributed little to the overall urban economy. Yet the coastal towns of Finland did prove remarkably resilient and ready to seize any chances that came their way. Even before the final freeing of trade after 1766, the Ostrobothnian towns had developed a sizeable shipbuilding industry. Between 1765 and 1804, over three hundred large seagoing vessels were built in the yards of Oulu, Kokkola, Pietarsaari, and Vaasa, far more than in any other region of the realm. The labour force was largely recruited from the surrounding countryside, and the work was carried out during the winter months, allowing the peasant shipwrights to return to their farms for the haymaking. This seasonal work-force was cheap to employ, and this gave the Ostrobothnian yards a competitive edge. In much the same way, small combines of peasant-traders all along the coast were able to build small boats, crew them for a pittance, and run profitable trips supplying the capital with fish, butter, and other items made, gleaned, or garnered on the eastern shores of the kingdom. As a contemporary French observer was quick to note soon after the final transfer of Finland from Sweden to the Russian empire in 1809, the acquisition of so much maritime expertise, and especially a sizeable merchant marine, was a valuable asset for a state with few such resources.

Ready access to the major markets of the eastern Baltic not only enabled the coastal regions to sell their firewood, butter, fish, hides, and even specialist products such as wooden bowls or lace, but also drew them into the global expansion of trade. By the end of the eighteenth century, Finnish-owned vessels were actively involved in the Mediterranean carrying trade, and merchants in the small coastal towns anxiously followed the fluctuations of current prices and premiums. Trade brought a modicum of prosperity, allowing the townspeople to rebuild their churches and erect solid town halls in addition to adorning their own houses. They also bought books, mostly prayer books and religious tracts, although treatises on political economy, natural law, and medicine, dictionaries, and even works of fiction and poetry also crop up in the inventories of their possessions. Clergymen and the leading citizens of the town often had sizeable libraries: that of Anders Gottlieb Herkepaeus, burgomaster of the tiny town of Naantali and a member of a long-established leading Finnish family in the region, who died in 1787, contained works in German, French, Dutch, English, and Swedish. Even the very poor might own a hymnal or prayer book.

Scattered throughout the country, and more numerous in the south and south-west than in the deep hinterland, were the persons of quality *(säätyläiset, ståndspersoner)*, some fifteen thousand in total (of whom fewer than two thousand were members of noble families) by the end of the eighteenth century. These were the *herrat*, or gentry, who administered, collected taxes, dispensed justice, staffed the officer ranks of the Finnish regiments, measured the land, taught the young, and ministered to the spiritual needs of the populace. Service to the crown was what distinguished and defined a gentleman. A title was a social necessity, an indication of status which has prevailed in Finnish society to the present day. Although holding office did not exclude the office-holder from

Plate 8 Rank and title: Hietaniemi cemetery, Helsinki. Rank and title, often acquired by dint of much personal effort, have had and continue to have great resonance in Finnish society. The highest level of achievement is the coveted title of 'councillor' (*neuvos, råd*), initially confined to those who distinguished themselves in administration, but over time granted to industrialists, entrepreneurs, and farmers. University education also confers status, either in the level of degree awarded (usually master or above) or in the particular qualification conferred (for example, 'ekonomi'). As the Finnish sociologist Veli Verkko observed in 1947, title and its strong associations with a society of rank dominated by nobility is still eagerly sought and coveted in the republic of Finland. Cemeteries and graveyards in Finland, as in other countries, offer a wealth of visual and semiotic material for genealogist and historian alike. Title is by no means confined to the successful, as in this illustration: there are farmers, bakers, traders, and shopkeepers, even the widow of a switchman, to be found immortalised on their headstones.

pursuing other profitable activities – farming, for the most part, though a number also engaged in trade – office was deemed more precious than any other livelihood. Over four-fifths of the persons of quality in eighteenth-century Finland held some form of office, a proportion that declined gradually to three-fifths by 1870.

Contemporary critics worried about the seeming profusion of offices, and urged the gentry to return to living on and farming the land, where their more affluent lifestyle would serve to support traders, artisans, and manufacturers. But in fact, the number of posts in state service failed by a considerable margin to keep pace with the growth in the population, which more than doubled between 1749 and the end of the century. This unprecedented increase in population (which occurred throughout the kingdom, though it was higher in the Finnish than the Swedish half) was famously attributed to 'peace, potatoes and vaccination'. Demographers have been more circumspect in their judgements, though there can be little doubt that much of the growth can be ascribed to the process of recovery from the years of famine, plague, and the ravages of war at the beginning of the century. Disturbed by the results of the first national census of 1749, the government sought in subsequent years to improve the nation's health by instituting a basic medical service, encouraging vaccination, and decreeing that each parish should have its own midwife. Between the intent and the execution there was, inevitably, a wide gap, and it is unlikely that the exhortations and decrees of officialdom had more than a marginal effect. As for potatoes, their cultivation and consumption was strictly limited well into the nineteenth century in most parts of the country; barley, oats and above all, rye, provided the basic sustenance for all but the few who could afford a more varied diet.

Population growth was uneven, though far more rapid in the countryside than in the towns, and greater in the hinterland than the coastal regions. Not unnaturally, it put great pressure on limited land resources. Anxious to promote improvements in agriculture that would increase the national wealth, the government authorised land enclosure in 1757, a process that was not finally completed until the 1950s. The crown also relaxed regulations on the partition of farms from 1747, and endeavoured from 1775 to create new farms from surpluses created during the process of enclosure. In this it was far less successful than the activities of individuals whose tireless efforts created small leasehold farms, or crofts (*torpat*). From a few thousand in mid-century, the numbers of crofts multiplied to over twenty thousand by the beginning of the nineteenth century, and continued growing until the 1860s, after which time the gradual adaptation of the peasant household to modern farming techniques and to the market prompted a movement to maximise income from leased land.

One of the more far-reaching changes of the last decades of Swedish rule was incorporated in Gustav III's imposed constitution of 1789, the act of union and assurance. This granted owners of heritable land the same full rights of ownership as those of noble, or *frälse* land, and gave peasants on crown land rights of inheritance. Security of tenure had come under threat in earlier decades, especially after the turmoil of war, when many farms had been abandoned, and farmers seem to have taken the law of 1789 as a signal to buy out their farms from the crown. The difference between the high levels of freehold heritable land holdings by the beginning of the nineteenth century in the western half of Finland – where the great majority of manorial estates were also to be found – and eastern Finland, where burn-beat cultivation was still prevalent, and the process of land enclosure had hardly begun, is striking, however, and yet another indication of the contrast between the coastal plains and the deep, forested hinterland.

In those parts of the country where population pressures resulted in a big increase in the numbers of the landless – eastern Finland and southern Ostrobothnia – there was also a high incidence of homicide, a phenomenon that has attracted the attention of historians in recent decades. In both instances, weak local authority and a low conviction rate (the law required the concurrent testimony of two competent eyewitnesses or a confession by the accused, neither of which was easy to obtain) were contributory factors, as was the widespread and excessive consumption of alcohol at social gatherings, such as weddings in Ostrobothnia, and a degree of frontier lawlessness in areas adjacent to Russia. Likewise, the murder weapon was invariably what lay to hand, a large stone or piece of wood.[3] Growing discrepancies in wealth and status in Ostrobothnia, a region where the population almost trebled between 1749 and 1805, were without doubt a cause of tension that could lead to violence. Violence also flourished where social restraints were weak and the powers of law enforcement were defective, and where the emergence of a proto-capitalist exchange economy created a different system of values, stressing enterprise and demanding of the individual evidence of ability or strength. Impoverished, isolated, and neglected ('the Swedish Siberia' for polite society in Stockholm), the frontier regions of northern Savo and northern Karelia suffered from the depredations of war and the activities of outlaws and bandits as well as the propensity of the frontiersmen themselves to fall into internecine feuding whenever war broke out. Here, demographic and economic pressures contributed to tensions within the extended family unit, and clearly account for a significant number of the inter-family homicides, including the startlingly high proportion of fratricides.

The response of the state to the social dislocation caused by war and disease in the early decades of the eighteenth century, and as a result of rapid population growth from the 1740s, was usually to restrict and control, although a more enlightened approach began to make itself felt from the 1760s. One of the more intractable problems was the excessive production and consumption of distilled alcohol (*viina*). Attempts to curb production, and thereby prevent wasteful consumption of precious grain stocks as well as reduce social disorder, culminated in the temporary banning of distillation and sale of alcohol in 1756, at a time of acute grain shortage. The estate of peasants, which had most to lose from the ban on an activity which was often very profitable for the farmer, consented reluctantly and was able to insist on a ban on imports of luxury goods such as tea and coffee, consumed largely by persons of quality. The ban on distillation was ended in 1760, but the problem remained, and was not solved either by Gustav III's efforts to impose a state monopoly via a network of crown-owned distilleries. The right to distil was strongly defended by the farmers, though they also wished to restrict that right to themselves. Alcohol produced by the farmer was a valuable commodity, and came to play an increasingly important role in the relationship between the farmer and his farmhands. In many areas, distilled liquor replaced beer. It was an essential ingredient in all celebrations from christenings to funerals. It also contributed to destitution and misery, as moralists and reformers pointed out. The efforts of the authorities to deal with the economic and social consequences of distillation during the eighteenth century prefigure the range of policies tried in more recent times: in like manner, many of the attitudes and habits associated with the consumption of strong drink in agrarian

Finland have survived to the present day. As the historian Heikki Ylikangas observes, 'Finnish drinking habits are, or rather have been, marked by the desire to get drunk as rapidly and completely as possible. The large numbers of those who die from excessive alcohol consumption or are victims of killings committed by someone who is drunk show that the concept of the Finnish way of drinking is not a mere myth.'

The fight against drink was to become a major theme in the Finnish nationalist drive to elevate and 'improve' the people. Improvement was also on the agenda in the latter half of the eighteenth century, though the motivation and underlying philosophy were somewhat different. The desired objective was the prosperity and contented well-being of the community as a whole. But could this be achieved without upsetting the established social order? On the whole, that question was rarely asked, and although reforms were undertaken that did indirectly loosen the ties, other measures were put in place that were specifically meant to tighten them – for example, legislation governing the relationship of master and servant or controlling the supply and direction of labour. Those who did venture to voice radical opinions could find themselves in trouble. The humble chaplain from Ostrobothnia, Anders Chydenius, for example, was hauled before the secret committee of the *riksdag* in 1766 as a result of the outspoken criticisms expressed in his pamphlets, and he found himself excluded from the estate of clergy to which he had been elected. Chydenius has been hailed as an early exponent of economic liberalism, but his arguments were mainly inspired by a desire to overthrow the restrictions on trade that hampered the commercial development of the Ostrobothnian port towns, and were fuelled by a deep suspicion of the luxury and wastefulness of the privileged mercantile elite whose interests were upheld by these very restrictions. Although he wrote with much compassion about the plight of farm servants, and was an ardent supporter of press freedom, Chydenius was a social moralist rather than a political liberal.

Chydenius was by no means the only Finn who contributed to the debates that so enlivened Swedish public life during the Age of Liberty. The rights of the non-noble members of society, including the right to be considered for the higher offices of state, jealously guarded by the nobility, were advocated by the Finnish clergyman Peter Forsskål in his anonymous 1759 pamphlet *Tankar om borgerliga friheten* (which in modern translation might be read as *Thoughts on Civil Liberties*) and in the memorial on civil rights presented to the *riksdag* of 1770 by Alexander Kepplerus, the burgomaster of the impoverished new town of Loviisa on the Russian frontier.

Recent research has studied the networks linking political activists, and has drawn attention in particular to the formative role of schools and the university. Peripheral and poor Finland may have been, with just over twenty secondary schools, compared to over five times as many in Sweden, but its contribution to what might be termed the Swedish Enlightenment was an important one. The list would include the historians Johan Arckenholtz (1695–1777), who was imprisoned in 1741 for his part in opposing the policy of waging a revenge war on Russia, and who, twenty-five years later, advised Chydenius in the composition of his pamphlet on press freedom; Henrik Gabriel Porthan (1739–1804), whose contribution to the creation of a Finnish identity was seminal; and a clutch of natural scientists, of whom Pehr Kalm (1716–79) and Pehr Gadd (1727–97) were outstanding examples, who inspired and led a rich outpouring of research at the university in Turku.

The university ceased its activities when most of its staff and students fled before the Russian occupation in 1714, and reopened its doors in 1722. It drew its students from all parts of Finland (though more from the western than the eastern half), as well as a small number from Sweden, mostly from the region of Småland. A significant proportion of the student body (which averaged between 180 and 200 throughout the period 1640–1808) were sons of the clergy, though farmers' sons began to take the places of the offspring of the nobility during the course of the eighteenth century, and made up between a quarter and a third of the Småland contingent. Most ended up as clergymen, though there is a noticeable diversification in the careers subsequently pursued by the graduates of the university from the 1760s.

The university in Turku was not only a training-ground for the Lutheran clergy and civil servants who ran the affairs of the kingdom of Sweden; it also became a meeting-ground for ideas and

Plate 9 The grammar school in Porvoo. After the loss of Viipuri to the Russians in 1721, the cathedral chapter and grammar school were moved to the small town of Porvoo, some fifty kilometres to the north-east of Helsinki. It was the only *gymnasium* in Finland (there were eleven in Sweden, which was also substantially better endowed with schools than the eastern half of the kingdom). This three-storey building, erected between 1753 and 1760, provided a classical education for the next century, and was also the setting of the opening and concluding sessions of the diet convened in 1809 by Alexander I.

sentiments, an intellectual centre which generated new notions of patriotism and identity. To a very large extent, this patriotism was fired by an enthusiasm for knowledge and founded upon the eudæmonic principles of the age, which believed that the happiness of the nation could be ensured through improving the people's well-being. Thus, of the Chydenius brothers who enrolled at the university in the 1740s, the eldest, Samuel, contributed to the discussion on ways to improve the navigability of the inland waterways and how to strengthen Finland's frontier defences; the youngest, Jacob, wrote on trade in Ostrobothnia and on the town of Kokkola; whilst Anders wrote his graduation dissertation on the birch-bark canoes of the natives of North America (and according to local legend, later attempted unsuccessfully to adapt their construction to Finnish waters). All three were deeply influenced by the new currents of thought, inspired by the great botanist Carl Linnaeus and disseminated by his disciples, men like Johan Browallius and Karl Fredrik Mennander, who directed studies in the natural sciences in Turku in the 1740s, and Pehr Kalm, appointed the first professor of economics at the university in 1747. In order to make their findings more accessible, these men encouraged their students (whose dissertations were in fact often written by the professors themselves) to publish in Swedish, rather than Latin, and to investigate the wonders of the natural world in order to bring benefit and happiness to mankind. In the poem of greeting which prefaced his lectures on mineralogy of 1731, Herman Didrich Spöring urged the students to search for precious metals in Finland's hills, the discovery and extraction of which would lead to a golden age for Finland. The underlying message of this poem, as indeed of other endeavours to promote the Finnish economy, is that increased prosperity would strengthen loyalty to the crown.

At one level, then, the patriotism that emerged out of the university of Turku was basically an awareness and love of one's own defined region, and an interest in promoting its prosperity and thereby the well-being of the kingdom as a whole. Towards the end of the century, there also developed an interest in the people themselves, their customs, history, and culture, inspired by the growing enthusiasm for rescuing, refurbishing, and, in some instances, inventing the past of the ancient and hitherto neglected peoples of Europe. A tireless and lively correspondent, collector, and bibliophile, appointed professor of rhetoric at the university in Turku in 1777, Henrik Gabriel Porthan did much to bring these new currents to Finland. In his *De poesi fennica*, published in five volumes between 1766 and 1778, he laid the foundations for future collection of and research into Finnish folk poetry. Much was also achieved by Kristfrid Ganander, a contemporary and friend of Porthan, in spite of his reduced circumstances as curate of a remote country parish – a dictionary, an index of Finnish mythology, collections of riddles, sayings, stories, and poems, as well as handy tips on curing ailments of man and beast. Another country parson, Anders Lizelius, produced a short-lived newspaper in Finnish, designed essentially to convey useful knowledge to

Plate 10 Daniel Juslenius, an early Finnish patriot. *Aboa vetus et nova*, or 'Turku Old and New' was submitted in 1700 for public examination at the Royal Academy, or university, of Turku as part of the process of gaining a master's degree by the twenty-four year old Daniel Juslenius. Born at Mietoinen, a parish some thirty kilometres north of Turku, Juslenius went on to present his master's thesis, a 'defence of the Finns' (*Vindiciae Fennorum*) in 1703, and to become professor of Greek and Hebrew at the university when it reopened in 1722. *Aboa vetus et nova* was written within the established tradition of local histories, of which the *Oratio de encomio Aboæ* (1657) of Johannes Rauthelius was one of the earliest. It also drew upon the earlier historiographical tradition that had sought to reflect Sweden's present greatness in an equally glorious distant past. Characteristic of Juslenius' work is his positive image of and strong identification with the Finnish nation, which he is at pains to distinguish from the Swedish nation. He is convinced, for example, that 'our countrymen' of old possessed their own literature, but that it was destroyed as pagan by the Swedish victors. As a good Christian he cannot, of course, but welcome the release of 'our forefathers' from idolatry, but he is also careful to point out that no people is so primitive and barbarous as not to possess a god, and that 'our forefathers' also had their own religion, even if it is difficult to ascertain what it was due to lack of written sources. Juslenius ended his career as bishop of Skara in central Sweden, where this portrait was painted.

countrymen, but also following major events in the world such as the American War of Independence.

A pride in the Finnish contribution to the well-being of the realm, and a fierce determination to ensure that this was known to posterity was perhaps fuelled by resentment of disparaging comments made in smart circles about Finnish backwardness and barbarity. Unlike other distinctive regions such as the island of Gotland and Skåne, which only came under Swedish rule in the seventeenth century, the part of Finland that constituted the see of Turku had been an integral part of the kingdom that began to take shape on the central plains of Sweden and the shores of the two gulfs of the eastern Baltic from the eleventh century onwards. Loyalty was part of that historical continuity; and if the crown's inability to protect Finland from the ravages of occupation raised doubts and questions, that loyalty was not seriously challenged before the 1780s.

Gustav III's bloodless revolution of 1772 was in fact generally welcomed in Finland. The king relied heavily on the active support of a group of young Finnish army officers, who believed an end to party strife and a vigorous, Swedish-born monarch bearing an illustrious name would restore Sweden's fortunes. A country of scattered and widely divergent provinces such as Sweden could never be governed by a parliamentary system, argued one of these officers, Göran Magnus Sprengtporten, in a series of 'letters to a friend', published a year after the coup. As an ardent supporter of the restoration of royal power, and as a highly competent soldier, Sprengtporten was given charge of the newly formed Savo brigade on the eastern frontier. In this post, he was responsible for training his men in fighting tactics suited to the wooded and rocky terrain, and he also laid the foundations of the Finnish cadet school. Quick to take offence, ambitious, and with a deep sense of inferiority that provoked fits of jealous rage, Sprengtporten felt himself and his work to have been neglected by the king, and drifted away from royalism into the growing ranks of the opposition. In 1786, he entered Russian service, having in the previous months presented the Russian ambassadors to The Hague and Stockholm with a proposal for Finland's separation from Sweden, with Russian assistance. Sprengtporten clearly hoped and believed that his fellow-officers of the Finnish army and other influential people in Finland would support the idea of independence, though Henrik Gabriel Porthan's conclusion that, with the exception of a few madcap adventurers, he secured few adherents, is almost certainly correct.

What distinguished Sprengtporten from other army officers who grumbled about pay and conditions, mocked the king's penchant for lavish theatrical spectacles, or who made oppositional utterances in secret societies such as the Walhalla Order on the fortress of Sveaborg, was his determination to secure the separation of Finland from Sweden and his subsequent activities in Russian service to achieve that objective. He lived long enough to witness the realisation of his wish, and did indeed briefly hold the post of governor-general of Finland. Characterised as an embittered old man consumed by an irrational hatred of Sweden by Carl Erik Mannerheim, one of the key members of the Finnish delegation summoned to St Petersburg to meet Alexander I in 1808 and himself a former Anjala confederate, Sprengtporten was and remains a controversial figure, a self-seeking traitor to some, an early champion of Finnish independence for others. His aims and objectives have been interpreted by historians writing in times which bore rather uncomfortable similarities to Finland's situation in the late eighteenth century, and there are very strong undertones of the long-running feud between the Swedish-speaking Finns who proclaimed the 'western' and constitutionalist roots of their patriotism in contrast to what they held to be the propensity of the Finnish nationalists to look to the east for inspiration and protection.

There is little to support Carl Erik Mannerheim's belief that Sprengtporten was responsible in part for the Russian attack on Sweden in 1808 which brought about Finland's separation; his influence in imperial court circles was never as great as his ambition. His importance lies more in the fact that he gave a political dimension to the question of national identity by daring to advocate separation from Sweden. Hatred of Sweden and a personal animosity towards the king may well have driven Sprengtporten to consider the idea of an independent Finland, but his thoughts and principles were guided rather more by the interests of his class than an interest in Finland and its people, of the kind fostered in

academic circles in Turku. Although he was clearly aware of the
new notions of representation and sovereignty current in the world,
there is little evidence in his writings to show that he incorporated
them into his plans. He justified the notion of Finnish independence
not as an inalienable right of a sovereign people, but as a geopoli-
tical necessity, which would end strife and conflict between Sweden
and Russia. The realisation of that independence was, moreover,
contingent upon the active assistance of Russia. His proposed constitution for Finland drew upon the Dutch model in its federal
aspects, but was in all other respects a recreation of the *riksdag*,
with the congress functioning much as the secret committee.
Nowhere is there any mention of a sovereign people, and in fact,
Spengtporten's independent Finland would have been nothing more
than a semi-autonomous land under Russian protection, much as
envisaged in Tsarina Elizabeth's manifesto of 1742.

The final loss of great power status in 1721, and more concretely,
of the Baltic provinces and the Karelian frontier established as
long ago as 1323, had a serious and lasting effect on the relationship of the western and eastern halves of the Swedish kingdom. The
shift of power from the absolutist monarch to the estates at the
same time implied a move away from an 'imperial' to a more
narrowly national perspective. The various proposals made to
encourage Swedes to settle in Finland, and Finns in Sweden, and
the exhortations to Finnish peasants to at least have their children
educated in Swedish are symptomatic of a growing intolerance of
linguistic diversity. As the Swedish bishop Anders Rhyzelius
observed to his colleague Daniel Juslenius, after six hundred years
of being part of Sweden, the Finns surely had a duty to become
Swedish. Officialdom did show itself to be responsive to the
demands of the peasantry for persons competent in Finnish to deal
with their affairs and for translations to be made of important
documents, and no measures of swedification were ever instituted
(as they were in areas taken from Denmark in the mid-seventeenth
century); but there are indications that the language spoken by
the majority in Finland was held in low esteem. Porthan, though
intensely loyal to Sweden and in no way desiring to challenge the
use of Swedish as the language of state and of polite society, felt
quite strongly that Finnish had been unjustly neglected. This point

was stated even more bluntly, and in Finnish, at the presentation in 1767 of a dissertation on the relationship between Finnish and Hebrew (a seventeenth-century notion that persisted, even surfacing in the introduction to *De poesi fennica*). Amongst the reasons for the undeveloped state of the Finnish language, it was claimed, was the fact that so few members of the higher orders, 'hold this language in the esteem that the honour of the people demands'. Even the Swedish spoken in Finland was considered uncouth. Sprengtporten remembered with evident bitterness the teasing he endured as a boy on account of his accent and provincial manners at the cadet school in Stockholm, and Porthan complained in 1798 that the gentry in Finland preferred to hire home tutors from Uppsala, even though equally competent ones – if not as conceited, fawning, or boastful – were be found in Turku. Porthan also noted the declining use of Finnish as the language of the home amongst the upper classes, and there are signs that those ascending the social ladder, even humble craftsmen, recognised the advantages of having Swedish – though there is also evidence of persons of quality who chose to farm in Finnish-speaking regions abandoning Swedish, and of Finnish-speaking peasants showing no desire to learn Swedish or adopt the customs of their Swedish-speaking neighbours, with whom they otherwise lived in perfect harmony.

Language and culture were distinctive, but not defining features of identity. Patriotism was grounded in a strong sense of place, and fuelled by an ardent wish to do one's best for that place and all its inhabitants, irrespective of status or language. That strong sense of attachment and duty was well expressed in the poem composed by Henrik Gabriel Porthan and Pehr Gadd, and published in the first number of the journal issued by the group of savants who came together in Turku in the 1770s to form the Aurora Society. The poem outlined the task of rescuing from the night of oblivion the treasures of Finland's past, but it also stressed the importance of working to develop its economy and future prosperity. Rescuing the treasures of Finland's past was to be the goal of the scholars of the university who followed Porthan, the so-called 'Turku romantics'; the promotion of the country's well-being was taken up by the Royal Finnish Economic

Society, established in 1797, and adapted in numerous projects which sought to tame wild nature and bring it into fruitful use. It is this combination of scholarly enquiry and utilitarian research, together with a respect for frugality and living within one's means, and for higher authority, that marks the Finnish patriotism of the late eighteenth and early nineteenth century.

3

From Stockholm to St Petersburg, 1780–1860

In the summer of 1788, having staged a frontier incident as a pretext for declaring war, Gustav III launched an attack on Russia. The success of this venture hinged upon the ability of the Swedish fleet to land a sizeable force within forty kilometres of St Petersburg. A major naval engagement off the island of Suursaari in the Gulf of Finland on 17 July, although indecisive, effectively nullified that part of the plan. Neither the main army nor the Savo brigade achieved their objective of capturing the fortress towns of Hamina and Savonlinna respectively; by early August, both had retired to defensive positions. The mood of discontent and opposition towards the king, which was rife within the officer corps, now burst to the surface, culminating in the formation of a confederation in the army camp at Anjala. This confederation was designed to force the king to make peace and to bring about a new constitutional order in Sweden. The statement issued on 13 August, signed by over a hundred officers headed by the commander of the Finnish army, Major-General Carl Gustav Armfelt, justified the extraordinary action of sending an emissary to the Empress Catherine to sound out the prospects for peace by claiming that Sweden appeared to be the aggressor, in contravention of the constitution which required the consent of the *riksdag* for an offensive war.

That emissary was Major Jan Anders Jägerhorn, who bore with him a note drafted in the village of Liikkala and signed by Armfelt and six other senior officers of the Finnish army. According to some versions of this note, its purpose was to bring to Her Imperial

Majesty's attention 'the heartfelt and general desire of the whole nation, and in particular the Finnish, for the preservation of a permanent peace and frontier harmony between both states, which now to our distress has been broken by the machinations of some unruly persons in the state, who under cover of the general good conceal selfish motives'. There is no mention in any of the extant versions of the note of any separate status for Finland. Armfelt later claimed that his intention in signing the note had been to extricate the king from a disastrous war. In a letter to the king dated 1 September 1788, Jägerhorn advanced the same line of argument, adding rather disingenuously that, as citizens, they were only doing what His Majesty as self-proclaimed first citizen amongst a free people saw as the highest honour, the promotion of the welfare of the common fatherland.

Jägerhorn was by all accounts the moving spirit behind the Liikkala note, and although several of the seven who signed it had doubts about the wisdom of entrusting it to a well-known intriguer and deviser of grandiose plans, Jägerhorn's connections in Russia and friendship with Sprengtporten seem to have won the waverers over. Flattered by the attention he received in Russia, where he had to interpret the text and meaning of the note in French, a language in which he expressed himself even more ambiguously than in his native Swedish, Jägerhorn seems to have taken it upon himself to negotiate. His six-point programme for the restoration of peace would have involved a return to the pre-1772 Swedish constitution, with self-government for Finland, to which Russia would graciously return the territory ceded by Sweden in 1743. The idea of an independent Finland under Russian protection was promoted by Sprengtporten, now in Russian service and called in to assist in the negotiations, rather than by Jägerhorn, who seems to have envisaged a relationship between Sweden and Finland rather similar to that which existed at the time between England and Ireland.

For the Russians, fully engaged in a major Turkish war, this note was a very welcome opportunity to weaken their opponent. The unsigned reply of the empress, which demanded evacuation of all Russian territory and sought further to split the Finnish forces from the Swedish, was, however, received badly by the confederates, most of whom now began to seek to make their peace with the king. Although the situation from the king's point of view remained critical, any plans for Finnish independence – which seemed to rely upon Russian support – were now dead in the water. At the end of the year, the king ordered the arrest of the leading conspirators. Jägerhorn and a handful of other conspirators fled across the frontier, where they continued their intrigues. A Russian offensive in Savo was repulsed in 1789, and a Swedish victory at sea in July 1790 helped bring an end to a war that could so easily have brought disaster to Gustav III. Instead, he was able to make peace on honourable terms, with no territorial changes, and he used the discomfiture of the noble opposition to push through a new constitution which, although seemingly confirming the legal and political rights of all citizens, considerably strengthened the king's powers to govern and defend the kingdom.

Although there was certainly an undercurrent of discontent in Finland in the 1780s, partly occasioned by unpopular agricultural policies and poor harvests, and by a growing feeling that Finland was condemned to be the poor relation, neglected and held in contempt by the grandees in Stockholm, this was far from constituting the kind of situation that might have led to an outbreak of open rebellion in the American or Dutch manner. The activities of the Anjala confederation aroused much contempt and anger amongst the common people, who, in Porthan's words, 'hate the Russians from the very bottom of their heart'. A former close acquaintance of Sprengtporten declared in the autumn that the despicable actions of the leading officers of the Finnish army were condemned on all sides as treasonable, whilst Porthan assured a colleague that the idea of independence was regarded with distaste by every member of the university and indeed of the whole nation, 'perhaps with the exception of a few weathercocks amongst our nobility, who seem to entertain the delightful idea of changing our citizens into slaves in the Livonian or Courlandish manner, and treating them like cattle'.

Open distrust of the 'gentry' (*herrat*) amongst the common people continued to surface after the summer of 1788. Fears of Russian troop movements in 1796 and 1803 prompted the partial mobilisation of the Finnish army; in the ensuing confusion, rumours began to circulate of further noble treachery. Suspicion of the upper classes was matched by a strong loyalty towards the monarchy and a general eagerness to fight the invader. The fierce bellicosity of the Finnish peasantry was however in marked contrast to the resigned mood of many leading members of society. The assassination of Gustav III in 1792 by a small group of discontented nobles, and the erratic policies of his successor Gustav IV Adolf, did nothing to dissipate the political tension. A leading Finnish nobleman who had enjoyed the confidence of the assassinated king, Gustav Mauritz Armfelt, was accused of plotting against the regency and obliged to flee to Russia in 1794.[1] Although later pardoned, and entrusted with diplomatic and military responsibilities by Gustav IV Adolf, Armfelt's years in Russia were to provide the link that allowed him to emerge after 1811 as the undisputed leading figure in Finnish public life.

Armfelt's rather cynical advice to friends in Finland in 1803 to 'get in stocks of brandy-wine, which mixed with water is called vodka and is the Russians' favourite drink' in the event of a Russian attack is not untypical of the mood of pessimism prevalent amongst the upper classes. The invasion of Finland launched by the Russians in February 1808 seemed to bear out the worst fears of Swedish unpreparedness and military incompetence. Within three months, southern Finland had been overrun, the fortress of Sveaborg surrendering without a fight. The army, having retreated to Ostrobothnia, showed itself capable of defeating the pursuing Russian forces in a series of battles during the late spring and summer, but was unable to regain the conquered southern territory. A reinforced Russian army gained the upper hand in the autumn, and the forces remaining in Finland were obliged to withdraw to Sweden by the terms of the truce signed at Olkijoki in northern Ostrobothnia on 19 November. Although the war was not formally brought to an end for another year, Finland was to all intents and purposes separated from Sweden, where the shock of defeat helped precipitate a military revolt that led to the forced abdication of the king and the proclamation of a new constitution by the estates in the summer of 1809.

The Russian attack on Sweden was a consequence of a much greater conflict in Europe. In the summer of 1807, the Russians had suffered defeat at the hands of the French armies campaigning in Prussia. Bereft of allies, Alexander I had entered into a peace agreement with the emperor Napoleon at Tilsit, which, amongst other things, obliged him to try and persuade Napoleon's last remaining enemies to sue for peace. The fiercely anti-Napoleonic king of Sweden, encouraged by the British, rejected all peaceful efforts at persuasion. At the end of 1807, Alexander decided upon a military operation to resolve matters. Sprengtporten, who had spent the previous two decades in Russian military and diplomatic service, laid out a plan for a winter campaign which would allow the Russians to advance rapidly and would also prevent the powerful Swedish fleet leaving the frozen harbours. He also urged the emperor to issue a proclamation, guaranteeing the liberties and privileges of the Finnish people, and summoning the estates to deliberate upon Finland's future. The summoning of the estates and the taking of Finland, with its existing liberties and privileges, under the emperor's protection 'for the time being', was indeed included in the proclamation to the Finnish people, issued by the commander of the Russian forces, General Friedrich Wilhelm von Buxhoevden, on 18 February. The official declaration of war on Sweden, however, promised to end the Finnish campaign if Sweden agreed to join Napoleon's Continental System, intended to deny British goods access to European markets. This suggests that Alexander I wished at this stage to keep his options open. The rapid occupation of southern Finland, and uncertainties on the international horizon, encouraged the emperor in the spring of 1808 to favour shifting the Russo-Swedish frontier to the river Tornio. This was made clear in a note to foreign powers in April, and in Alexander I's manifesto concerning the union of Finland with the Russian empire, issued on 17 June. This manifesto made no mention of an assembly of the estates, or of any special status for Finland other than the maintenance of the country's ancient laws and privileges. Sprengtporten's notion of an assembly of the estates, which would conclude a settlement for Finland with the emperor, enjoyed little support in Russia or in Finland. Buxhoevden, responsible for civil administration as well as the command of the army, was more concerned to secure an oath of loyalty from the inhabitants; the foreign minister, Nikolay Petrovich Rumyantsov, dismissed the idea of an assembly of the estates as unnecessary, and was supported in this by another former Anjala conspirator now in Russian service, Karl Henrik Klick. Leading Finns, such as the bishop of Turku, Jakob Tengström, argued that the convening of the estates whilst the outcome of the war remained undecided would be a premature action likely to arouse passions and stir up factions.

In spite of a good deal of active resistance to the Russians in Savo and Ostrobothnia, and rumbles of discontent in occupied southern Finland, Bishop Tengström's policy of compliance with the occupying authorities' wishes prevailed. The inhabitants of occupied areas had sworn an oath of loyalty in 1742 as a means of ensuring the protection of the occupying forces, and this precedent was followed in 1808. Although some such as Tengström conceded privately that the fate of Finland had probably been decided, the successful counter-offensive of the Swedish–Finnish forces in Ostrobothnia and Savo during the summer of 1808 heightened the mood of uncertainty and caution. There was some reluctance amongst the Finns of the occupied areas to elect delegates to the deputation which Buxhoevden was ordered on 21 June to organise, since they feared the delegates would be treated as negotiators. The memorandum drawn up by Carl Erik Mannerheim, who emerged as the leading figure of the deputation that conferred with the emperor in St Petersburg at the end of the year, made plain that any advice offered must in no way be seen as the resolve of the nation, nor used to alter any laws or institutions, which should remain inviolate and in force until it pleased the emperor 'to convene the estates according to the lawful procedure of the land, graciously to hear them on the matters which His Majesty's fatherly concern for their well-being may find necessary'. Alexander reassured the deputation that he recognised they were not empowered to deliberate as he had initially wished, and that he had decided therefore to call the estates.

The convening of the estates in the small southern Finnish town of Porvoo in March 1809 was an important step, and that meeting has subsequently been elevated into pride of place in the history of Finnish nationhood. But there is more reason to see the establishment of a governmental structure for Finland by the emperor on 1 December 1808 as the real foundation of a Finnish state. It was also a final triumph for the septuagenarian Finnish exile who had bombarded the emperor and his ministers with plans for Finland's future, for, although a number of the features of Sprengtporten's plan for a provisional government for Finland submitted to scrutiny by a three-man committee (the minister of war Arakcheyev, the future commander of forces in Finland, von Knorring, and Sprengtporten himself) were not realised, his wish to ensure that Finnish affairs did not fall under the control of the ministries in St Petersburg was given imperial sanction. In confirming the committee's proposals on 1 December, the emperor decreed that Finnish affairs should be presented directly to himself. The task of preparing Finnish affairs was to be entrusted to a state-secretary for Finland, and Alexander nominated his influential adviser Mikhail Speransky to be the first holder of that post, and a governor-general, who was to chair a governing council. The first holder of that post was to be Sprengtporten himself, although his tenure proved to be short-lived, the emperor accepting with ill-disguised relief his resignation in the spring of 1809.

The main reason for convening the estates was to secure a binding oath of loyalty and to obtain useful advice on a range of matters, including taxation, the future of the Finnish armed forces, and the composition of the governing council. It was not envisaged that the Diet should have decision-making powers, or become a permanent institution. At a time when Alexander I and his principal adviser Speransky were much concerned with reforming the administrative structure of the empire, Finland did, however, offer a timely exemplar of the well-ordered monarchical state. This was acknowledged by Alexander himself in conversation with Gustav Mauritz Armfelt, when the emperor averred that he felt much more comfortable working with rules and regulations in Finland, since they provided him with the necessary knowledge to govern; in Russia, he was surrounded by uncertainty and customs instead of laws. It was this administrative efficiency that the emperor and Speransky wished not only to preserve and develop, but also to adapt to the rest of Russia.

In this sense, Finland was in Speransky's words, a state, and not a mere *guberniya*, or province of the empire. Speransky believed it had an ancient constitution, which owed nothing to the machinations of cabinets or the graciousness of sovereigns, but was essentially a kind of corporate entity, similar to that of the Russian peasant commune, which through representation could act as means of enlightening the ruler about the state and needs of his subjects. This interpretation would not have sounded unfamiliar or unwelcome to the spokesmen for Finland, who tended to see the constitution as a framework of laws which guaranteed the rights of the subject according to their status or estate. In the words of the leading Finnish scholar on this subject, Osmo Jussila, 'traditionalism had been a characteristic feature of constitutional thinking during Swedish times; Finland's new position merely increased this deep conservatism and the need to preserve everything as it was'.

What Alexander I did or did not confirm at the Diet of Porvoo was to become the subject of fierce debate at the end of the nineteenth century, when Finland's separate status within the empire seemed threatened by centralising tendencies. Leo Mechelin, professor of jurisprudence and member of the Finnish Senate, or government, set the cat amongst the pigeons with his *Précis du droit public de la grand-duché de Finlande*, published in 1886. This slim volume, which was intended to proclaim Finland's rights to a European audience, claimed that Alexander had confirmed the Finnish constitution, and in hailing him as the grand duke of Finland, the estates had in fact concluded a treaty, which allowed the emperor of Russia and his successors to exercise the powers of government in the Grand Duchy of Finland on the basis of the confirmed constitution. Finland was therefore a constitutional monarchy, a state in a real union with Russia. This was immediately challenged on the Russian side by K. F. Ordin, whose two-volume history, *Pokorenie Finlyandii* (*The Conquest of Finland*, 1889) rejected the whole idea of a solemn agreement having been concluded at Porvoo by the autocratic ruler of an empire that had conquered Finland. The debate rumbled on for the next twenty years or so, as the storm clouds which Armfelt had feared in his worst moments of doubt began to obscure the political horizon.

This debate is significant less for any light it might throw upon the motives and objectives of the emperor and his advisers in 1809 than for its capacity to generate and sustain belief in Finnish statehood. As we shall see, the belief that Finland was in fact a constitutional state united to an empire merely by virtue of a solemn promise made by the autocratic ruler of that empire became a vital building-block in the process of nation-building in the early twentieth century, and it remained deeply embedded in the historiography until recent times. The modern consensus is that Alexander was mainly concerned to ensure the loyalty of his new subjects, and that his assurances to respect and uphold the rights and privileges that prevailed in Finland were very much in line with other solemn declarations made by his predecessors upon entering into possession of conquered territories on Russia's western frontier. The emperor did, however, consider himself an enlightened ruler, familiar with many of the latest doctrines, and he was eager and willing to experiment with reforms that might result in a more efficient and better-administered state. He was also, it must be said, a very shrewd politician, who managed to win over many leading members of Finnish society by his charm and generosity. As he himself wrote in 1810 in his instructions to the new governor-general, Fabian Steinheil, 'my intention has been to give the people of that country a political existence, so that they would not consider themselves conquered by Russia, but joined to it by their own self-evident interests'.

In appealing directly to the eudæmonic instincts of those who actually enjoyed rights and privileges in Finland, such as the army officers who retained their salaries and homes, even though the army was disbanded, and office-holders or would-be aspirants to a job in the judiciary or bureaucracy, who could now see not only opportunities to advance their careers in a self-governing Grand Duchy, but also – if they chose to – within the vast Russian empire, Alexander I struck the right chord. Amongst the Finnish elite, there was a deep sense of having been let down by Sweden. Many were disturbed by the revolutionary sequence of events in Sweden, and were reassured by the emperor's commitment to uphold the existing order that the Swedish estates seemed intent on destroying. There were plenty of misgivings about Finland's future under the imperial eagle, and much affection for the former motherland, but there was also a clear determination to seize the opportunities offered by Alexander I. From a very early stage, the Finns realised the value of lobbying in St Petersburg, and there can be little doubt that seeing the emperor's receptivity and willingness to act was in marked contrast to the frustrations of being a peripheral and seemingly neglected province of a state in decline. This was very much the experience of Gustav Mauritz Armfelt, who moved from strife-torn Sweden to Russia in 1810, hoping to show Alexander how he might bring happiness to his country and himself by doing justice to the Finns. Although he did not escape the snares of jealous intrigue (and he was himself no mean practitioner of that art), he was captivated by the emperor and, as his advisor, was allowed scope to present a number of wide-ranging proposals for the future governance of Finland. Armfelt had few illusions about the harsh and oppressive nature of life in Russia, and in a letter to a colleague written just before he left Sweden, had expressed fears that devastation and slavery would be the fate of Finland, too. But he was sufficiently convinced of the emperor's goodwill to believe that there was no intention to impose Russian rule. 'The emperor will have us as Finns', he wrote to a colleague in 1811, 'and let us in God's name fulfil our destiny.'

What His Imperial Majesty did not foresee, however, or did not understand was that, in giving the Finns a 'political existence' and publicly declaring, in his speech at the conclusion of the Diet of Porvoo, that Finland had been 'placed from this time on amongst the rank of nations', he was more likely to encourage further aspirations than merely persuade his new subjects to 'remember nothing of past domination'. Fine assurances were one thing, but for a people accustomed to their rights and privileges being spelled out in writing, not quite enough.

The abiding worry of the Finnish elite was that the solemn promise made by Alexander I in his charter to maintain inviolably and in full force 'the Christian faith and fundamental laws as well as the liberties and privileges which each estate in the said Grand Duchy in particular and all the inhabitants in general, both high and low, have hitherto enjoyed according to the constitution' would not be honoured by his successors, or would in some way or other be undermined by those in the Russian empire who were hostile to Finland's special status. The peace treaty concluded in Hamina in September 1809 absolved the king of Sweden of any responsibility for ensuring the interests of his former subjects, since Alexander had already 'of his own accord' assured them of the free

exercise of their religion, rights to property, and privileges. Nothing
was said of the part played by the Finnish estates, and indeed, no
mention was made of Finland at all – the king of Sweden simply
relinquished 'all privileges and title pertaining to the provinces hereafter enumerated, which have been conquered from the crown of
Sweden in the late war by the arms of His Imperial Majesty'. There
was much concern that, ignorant of the fundamental laws of the
land, the emperor might issue decrees or orders that violated these
laws. For this precise reason, the Finns objected to the regulations
governing the powers of the governor-general and the chief law
officer of the Finnish government, issued in 1811, and succeeded in
persuading the emperor to make the necessary changes. The replacement of Speransky by Robert Rehbinder as state-secretary for
Finnish affairs in the same year, and the reconstruction of the Committee for Finnish Affairs set up to advise the state-secretary was a
decisive breakthrough, giving the Finns direct and regular access to
the emperor. The highly labile international situation probably
helped the Finnish cause, for until he finally secured an alliance in
1812 with Napoleon's former marshal, Jean-Baptiste Bernadotte
(from 1810, the elected heir to the Swedish throne, and from 1818
to 1844, King Carl XIV Johan), Alexander faced the very real prospect of a French-backed war of revenge from Sweden. It was thus
prudent for him to heed the Finns' wishes, though his project for the
creation of a Grand Duchy of Lithuania, based on the Finnish model,
would suggest that his enthusiasm for experimental reform outside
the confines of Russia remained undiminished, at least before the fall
from grace of Speransky in 1812.

The lack of any recognised written constitution clearly concerned
the Finns. Without this, declared Carl Erik Mannerheim in 1819,
Finland was a house built on sand, which might fall in the next bout
of stormy weather. The granting of a constitution for the kingdom
of Poland in 1815 encouraged hopes that the emperor might do the
same for Finland, and probably inspired the Committee for Finnish
Affairs to ask Alexander for a written constitution, which would
include provision for regular meetings of the estates. Alexander
seemed favourably disposed, even announcing during a visit to his
new Finnish capital of Helsinki in 1819 that he would soon
be summoning the estates. Worries about revolutionary unrest in

Germany, together with a waning enthusiasm for experiment, may have caused the emperor to have had second thoughts. No diet was called, nor any written constitution graciously given to his Finnish subjects.

Russia had, of course, acquired territory in eastern Finland on two earlier occasions. Organised in 1744 as the province or *guberniya* of Viipuri, but better known by its nineteenth-century designation of 'Old Finland', this territory comprised three different parts. The fortress city of Viipuri and the surrounding area, ceded in 1721, and the land lying immediately to the west, including the strong points of Hamina, Lappeenranta and Savonlinna, ceded in 1743, had been part of the kingdom of Sweden since medieval times, but the region of Käkisalmi on the north-eastern shores of lake Ladoga had been acquired by Sweden in 1617, and had never been incorporated into the realm. Although in practice the privileges and rights of the inhabitants of these lands were kept in force, no formal agreement of the kind made by Peter the Great with regard to his new subjects in Estonia and Livonia was made. Administratively, they were placed under two departments overseen by Peter the Great's creation, the imperial Senate: the justice college for Livonian and Estonian (and after 1762, Finnish) affairs, and the finance office for Livonian and Estonian affairs. These organs were staffed largely by Baltic Germans, and their desire to preserve as much autonomy as possible for the Baltic provinces also sheltered the province of Viipuri from closer incorporation into Russia. The extensive reforms introduced in 1783–84 by Catherine the Great threatened to break down that barrier and bring nearer the stated objective of the empress to bring these provinces to the point where they became Russian and ceased to hanker after their previous allegiance. These reforms were scrapped by her successor, Paul I, but certain features, such as the *guberniya* administration set up in Viipuri, remained in place.

With its odd mixture of institutions, practices, and even law codes (the 1734 Swedish law code had been implemented in the areas ceded in 1743, for instance), and cursed with the consequences of an imperial policy of rewarding officials, soldiers, and favourites with lands in the crown's possession – the so-called 'donation lands', where the harsh terms of servitude affected almost a third of the peasant population – Russian Finland left an unfavourable impression on those from 'the other side' who visited it immediately after Swedish Finland passed under the imperial crown. In the words of Carl Stjernwall, appointed governor of Viipuri after the reuniting of Old and New Finland at the end of 1811, 'Russia has spoiled the simple customs of the people here; Asiatic excess and luxury alongside poverty, oppression and misery'. Robert Rehbinder, minister state-secretary for Finland from 1811 to 1841, found Viipuri an alien and hostile place during his stay there in the autumn of 1808 as a member of the delegation to St Petersburg, and he opposed the reunion, arguing that the province of Viipuri would be the rock upon which Finland's autonomy would be stranded. Rehbinder even proposed in 1824 that the easternmost parishes of Old Finland, where these landowners were most numerous, be detached from the Grand Duchy and returned to Russian rule.

Rehbinder and others who opposed reunion were right to be concerned, for it caused a groundswell of resentment in Russia, where it was widely felt that, having just been conquered by Russia, Finland now seemed to have taken over a part of Russia. That the emperor had been persuaded to issue the decree was due largely to Gustav Mauritz Armfelt, who argued passionately for the reunion as an enlightened, just cause that would reinforce the bonds of loyalty between the emperor and his new subjects. Like his principal adviser Speransky, however, Alexander I was quite willing to bring to an end the state of administrative and legal confusion in the province of Viipuri, and to allow the bureaucrats of Swedish Finland to bring order and justice.

The reorganisation of the administrative structure of Old Finland after 1811 did indeed replace most of the local officials with 'dogs from the other side', as the men from New Finland were rudely called. By the 1840s, it was to the Imperial Alexander University, (the seventeenth-century foundation was moved from Turku to Helsinki and renamed in 1828), rather than Tartu or St Petersburg, that the aspiring youth of the region were tracing their steps. Old Finland did nevertheless preserve a distinctive character within the enlarged Grand Duchy. Its two hundred thousand inhabitants had the inherited experience of living within the Russian empire, and

Plate 11 Imperial Helsinki: Senate Square. The city of Helsinki owes its
existence to the wishes of two rulers, Gustav I Vasa of Sweden and
Alexander I of Russia. It was Gustav Vasa who ordered a new town to be
built on the river Vantaa, as part of his drive to increase trade and
prosperity in his kingdom. That settlement did not prosper, and was moved
further towards the sea, to a promontory protected from the sea by a string
of islands, upon which the fortress of Sveaborg was built in the middle of
the eighteenth century. The largest town in Finland was Turku, with its
cathedral, university, and high court. From a Russian point of view,
however, it was too close to Stockholm, and in 1812, Helsinki was named
the new administrative capital of the Grand Duchy. A town of modest size
with no imposing public buildings, Helsinki had its central area completely
redesigned and rebuilt during the first decades of the nineteenth century.
The work was planned and supervised by a nobleman, Johan Albrecht
Ehrenström, with the German architect Carl Ludvig Engel responsible for
designing the neo-classical buildings which still form the core of the city's
administrative and intellectual centre. The northern side of the imposing
Senate Square is dominated by the Nikolai church, whilst the eastern and
western flanks of the square are occupied by the senate building and the

within close proximity of the imperial capital of St Petersburg, which had provided work and career opportunities for over a century. Not a few bright young men, such as the brothers Alopaeus, who served as ambassadors under Catherine the Great and her successors, made a glittering career in imperial service. Although the influx of 'damned Swedes' from New Finland significantly reduced job prospects in the local bureaucracy after reunion, men from Old Finland, with their connections in St Petersburg and their better knowledge of Russian, often occupied posts at the interface between the Grand Duchy and the empire – in the chancery of the governor-general, or in the office of the state-secretary for Finland. Many of the sons of the German-speaking merchant families of Viipuri found work in the capital as copyists and clerks as part of their commercial education, and the expanding metropolis had constant need of building workers, domestic servants, suppliers of comestibles and fuel, even of wet-nurses – not to mention prostitutes. St Petersburg proved to be an ever more powerful magnet in the nineteenth century. There were over ten thousand Finns resident in the city in 1840, far more than the population of most Finnish towns of the time, and that number more than doubled over the next forty years to reach a peak of 24,374 in 1881.

The frontiers of the Grand Duchy were not only extended eastwards with the return of Old Finland; the peace treaty of Hamina had also created a new frontier with Sweden, bringing under Finnish civil and ecclesiastical administration a large area east of the river Tornio and north of the river Kemi that had hitherto been considered part of Sweden. Great care was taken to delineate the frontier; those carrying the post or otherwise travelling by sea crossing from Sweden to Finland were soon to be confronted by an imposing customs and post office in the approved neo-classical imperial style on the windswept shores of the Åland islands, an unequivocal

Caption for Plate 11 (*cont.*)
main building of the university respectively. The statue of Alexander II in the centre of the square was erected in the 1880s; during the stormy period of the Finnish–Russian relationship in the early twentieth century, it became a focal point for demonstrations and protests.

reminder that they were now entering an empire. The public emphasis placed upon Finland as a Grand Duchy and the erection of fine public buildings in the new capital, Helsinki, were prominent reminders of the imperial sceptre now protecting the land. The bonds of loyalty between the emperor and his new subjects were carefully fostered. Alexander I undertook an extensive tour of Finland in 1819, deliberately including southern Ostrobothnia, where there were still bitter memories of the fighting and the damage done by Russian troops in the summer of 1808. He was well received, and left a good impression, which survived in folk memory (though his failure to call the estates did little to lighten the gloomy mood of the elite). The Russians had learnt during the war to use the clergy as intermediaries with the population at large, and this policy was assiduously continued by Alexander I, who saw to it that his victories were celebrated and his actions explained through officially drafted proclamations read out to the congregation by the vicar. In addition to this traditional channel of communication from ruler to subject, the official newspaper in Finland was also used to portray Russia and Sweden as allies against Napoleon, who, far from returning Finland to Sweden, would impose tyrannical French rule (subtly contrasted with the mild and benevolent rule of Alexander I) upon the Finnish people. The head of the church in Finland, Jakob Tengström, was intensely involved in the politics of his time, and played a vital role in the policy of pacification and subsequent accommodation to imperial rule. The emperor for his part appreciated the value of the church as a disseminator and upholder of loyalty, and went out of his way to assure its leaders that the Lutheran faith would remain inviolate. However, by issuing directives for the reorganisation of church administration within the new frontiers of Finland and by creating an archbishopric in 1817, Alexander not only drew a clear line of separation between Finnish and Swedish ecclesiastical administration, but also reinforced the power and authority of the state to direct and control the church and its clergy.

To administer the civil affairs of his new Grand Duchy, Alexander I established a governing council (*conseil de régence, hallitus-raati*). It was to consist of two divisions, one for the administration of the law, the other for the direction of the national economy, and was to have fourteen members. The instructions for the establishment of this council issued by the emperor on 18 August 1809 were careful to reserve the imperial prerogatives and explicitly forbade the council to levy new impositions or taxes, or to initiate new laws. As Markku Tyynilä observes in his authoritative study of this body, 'the governing council was not initially set up as a government for Finland, but as a local high court and administrative office, and its task was to look after the routine business of justice and administration'. For much of the reign of Alexander I, it occupied a subordinate position to the Committee for Finnish Affairs, which had direct access to the emperor. The committee was dominated in its early years by men loyal to the memory of Gustav III, and on two occasions – in 1812 and 1819 – made proposals to restructure the administrative and judicial apparatus in Finland along lines reminiscent of the Gustavian model of government. These proposals were not implemented, although Alexander was not unfavourably disposed towards them. Despite the sneers of grandees such as Armfelt, who thought its members were incompetent and pettyminded, and the fact that it was excluded from discussions about reform and not even consulted about the transfer of the seat of government from Turku to Helsinki or its renaming in 1816 as the Imperial Senate of Finland, it was the governing council, and not the Committee for Finnish Affairs, that provided the foundation upon which government in Finland developed. Much of this can be attributed to the positive contributions of the first two governors-general, who by virtue of their office presided over the council. By allowing the two divisions to meet in plenary session, Governor-General Mikhail Barclay de Tolly (1809–10) encouraged a sense of collective responsibility to grow. He was also largely responsible for creating the post of procurator, whose task it was to ensure that correct legal procedures were being followed. His successor, Fabian Steinheil (1810–23), proved to be a conciliatory and helpful president of the council. It was his proposal to increase the size of the economic division and to subdivide it into two sections to expedite business and to approve the nomination of vice-chairmen for each of the two divisions that won the approval of the emperor in 1820–22, rather than the plans of the Finnish committee to cut down the role of the Senate and place its actions under the scrutiny of the estates.

The governing council had also dared to speak up for itself, successfully challenging the procedural regulations proposed in 1811. In 1825, with the Committee for Finnish Affairs remaining largely passive, the Senate challenged the attempt of the new governor-general, Arseny Zakrevsky (1823–31), to bypass it. The challenge was unsuccessful, but the Senate did obtain powers to make decisions on a range of issues hitherto reserved to the emperor. The abolition in 1826 of the Committee for Finnish Affairs, which was replaced in St Petersburg by a non-advisory state-secretary for Finnish affairs, shifted the balance decisively to the Senate in Helsinki. Zakrevsky may have won the right to present directly to the emperor matters relating to Finland, but he also obtained permission to absent himself from the sessions of the Senate (which, unlike the multilingual Steinheil, he was unable to follow without the aid of an interpreter) and as minister of the interior from 1828, he resided in St Petersburg. His successor, Prince Alexander Menshikov (1831–55) also held high office in the empire, and resided in St Petersburg rather than in Helsinki. Their insistence on presenting Finnish affairs directly to the emperor undermined the position of the state-secretary for Finnish affairs, though the holder of that post was able to act as the eyes and ears of the Finnish Senate in the imperial capital: but no longer in day-to-day contact with the Senate in Helsinki, Zakrevsky and Menshikov relied heavily on their heads of chancery, who supplied them with information and advice – and these men were part of the small, intimate circle of the Finnish ruling elite.

Kinship and connection in fact permeated all levels of public service in Finland. Even though access to office was conditional upon obtaining the necessary qualifications from the Alexander University in Helsinki, advancement without the right marriage or family ties was difficult. The upper echelons of the bureaucracy resembled the branches of family trees, interwoven through the trellis-work of the rank system. Thus, Casimir von Kothen, whose father was a member of the Senate from 1820 until his death in 1851, was named head of the governor-general's chancery in 1840, after serving with distinction in the imperial Russian army. Made a member of the Senate in 1853, von Kothen sat alongside his brother-in-law, Lars Gabriel von Haartman, son of another former member of the Senate, and, by virtue of marrying two daughters in succession, son-in-law twice over of Carl Erik Mannerheim.

Laden with decorations and honours, rewarded regularly with 'gratifications' from the emperor, loyal, honest, and intensely conservative, this small coterie of men – fewer than two thousand in number for much of the nineteenth century – dispensed justice to and administered the affairs of a population that, with the addition of new territory, jumped from three-quarters of a million at the end of the eighteenth century to over one and a half million by 1850. Much of their work was low-grade by modern standards. The annual reports of county governors were preoccupied with control, and rarely addressed deep-seated problems; the mediation of petitions and requests to the governor-general, and the implementation of directives from higher authority, constituted the backbone of their weekly routine. The Senate's powers were severely circumscribed, although the sheer necessity of having to take action meant in practice that its committees did take decisions without reference to the ruler. The regulations issued by Alexander I in 1809, for example, had assigned control of schools to the chancery of the governor-general, but by the 1830s, the ecclesiastical department in the economic division of the Senate had effectively taken education under its wing. In 1841, the departments of the Senate's economic division were given formal powers to act independently. The finance department had been given separate status the previous year, with rights to employ its own staff and to report directly to the emperor. Although this was an exceptional case, brought about by the need for financial reform, and came to an end in 1842, it marked a distinct step on the path towards something approximating to ministerial government.

Finland nevertheless remained firmly in the grip of a conservative bureaucracy, and attempts to bring about change often encountered stiff resistance. Efforts to reform the school system were frustrated by the opposition of the cathedral chapters, which feared that their role would be diminished, and by the unwillingness of the Senate to support the proposals produced in 1826 by the school commission. Pressure later brought to bear on State-Secretary Alexander Armfelt and the emperor himself by the procurator and Archbishop Erik Gabriel Melartin brought results, but Nicholas I's decision in 1841 merely laid down general principles, and left it to the Senate to put these into practice through legislation. Reforms could be pushed through by a determined and strong insider, such as Casimir von Kothen, made chair of the ecclesiastical department in 1853, but in general, the Senate was obdurately unwilling to spend money on schools, or to endorse anything that seemed to stray away from their fundamental belief that education was all about instilling loyalty and obedience into the heads of the emperor's young sub-jects. The programme for elementary education outlined by Uno Cygnaeus ran into opposition from conservatives, who were reluc-tant to go beyond the idea of a voluntary, church-run school, and who were suspicious of Cygnaeus' vision of an entire school system. With the support of the secretary of the ecclesiastical department, however, it became law in 1866.

The fact that a diet was not to be convened until 1863 and that Finnish affairs were effectively controlled by a small group of conservative bureaucrats, with tight controls upon expression of opinion, does not mean, however, that thinking about Finland's relationship with the Russian empire and its ruler remained static. By declaring in 1819 that in respect of its relations with foreign powers, Finland was united with and subordinated to the Russian empire, but that in its internal administration it had a special poli-tical existence, the members of the Committee for Finnish Affairs were clearly at variance with those Russians seeking reform for the empire as a whole, for whom Finland was distinct only insofar as it offered a model for efficiency and good administration for the rest of Russia. Once the other provinces had been brought up to these standards, that distinction would disappear. In seeking further to define and firmly establish that internal separate existence over the next four decades, the retired soldiers and lawyers who constituted the Finnish bureaucracy may have been motivated more by conser-vative self-interest than a vision of Finland as a constitutional mon-archy; but by the 1860s, the more liberal-minded of their successors could perfectly seriously claim that such was in fact the situation.

The memoranda heavy with lawyers' prose and the constant manoeuvring behind the scenes to win the emperor's approval were vital elements in the forging of Finnish statehood. It is, however, rare for any nation to place the efforts of its bureaucrats on a par with individuals whose words and deeds qualify them for a place in the nationalist pantheon. Finland is somewhat unusual in that the principal leaders of the nationalist movement, and indeed, of liberal opinion, were actually co-opted into the bureaucracy after 1860 (and were very quick to adapt to the methods and mind-set of the Senate); but in truth, there were never any serious rifts between those who undertook to administer the land in the emperor's name and those who sought to give meaning to the political existence Alexander I had spoken of at Porvoo. Unlike the Poles, the Finns did not revolt, and the oppositional spirit of young Finnish students never rose much beyond the level of poking fun at the authorities in rude songs and plays. Although some teachers at the university were forced to resign in the early 1820s, and others came under the surveillance of the authorities, the equivalents of Alexander Herzen and his fellow-students at the university of Moscow, imprisoned and exiled for their part in a supposed conspiracy in 1834, simply did not exist in Finland.

Voices more critical of Finland's position and circumstances were raised in Sweden, especially by the liberal opposition to the official policy of maintaining good relations with Russia. The claim made in 1838 by Israel Hwasser, a Swede who had occupied the chair of medicine at the university in Turku in the 1820s, that Finland had concluded a separate peace treaty with the emperor at Porvoo and as a consequence of this, had ceased to be a Swedish province and became a state with its own institutions and constitution may have been inspired by a conversation with the author's old friend Carl XIV Johan, in which the king voiced his wish for a contented Finland. Hwasser's pamphlet provoked much criticism in the liberal Swedish press, which entertained the view that Finland was groaning under the yoke of Russian oppression and longing to be freed. A pseudonymous response caused more concern in Finland, since by arguing that Finland had been conquered by Russia, and that no agreement or treaty was concluded at Porvoo, 'Pekka Kuoharinen' appeared to undermine any claim to special status. Another pseudonymous contributor to the debate, 'Olli Kekäläinen', attempted to reconcile the differences, and concluded that the treaty had indeed been concluded at Porvoo by virtue of the victorious emperor graciously confirming Finland's ancient fundamental laws. That treaty, characterised as a *pactum beneficiarum* or *donationis*, was also deemed to be binding not only upon Alexander I, but also his successors.

The pseudonymous author on both occasions was in all probability Adolf Iwar Arwidsson, who had been obliged to leave his post at the university in Turku in 1821 after he was exposed as the anonymous author of an article critical of conditions in Finland that had appeared in the Stockholm press. His second intervention in the debate owed much to the advice of Professor J. J. Nordström of the Alexander University in Helsinki. Influenced by the new thinking, emanating from Germany, on the state as an organic and purposeful entity, Nordström postulated that, having been incorporated into the Russian empire by virtue of military conquest in 1808, Finland as a result of the emperor's assurances and actions in 1809 'had to be a state in itself, with its own constitution, under the protective overlordship of Russia'.

Nordström had begun lecturing on public law in 1836, spurred by an awareness that, in his own words, a growing national consciousness necessitated a knowledge of the law pertaining to the state. The term *valtio*, the Finnish equivalent of the Swedish *stat*, began to appear from the mid-1840s, and was used in the Finnish-language designation of the Diet, which was convened regularly from 1863 onwards.[2] *Valtio* and its derivatives is a central concept in Finnish political thought and is indeed the very foundation of authority and legitimacy. On a day-to-day level, the centrality of the state and its institutions in Finnish public life owes rather more to the long experience of bureaucratic government than to the lectures of Nordström or even the publication in 1842 of Johan Vilhelm Snellman's doctoral thesis *Om statsläran* (*On the Doctrine of the State*). But Snellman's belief that the state, seen in Hegelian terms as an organic, dynamic force, was an instrument of power to be conquered and used to ensure that the aspirations of the people (*kansa*) were fulfilled was to become a major component of Finnish nationalist thought. And as we shall see, leading and guiding the *kansa* to its destination proved to be deeply problematic, which in turn made more attractive the idea of a strong state founded upon constitutional laws which, far from drawing inspiration from ideas of popular sovereignty, had reinforced the authority of the ruler.

'Which is now my fatherland, Sweden or Finland?' a question posed in his private musings by Major Berndt Aminoff some time in 1810, troubled many others in the first years of separation from Sweden. There still remained many close ties with Sweden, and although Alexander I acted swiftly to satisfy the worries of those whose jobs and pensions were threatened, the inheritance of centuries was not easily forgotten. The elite fretted about the apathy and passivity of the people, who, as Armfelt put it in a letter to Carl Stjernwall at the end of 1812, did nothing themselves for the common good and regarded society and government as created for their private benefit. Reflecting in 1813 on whether there existed a national spirit in Finland, a member of the Committee for Finnish Affairs, Carl Johan Walleen, concluded that the uncultured masses remained conservatively passive, whilst the enlightened minority did not even deserve to be called a nation, since 'they have nothing of their own, nothing that is characteristic, which distinguishes them from other peoples and on the whole, they possess so little true attachment for their fatherland, their language and their government, and they surely within a fairly short time will completely disappear and be absorbed into their conquerors, if this is not forestalled by other circumstances'.

The men entrusted with the affairs of the Grand Duchy were acutely aware of the need to create a national spirit that would prise Finns away from residual loyalties towards Sweden, but also distinguish them politically from the other inhabitants of the Russian empire. In a letter to Rehbinder in July 1811, Armfelt observed that 'our peace and welfare depend upon us *de bonne foi et de bon coeur* becoming Finns, since it is now as unlikely for us to be allowed in political terms to dabble with Swedish ideas as it is *en fait d'honneur et de sentiment* acceptable for us to be Russians'. In this, the cosmopolitan aristocrat Armfelt came very close to formulating the celebrated syllogism posterity attributed to the exiled academic, A. I. Arwidsson: Swedes we are no longer, Russians we cannot be, therefore let us be Finns. In the end, however, being Finnish for those steeped in the eudæmonic spirit of the late Enlightenment (and this included as much the 'Gustavians' such as Armfelt and J. A. Ehrenström who opted to return to Finland after 1809 as the 'anti-Gustavians' such as Sprengtporten and Jägerhorn who returned to Finland with the Russian army in 1808) was a compound of political self-interest, loyalty to the new ruler and obedience to the old pre-revolutionary social order. Beyond vague generalisations about the character of the people, they had neither understanding of nor sympathy for Finnishness as a cultural concept.

It was amongst a small circle of academics during the last years of the university's activities in Turku that a rather different notion of Finnishness emerged. An interest in the past of the Finnish people had been awakened there, and continued to draw sustenance from the general enthusiasm for collecting and publishing folk poetry and writing the histories of the peoples of Europe. The changes effected in 1809 gave to this scholarly interest a new, political dimension, which surfaced in discussions in learned societies and the press, most notably in Arwidsson's short-lived newspaper *Åbo Morgonblad*, and the Finnish-language newspaper, *Turun Viikkosanomat*. The advancement of the language was seen as a crucial element. The philosopher and nephew of the archbishop, J. J. Tengström, argued that Finnish would never prosper unless the elite also learnt and used the language. An even more radical idea was advanced by E. G. Ehrström, who wanted Finnish eventually to replace Swedish entirely as the language of the country.

These bold thoughts were eventually to constitute the foundations of a political programme for Finnish nationalism, but during the first three decades or so of imperial rule, *fennomani* – a term that seems to have been coined in Sweden in 1810 – betokened an interest in the past of the Finnish people, which could be and was shared by many in Finland and abroad who did not necessarily envision the trans-formation of that people into a politically conscious nation seeking to fulfil its destiny. It was something that the imperial authorities were willing to support and even encourage, since the strengthening of a loyal Finnish identity would serve only to distance the people as a whole from their Swedish attachments. The career of Anders Johan Sjögren, the son of a village cobbler, who rose to become director of the museum of ethnology of the Academy of Sciences in St Petersburg, and who enjoyed the support and patronage of highly placed members of the Russian aristocracy, was perhaps exceptional in that most Finnish searchers for cultural roots in the Russian

Plate 12 Väinämöinen playing his lyre. One of six neo-classical reliefs executed in plaster by the Finnish-born sculptor Erik Cainberg for the ceremonial hall of the university in Turku around 1814, this is an early depiction of the central figure of the *Kalevala*, Väinämöinen, and reflects the growing interest in the customs and culture of the Finnish people amongst the generation of intellectuals influenced by the German thinker Johann Gottfried Herder (1744–1803), and professor Henrik Gabriel Porthan (1739–1804). Porthan, a leading figure in university circles in Turku during the latter decades of the eighteenth century, had laid the foundations for the collection and study of Finnish folk poetry in his seminal work, *De poesi fennica* (1778). It was, however, the small group of students at the university in the second decade of the nineteenth century, the so-called 'Turku Romantics', who were to push forward the work initiated by Porthan and his disciples, undertaking lengthy trips through the woods of Karelia or amongst the Finnish settlers in the forests on the Swedish–Norwegian border to collect poems, and actively seeking to promote their work through publication. The founding of the Finnish Literature Society in 1831 was a definite milestone, as was the adoption in its seal of the *kantele*, the traditional stringed instrument that accompanied the singing of folk verses. It is in fact a *kantele*, rather than a lyre, that the classically draped Väinämöinen is playing in Cainberg's relief. The bear in its various manifestations, alive or skinned, is an interesting motif in Finnish representational art, deserving of more attention.

hinterland preferred to make their careers on the more modest domestic stage; but it is a good indication of the generally positive attitude towards such endeavours that prevailed in the empire in the first half of the nineteenth century.

Sjögren had struck the correct note in the introduction to his book *Ueber die finnische Sprache und ihre Literatur (On the Finnish Language and its Literature, 1821)*, when he declared that Finnish–Russian co-operation in investigating the past could only be for the good of a common fatherland. Sjögren was not the first academically trained Finnish scholar to make extensive research trips in Karelia, for Erik Laxman, a former student of Pehr Kalm at the university in Turku and later member of the Academy of Sciences in St Petersburg, had published in 1769 a survey of farming in the Olonets region, but he was the first to conduct serious ethnological investigations. Karelia attracted the attention of Russian scholars and writers – some, such as the poet Fyodor Glinka, sent into internal exile there as a result of their political activities – and Panslavists such as Lev Porovsky took care not only to include Karelia, but Finland as well within the great Slavic realm over which the tsar would rule; but it nevertheless remained very much on the outer periphery of Russian national consciousness. For Finns, however, Karelia came to assume immense significance as the cultural cradle of Finnishness, where the ancient poems and traditions of their forefathers had somehow been magically preserved by simple folk. It was, of course, fortunate that Karelia was located across the eastern border, its inhabitants were Orthodox, and, as loyal subjects of the tsar for hundreds of years, not unnaturally saw the 'Swede' (which in practice often meant their Lutheran Finnish neighbours across the border) as an arch-enemy. This fitted neatly into the doctrine of 'official nationality', a fusion of Orthodoxy, autocracy, and the people (*narodnost'*) proclaimed by Sergey Uvarov, the minister for education in the reign of Nicholas I. As long as the Finnish interest in Karelia did not challenge this doctrine, but served merely to draw the Finns away from their attachment to Sweden and the wiles of the Pan-Scandinavianists (who were at times also inclined to dream of Karelia as a part of their Nordic superstate), imperial Russia stood to benefit.

'From beyond the night of centuries, these poems speak to us words of our fathers' faith, their wisdom and their strength', was how the ethnographer Mattias Castrén began his series of lectures on the *Kalevala* in 1841; they were a treasure comparable to Homer, Ossian, and Edda. To produce a work that might rival the epics of the ancients had been the declared intention of the compiler of the *Kalevala*, Elias Lönnrot, who carried out five collecting trips in Karelia between 1828 and 1834. Subtitled 'old poems of Karelia from the ancient times of the Finnish people', *Kalevala* was published in 1835 by the recently established Finnish Literature Society. It was not an immediate success. Few copies were sold, and even enthusiasts confessed that they were unable to understand much of the language. Arwidsson accused Lönnrot of inventing the whole idea of a national epos called *Kalevala*, and the work was also sharply criticised by Carl Axel Gottlund, who had spent many years collecting folk poems amongst the Finnish-speaking descendants of seventeenth-century settlers in the upland forests of Sweden. Gottlund had published his first collection of folk poems as early as 1818, and had been active in founding a Finnish society in Stockholm in 1828. He returned to Finland in 1834, with an impressive list of publications to his name; but was effectively shunned by the Finnish Literature Society and ignored by Lönnrot. Jealousy and personal feelings may have played a part, but Gottlund's long association with Sweden and the fact that his researches had been conducted there, rather than across the eastern border, tended to isolate him. His promotion of Savo dialect as the true language of the people also clashed with the younger genera-tion's belief that the Finnish language should not be based upon any one dialect.

In her history of the Finnish Literature Society (*Suomalaisen Kirjallisuuden Seura*, hereafter referred to as SKS), Irma Sulkunen has laid great emphasis upon the way in which during his lifetime Lönnrot became elevated to the status of a founder of a religion with the *Kalevala* as his holy book. She has sought to demonstrate how the pioneering work of Carl Niklas Keckman, lecturer in Finnish at the university, and elected chairman of the SKS at the founding meeting which was held in his house, was virtually buried after his death, when a new generation headed by Mattias Castrén took the lead, and how those who appeared to challenge Lönnrot's authority were ostracised. Her history has also brought out the many tensions that flowed beneath the surface, tensions subsequently hidden in a nationalist historiography that saw only great men united in the common purpose of fulfilling the nation's destiny.

In many respects, the history of the SKS mirrors many unresolved conflicts of opinion and thought in nineteenth-century Finland. It was founded at a time when the authorities were especially watchful for any sign of activity that could be construed as disloyal, and the founding members were quick to secure patronage. Within a week of the first meeting, they had secured an assurance that the chancellor of the university and the Senate would look favourably upon their endeavours; to make sure, they also obtained a promise of patronage and protection from the vice-chairman of the Senate, a man known to be a favourite of the governor-general. The appointment as chairman of the Society in May 1831 of Professor Erik Gabriel Melartin, a former headmaster of the grammar school in Viipuri entrusted in 1811 with the task of integrating the school system of Old Finland into that of the rest of the Grand Duchy, satisfied not only the etiquette of seniority and rank, but was a further assurance that the SKS was being led by a loyal and trusted member of the elite, who was to succeed Jakob Tengström as archbishop in 1833.

Finnish scholars have also contrasted the more scholarly tradition of the 'Turku Romantics' that saw the SKS primarily as a vehicle for promoting Finnish culture in western Europe through the medium of translation, with the more radical and populist currents emanating primarily from eastern Finland. In this respect, it is instructive to compare the Finnish Literature Society in the capital with that founded in Viipuri in 1845. The Finnish Literature Society in Viipuri was founded by a fairly diverse collection of individuals, including local landowners, office clerks, and teachers of the local grammar school. It declared itself open to all men and women, irrespective of social background. Although it later recruited members of the leading merchant families and bureaucracy of the town and county, it was also active in attracting farmers, over a hundred of whom were invited to join the society between 1845 and 1850. By contrast, the SKS, which levied much higher membership dues, had managed to recruit only two farmers by 1843, and fewer than twenty by 1850. The use of Finnish as the language of record was soon abandoned by the SKS, and did not replace Swedish until 1861. The active promotion of popular education was a prime objective of the Viipuri society, which openly declared its desire to bridge the gap between the lower social orders and the upper classes. Where the SKS chose to translate for popular consumption Heinrich Zschokke's *Goldmacherdorf*, with its emphasis upon loyalty and obedience to higher authority, the Viipuri society's first publication was a cheap primer, which ran through sixteen reprints and managed to sell almost half-a-million copies over the next half century. In the first fifteen or so years of its existence, the SKS preferred to bend its energies to publishing folk poems and other memorials of the Finnish past. Its leaders, most of whom had had to acquire a knowledge of Finnish, living and working in a Swedish-speaking milieu (the capital Helsinki had a largely Swedish-speaking hinterland), were far more hesitant about the promotion of Finnish before it had been suitably refined and given cultural respectability. This was far less of a problem for the members of Viipuri society, who were more at ease with a language they regularly heard and used. They were also acutely aware of the poverty and oppression of much of the rural population, subjected to the harsh conditions imposed by their landlords, who were usually Russian, and this gave their activities a distinctly social-reformist character.

Fennomani entered a period of major change in the 1840s. In a Europe where the ardent demands of nationalism echoed from Young Italy to the Panslavists, the articulation of a Finnish national idea was not unexpected. Broadly speaking, it comprised four main elements: the discovery and description of the country's history, geography, and natural history; the creation of national archetypes; the promotion and development of the Finnish language; and the definition of Finland's constitutional position. Although the last-named rarely, if ever, featured on the programmes of Finnish-minded associations or societies, and was indeed pursued largely by jurists and the bureaucrats who ran the country, it was arguably the most important in that it helped lay the foundations of a national state. The other three elements were all essential components of the process of building a distinctive national identity.

A respectable number of local studies had been produced in the eighteenth century, but much of the information required for a comprehensive and authoritative national guide was lacking. It was not until the 1840s, for example, that the first specifically Finnish, as opposed to Swedish, guide to the country's flora appeared. The seeming lack of a history was also a concern. 'The Swedes well know what they have done for humankind, as do the Germans and French – that is the foundation of their national feeling. But who has written a Finnish history from a *Finnish* point of view?' lamented Robert Tengström in 1845, concluding 'let us therefore first search for national elements and national memorials, wherever they might be found, and let us make of them a picture, so that the people may look at each other face to face!'. Reviewing in 1847 J. F. Kajaani's *Suomen historia*, a history of Finland in medieval times, Johan Vilhelm Snellman bemoaned the fact that Finnish history was not taught in schools. The main reason for this, he continued, was that there was no clear idea of what a Finnish history was; historians had even claimed in recent times that Finland possessed no history before 1809.

Separating Finland from its Swedish past was a long and complex process, and it should be noted that for the reading public of both lands, Swedish-language literature published in Sweden and Finland was generally regarded as part of a common heritage. Zachris Topelius, whose tales for children are a good example of that common heritage, sought in the 1840s to outline how Finland should seek to define itself – as a young nation, whose independent history began only in 1809, which would only shake off foreign influences by turning to the wilderness (*erämaa*) to find its true self. Poet, historian (he was the one who had claimed that, under Swedish rule, Finland had had no history of its own), novelist, and journalist, Topelius probably did more than anyone else of his generation to create an image of Finland. Many of his poems and stories were published in *Helsingfors Tidningar*, the newspaper he edited from 1841 to 1860. *Finland framställdt i teckningar*, which he brought out between 1845 and 1852, was an ambitious topographical survey, illustrated by the country's leading artists. In common with the poet Johan Ludvig Runeberg, Topelius portrayed Finland as a poor land, rich in natural beauty; but where Runeberg found his inspiration in the lakeland of the interior, Topelius was more the poet of the coast and the sea, from which, as he constantly reminded his readers, Finland was still emerging.

Both men wrote in Swedish, the language in which the educated class continued to communicate well into the nineteenth century. There were however peasant-poets and a few members of the educated class, such as the clergyman Johan Aejmelaeus, who wrote in Finnish. One of the most interesting and original of these poets was Jaakko Juteini. Born in central Finland in 1781 and educated at the university in Turku, Juteini was a domestic tutor in Old Finland when the war broke out in 1808, and later worked in Viipuri as a clerk to the magistrates. Juteini hailed the victory of Russia, whose ruler he regarded as more 'Finnish' than any Swede by virtue of his residence in his capital on the shores of the Gulf of Finland. Under Swedish rule, the Finnish language had been neglected, excluded from the academy and schools; in a striking phrase, 'the deaf had been made a judge, the dumb appointed as priest'. Now, under its 'Finnish-born' ruler, the Finns had a new opportunity, and Juteini urged the elite to adopt and develop the language and pressed for it to be used in the courts, schools, and university. In portraying Swedish as an alien and oppressive language, he went much further than the fennophiles in Turku and Helsinki, who were less than enthusiastic about adopting the language of the simple peasants whom they idealised. Juteini and the peasant-poets also eschewed the heroic myth-making of the Turku Romantics. The Finnish peasant of their verse is hard-working, tough, familiar with poverty and hardship, God-fearing, and respectful of authority; a saltier and more down-to-earth character than the rather saintly *Bonden Paavo (Farmer Paavo)* of one of Runeberg's most famous lyrical poems.

This image of the peasantry was in rather sharp contrast to their frequent portrayal in reports and articles as idle, feckless, and given to drunkenness. Lönnrot in particular was not backward in lambasting the poverty-stricken farmers of the Kajaani region of northeast Finland, where he worked for a time as district medical officer. Poverty as such was no disgrace: 'honest poverty' was elevated almost to a national virtue by Runeberg. What those who sought to elevate the people objected to was more often than not the evident unwillingness of the peasantry to conform to these ideals of patient and sober endurance. This in large measure lies behind the ferocious attack launched by a leading figure of the fennoman movement, August Ahlqvist, on the novel by Alexis Kivi, *Seitsemän veljestä* (*The Seven Brothers*, first published in 1870, and commonly regarded as the first great novel written in Finnish). In Ahlqvist's eyes, Kivi had wickedly slandered the common people of Finland in his portrayal of the crude, boisterous backwoodsmen. So powerful was Ahlqvist, professor of Finnish language and literature after Lönnrot, that few of Kivi's supporters dared openly contradict him, and the SKS, which had agreed to publish the book, immediately halted its distribution and only allowed sales to go ahead in 1873.

On the whole, the creators of an image of the Finnish peasantry paid little attention to or were faintly hostile towards those swept up in the great wave of religious revivalism that affected much of northern Europe at this time. Often inspired and led by lay people, such as the farmer Paavo Ruotsalainen in Savo, these movements fell foul of the strict laws on religious conformity, and there were a number of prosecutions, culminating in a series of mass trials in Ostrobothnia between 1838 and 1844. People moving about aroused the supicions of the authorities; Paavo Ruotsalainen was in no doubt that he was brought to trial because he travelled extensively, carrying the word of the Lord. But the 'awakened' were deeply conservative. 'We have no interest in republics, in autocracy or constitutionalism or anything like that', declared one 'awakened' clergyman in 1848, 'we leave those things to the world which imagines it has time for them. For our part, we are zealous for the kingdom of God, not in a political but in a religious sense.' The adhesion of clergymen to these movements ensured that they remained within the church, albeit with their own distinctive practices and even dress, which, as Lönnrot observed in the 1830s, set them apart from other folk. In achieving an intensely personal and emotional relationship with their creator, and in stepping outside and beyond the habits and customs of the peasant community, the 'awakened' developed a new group identity.[3] Deeply distrustful of the sinful world, the 'awakened' were also suspicious of gentlemen who came round collecting folk poems. They regarded the singing of secular songs a great sin, reported Lönnrot in 1828, and thought they had acquired great piety by forgetting the songs and poems they heard as children. A. W. Ingman was called a pagan for singing some of the verses of the *Kalevala* to peasants in Savo; such things were sung by their pagan forefathers, but were no longer acceptable to Christians. Both men encountered other difficulties in their attempts to approach the people. Ingman confessed that the locals had great difficulty understanding his Finnish, whilst Lönnrot, the son of a village tailor and fluent in Finnish, could not avoid being classified as a member of the gentry, even when tramping around the backwoods of Karelia.

By the end of the 1840s, the gulf between the elite and the people had been narrowed somewhat by the growth of a Finnish-language press and the publication and dissemination of popular reading material. The more vigorous approach to the promotion of popular education was largely the work of a new generation of students, many of humble background from the purely Finnish-speaking hinterland. The Finnish Society which they founded in 1847 became the core of radical *fennomani*, and their newspaper, *Suometar*, its voice. Many of these students had come under the influence of the philosopher and tireless activist for the Finnish cause, Johan Vilhelm Snellman, headmaster of the grammar school in the eastern town of Kuopio from 1843. Committed to the cause of bringing enlightenment to the people, Snellman edited a Finnish-language newspaper aimed at the rural population, and argued his case before the educated minority in the weekly journal *Saima* and, from 1847, the monthly *Litteraturbladet*.

A disciple of Hegel, Snellman brought a sharper edge to the debate on the language question, publicly calling for the dominance of Swedish to be ended. This alarmed many fennophiles, who questioned the wisdom of driving out Swedish when Finnish was still unsuitable for adoption as the country's official language, and worried about the attempts of the bureaucracy to make the Finns learn Russian. An imperial order of 1812 had stipulated that after a period of five years, all young people seeking employment in ecclesiastical, military, or civil service posts in Finland would have to demonstrate reasonable knowledge of Russian. Two decades later, Alexander Armfelt complained that nothing had been done to implement this, and laid down a series of proposals, including the setting up of a chair of Finnish at the university and the gradual elimination of Swedish as the language of instruction in schools in favour of Russian and/or Finnish. In this manner, Armfelt hoped, the barriers to a fusion of the Finnish and Russian nation would be broken down. His hopes were not to be realised. In the discussions on school reform in the 1850s, Russian was regarded as expendable, suitable only for those who intended to pursue a career in Russia itself. This was perfectly true. Few Russians moved to Finland, and those who stayed, such as the founder of the Helsinki brewery of Sinebrychoff, invariably became assimilated into Finnish society. The emperor's representative was surrounded by Finns, who manned his chancery and ran the national and local administration. Those who needed to know Russian to make a career in the empire – and there were many of these, from craftsmen to entrepreneurs, soldiers, sailors, and even bureaucrats – learnt it well enough; the great majority who remained at home found no need for it and their unwillingness to learn was the cause of much sorrow and frustration for those whose job it was to monitor the teaching of Russian.

Fearful that the sparks of the 1848 revolutions in Europe might land in what a French writer visiting the Grand Duchy in the 1830s described as 'a primitive country, whose antediluvian character has been faithfully protected by nature in the midst of human revolutions', the Russian authorities imposed severe controls over student life and restricted the publication of Finnish-language books to religious works and practical advice to farmers. This was justified on the grounds that such instruction was all that was needful for a peasant people. In general, however, the authorities continued to maintain a benevolent attitude towards Finnish. A law of 1841 made it a compulsory subject in boys' schools, and in 1843, it was included in the curriculum of all elementary and secondary schools. The philologist Mattias Castrén was appointed first professor of the Finnish language at the Alexander University in 1851. Governor-General Friedrich Wilhelm von Berg (1855–61) was a strong supporter of the adoption of Finnish as the language of instruction in the new elementary school system designed by Cygnaeus in the 1850s, and helped push through the reforms in the teeth of opposition from members of the Senate's economic division. The appointment of

Snellman to the Senate in 1863, and the issuing at his request of an imperial decree giving Finnish equal status with Swedish in all matters of direct concern to the Finnish-speaking population marked a significant breakthrough, in spite of much bureaucratic obstructionism in the working out of the details.

The outbreak of war in 1853 between Russia and the western powers, Britain and France, was the first serious test of Finnish loyalties. In Sweden, liberal Scandinavianist opinion urged intervention on the side of the western powers, with a view to regaining Finland. The heavy-handed imposition of controls upon student activities and the marshalling of the formidable forces of order to stamp out the least sign of subversion created discontent in the Alexander University and a mood of deep gloom amongst the leading 'Jacobins in Finnish homespun' (a description of the supporters of *fennomani* by one official), not least the 'communist' (as he was described by Governor-General Menshikov) Snellman, obliged to take employment as a clerk after being passed over for a chair at the university. In spite of the efforts of the authorities, including the church, to rally support for the war, there was a good deal of passivity, even hostility, most marked in southern Ostrobothnia, where the stationing of Russian troops revived painful memories of the bitter fighting there in 1808.

The widespread destruction in the port towns along the Gulf of Bothnia caused by British naval forces in the summer of 1854 prompted a wave of anti-British feeling, however, and an outburst of loyalty towards the emperor. Nicholas I was quick to take advantage of this, ordering the portrait painted of the farmer who had led the local resistance to the British assault on the town of Kokkola to be displayed in the governor-general's residence, and recruiting additional battalions of Finnish infantry for the defence of the country. With the possible exception of the Swedish-speaking Åland islands, where British and French forces captured and occupied the stronghold of Bomarsund and declared the islands free and under their protection, the war rallied popular opinion to the Russian cause, and strengthened the bonds of loyalty between subject and ruler. Amongst the elite, although there was general public condemnation of the Franco-British assaults, attitudes were more divided. Whereas Topelius adopted an ostentatiously loyal pro-war

PRISE DE BOMARSUND.

Plate 13 The capture of the fortress of Bomarsund by French and British troops, 1854. The outbreak of war between Turkey and Russia in the autumn of 1853 drew in the British and French, whose armies fought for two years against the Russians, for the most part on the Crimean peninsula. Fearful of attack by sea, and worried about the possibility of Sweden being persuaded to attack Russia in order to regain Finland, the Russians moved three naval squadrons and a total of 70,000 troops into Finland. There was some resentment of their presence in Ostrobothnia, where there were strong memories of the damage caused by Russian troops in 1808, and the capture or detention of almost half of the entire Finnish merchant fleet by the British cast much gloom in the ports along the coast. The destruction of property in the summer of 1854 in two of these ports, Oulu and Raahe, led to a wave of anti-British feeling, which the government in St Petersburg cleverly exploited by giving ample publicity to the Finnish resistance to a landing at the port of Kokkola. The war was a test of Finnish loyalty to their new allegiance. The busy period of reforming the economic and social structure of the country initiated by Alexander II in the 1860s may be seen as a continuation of Alexander I's intention to ensure loyalty by giving the country and its inhabitants a political existence, so that they would consider themselves joined to Russia by their own self-evident interests. These interests could however be interpreted in ways that caused alarm in Russian circles. When the prospect of war between Russia and Britain loomed once more in 1863, and again in 1885, for example, the liberal press in Finland began to advance the demand for Finnish neutrality in order to protect the Finnish merchant fleet from confiscation or attack.

stance in *Helsingfors Tidningar*, the liberal August Schauman argued the case for Finnish non-involvement in a war that was damaging to its interests in his newspaper, *Morgonbladet*. Snellman thundered against exiles who were doing Finland a grave disservice by calling for its reunification with Sweden, and urged his fellow-countrymen to abandon their sentimental attachments to the Swedish past in favour of a truly Finnish identity. Liberals such as Schauman and C. G. Estlander, who saw little good coming out of Russia, argued the cultural and political importance of maintaining close links with Sweden. Given the constrained circumstances of tight censorhip and strict surveillance, the debate was remarkably lively. In December 1854, Topelius had written to Schauman of his hopes that in the critical times Finland was living through, 'we must save for the morrow that which today is impossible'. The mood of change brought about by the new emperor Alexander II (1855–81), with his proposals for reform, seemed to promise that that hope would be redeemed.

4

The embryonic state, 1860–1907

In March 1856, Alexander II (1855–81) visited the Grand Duchy of Finland, and laid before the Senate a five-point programme of reform, designed to revive trade and stimulate the economy. This marked the beginning of a hectic period in which public life in Finland would escape from the narrow, cramped confines of the first five decades of imperial Russian rule, and the firm contours of a modern state would begin to take shape. The new emperor's visit took place at the end of a war which had revealed the necessity of modernisation throughout his sprawling domains. The Grand Duchy of Finland was thus not alone in going through the turmoil of change, which was ultimately to threaten the continued existence of favoured autonomous regions within an empire striving for uniformity and administrative centralisation.

Alexander II had probably less freedom than his namesake fifty years earlier to experiment in reform within the framework of an established political and legal system. In the first instance, as the emperor occasionally reminded his advisors on Finnish affairs, unrest at home occasioned by the emancipation of the peasantry in 1861 and the growing threat of revolt in the Polish lands compelled him to exercise caution. He also had to take account of the still tense international situation after the conclusion of the Crimean War in 1856, and of an emerging Russian nationalism that expressed critical opinions about Finland's status. The return of Finland to Sweden was still a popular cause in Sweden itself, especially amongst the students. Scandinavianism also appealed to the students at the Alexander University in Helsinki, much to the distress of their more cautious elders. And, if there was any truth in the conclusion of a leading member of the Finnish government that Finland was 'less Russian' in the 1850s than it had been in the 1820s, isolated behind a cultural barrier that had been built up over the centuries, seeing Russia as an alien land, there was yet more reason for the emperor not to encourage Finnish separatism with further concessions.

There were also many who urged caution upon the emperor, not least in Finland itself, where a section of the ruling elite feared that change would undermine their status. The attitudes and actions of the small coterie of men who ruled the country were in fact decisive. Public opinion, as expressed in the press, which entered upon a period of rapid expansion in Finland during the reign of Alexander II, and in the deliberations of the estates after 1863, may well have helped define an image of Finland, and of the status of the Grand Duchy within the empire, but the power and authority to effect change in Finland remained firmly in the hands of these men. They were more than a match for the emperor's representative, the governor-general. An active and energetic man like Friedrich Wilhelm von Berg, appointed to the post in 1855, could endeavour to implement his own programme, but he was sure to make enemies who would do their best to thwart him. Berg's enthusiasm for reform annoyed many in the Finnish government, or Senate, who had been used to running their own affairs without much interference from his predecessor Prince Menshikov. It was, however, possible to outfox him. The long-serving minister state-secretary for Finnish affairs, Alexander Armfelt, was able for example to persuade the emperor to reconstitute a Committee for Finnish Affairs in St Petersburg before Berg got wind of the idea. Although this committee, proved to be a less effective channel of communication from Finland to the ruler than its predecessor, it did strengthen the position of the Senate, which nominated two of its four members.

The Senate also showed itself well able to defend its position and authority against the challenge, real or potential, of the estates, when they began to meet on a regular basis after 1863. Various figures in Finnish public life from the rector of the Alexander

University to poets and journalists had made veiled or direct requests for the convening of the estates from 1856 onwards. Berg was generally thought to be the principal obstacle, though he was in fact favourably inclined towards the idea and managed to win over the emperor in 1859. Worries about Poland inclined the emperor to postpone the idea, though he was amenable to the suggestion of Fabian Langenskiöld, head of the finance department of the Senate, that a committee of the estates be elected and convened to deliberate upon government proposals preparatory to the calling of a Diet some time in the future. The manifesto authorising the election of this committee, issued in April 1861, caused some alarm in Finland, where it was feared that the committee would *replace* the Diet, and a further rescript clarifying the functions of the committee was needed to mollify opinion. Berg's replacement, General Platon Rokassovsky (1861–66), was authorised by the emperor to say that the Diet would be called as soon as the committee had finished its work. Fears of liberals using the committee as a platform for constitutionalist protests were quickly dispelled when the committee met and began its work in January 1862. The successful completion of that work encouraged the emperor to proceed with his intention to call the estates, in spite of the outbreak of revolt in the Polish lands. The Diet was ceremonially opened by the emperor on 14 September, 1863. In his speech, he observed that many of the provisions of the fundamental laws of the Grand Duchy were either no longer applicable or required greater clarity and precision. To remedy this, he proposed to have a draft bill prepared which would contain explanations and supplements to these provisions. This would be submitted to the scrutiny of the estates at the next Diet, which Alexander proposed to call in three years' time.

In addition to this implicit acknowledgement of the principle of regularly convened Diets, the emperor also promised to the estates more rights in matters of taxation and in the initiation of legislation. Addressing the estates at the opening of the Diet, Alexander placed himself within 'the principle of constitutional monarchy inherent to the customs of the Finnish people', but he failed to elaborate on this. A later attempt to have the emperor explicitly name the fundamental laws of the reign of Gustav III which were by now regarded as the foundation-stone of a Finnish constitution provoked a sharp response from St Petersburg, and the governor-general was instructed to say that no legislation existed which gave to the Finnish Senate the same rights accorded to the Swedish council of state in Gustav III's 1789 constitution. By explicitly reserving for himself rights accorded to the ruler in the laws of 1772 and 1789 in his confirmation of the act regulating the functions of the Diet in 1869, Alexander II did nevertheless go some way towards acknowledging these as constitutional laws. The real centre of power in Finland, the entire administrative structure of the country, was nevertheless still defined and regulated by administrative decrees, not constitutional laws.

Despite the best efforts of the liberals, the estates failed to obtain a measure of control or scrutiny over the Senate. It was the Senate that prepared the order of business for the Diet, and presented bills; the estates were allowed only limited rights of comment on statements and reports from the government, and were also obliged to send all petitions and propositions accepted by the Diet to the Senate, which would then give its opinion on how to proceed. The Diet Act of 1869 permitted few powers of administrative supervision or control, and although it included measures to overcome the clumsy and outmoded division of the four estates, decisions were still to be arrived at separately by each estate. A few modest adjustments which extended the right to vote or be represented to certain categories such as teachers at the university or tenants on crown farms in 1869 or to town-dwellers who paid local taxes in 1879 did not disguise the fact that Finland remained firmly rooted in the past as far as its representative institutions were concerned.

Conservative in comparison with the parliamentary reforms that had taken place in Denmark and Sweden (where the four-estate Diet was replaced by a two-chamber legislature in 1866), the Diet Act of 1869 was nevertheless a considerable achievement within the context of the Russian empire. It established the principle of permanency, in that the Diet was to be called every fifth year, with provision for extraordinary Diets should the ruler deem this desirable, and this principle was never seriously challenged in the remaining decades of imperial Russian rule. And although its powers were circumscribed, the Diet was actively engaged in the work of reform, and provided a forum for debate and discussion of national issues and aspirations.

In many respects the least contentious of the reforms of the 1860s and 1870s were those designed to modernise the Finnish economy, for it was this that had prompted the emperor to initiate the process in the first place; but even railway-building and currency reform could prove controversial. In 1849, Governor-General Menshikov had ordered the road and waterways transport board to investigate the possibilities of building a railway line between Helsinki and the inland town of Hämeenlinna, a measure supported eight years later by his successor and the emperor himself. Liberals supported the idea as a means of freeing the national economy from the cautious mercantilism of Lars Gabriel von Haartman, the head of the finance department of the Senate who had effectively directed economic policy since the 1830s. Nationalists such as Snellman saw the railways bringing civilisation and progress to Finland. Haartman on the other hand was a strong advocate of improving Finland's internal waterways. The completion in 1856 of a canal linking the Saimaa lake system of eastern Finland to the port of Viipuri owed much to his efforts, and proved to be a wise investment, paying off the high costs of construction within twenty years. Loyal bureaucrat that he was, Haartman strongly opposed the building of a railway line from Helsinki to Hämeenlinna, arguing that linking the capital to the Finnish hinterland would only serve to encourage the nationalists, whereas his own proposal for a line from Helsinki to St Petersburg would unite Finland more closely with the empire. That line was not completed until 1870, eight years after the opening of the Helsinki–Hämeenlinna line. The gradual extension of the railway network in Finland was largely a compromise between the demands of industry, the claims of towns and regions, and the strategic interests of Russia. In common with many other major infrastructural enterprises, it was largely state-directed and controlled.

The state had played a central role in the direction of the national economy in Swedish times, and that tradition was inherited by the men who were responsible for the administration of the Grand Duchy. Initially, the government had favoured agriculture and gave

little support to industry, but under Haartman's leadership, the
Senate adopted a more positive attitude. The stabilisation of the
currency from 1840 onwards and the strengthening of the bank of
Finland helped provide a firmer foundation for the economy, which
was also weaned away from excessive dependency on the Swedish
market by the phasing out of favourable trade and tariff agreements
and the opening up of new trading opportunities within the Russian
empire. In 1860, the emperor authorised the issue of a Finnish
currency, the mark, which was tied to the rouble. This was to cause
problems during the revolution of 1917, when the value of the
rouble collapsed, but it was an important step towards the creation
of a fully-fledged and autonomous financial system in Finland.

Economic growth was, however, hampered by excessive restrictions and regulations, and it was not until Haartman's resignation
in 1858 that the liberalisation of the economy could begin in
earnest. The removal of restrictions and general lowering of customs duties in 1859, following similar moves in Russia, helped
open the Russian market to Finnish exports hitherto denied access
or forced to pay high import duties. Restrictions on rural trade
were relaxed, depriving smugglers of a lucrative trade and bringing
shops and small businesses to the countryside. Steam-driven sawmills were permitted from 1859, and all restrictions on the cutting
of timber were abolished two years later. Between 1860 and 1877,
there was a sevenfold increase in the output of sawn timber, of
which the share of the steam-powered sawmills jumped from virtually nothing to 70 per cent. The timber industry was mainly in
the hands of the big commercial firms that also owned around a
third of the Finnish merchant marine. These well-established firms
showed themselves adept at spreading their investments, buying up
glassworks and foundries, branching out into pulp and paper manufacture from the 1880s, and developing new industries from the
by-products of timber-processing. They were better able to ride
out the crash of 1873 which forced many foreign entrepreneurs
in Finland to close or sell up, and they often bought up the
newly built and technically well-equipped sawmills of their ruined
competitors.

Notwithstanding the growth of the timber-processing industries –
sawn timber, pulp, paper and other wood products accounted

Plate 14 Main entrance to the company offices, Verla pulp mill. The beautifully adorned wooden façade of this building is typical of the architecture of the country villas built for the wealthy Finnish bourgeoisie at the end of the nineteenth century, though the grand spiral staircase adds an extra touch of elegance to a building intended to serve as company offices. The Verla mill, now a museum, was founded in 1870 by Hugo Neuman, a Swiss-trained engineer from the town of Oulu. Neuman introduced the latest Swiss technology to produce pulp by mechanical process. In 1881, Verla was bought by Gottlieb Kriedl, a master papermaker of Austrian origin. Kriedl subsequently added a factory for the production of pasteboard to the Verla site. In 1922, Verla passed under the ownership of the Kymi paper concern, and ceased production after the war. This is a not untypical factory complex, grouped around a suitable supply of swift-flowing water, with housing and other facilities provided for the workers. Although sizeable factory communities developed, for example, in the Kymi valley, there was no concentration of workers into the kind of industrial conurbations that developed in the Ruhr or Lancashire.

for three-quarters of the total value of Finnish exports by 1913 – agriculture was still regarded by most commentators as the only viable option for the foreseeable future. Farming entered something of a crisis during the nineteenth century, culminating in the catastrophic famine years of the 1860s. Productivity per hectare could not keep up with the rapid increase in population, which in some parts of the country doubled between 1810 and the mid-1860s; the only way of keeping up was to take new land into cultivation. Burnbeat cultivation fell into decline as the supply of suitable wooded areas began to diminish, a situation made worse by the privatisation of the forest in many areas as a consequence of enclosure. Ominously, it was one of the major areas of burn-beat cultivation, the stony lands of northern Savo, that saw one of the greatest increases in population. The more marginal arable lands of northern and central Finland were periodically afflicted by famine as a consequence of crop failure; 'hunger bread', made partially or wholly with ground birch-bark, was a staple item of consumption in many districts. In a still deeply religious society, these afflictions were seen as divine punishment for sinfulness; there remained a deep suspicion of anything that deviated from a life of 'honest poverty', such as an excessive addiction to perceived luxury items such as coffee. Hardship was the lot of the peasant, and was to be borne with patient fortitude, the message most famously epitomised by the poet Runeberg's poor farmer Paavo. Self-help and mutual support was the initial response of the local community to the failed harvest of 1867, though as the crisis deepened, sympathy towards the large numbers of people reduced to begging from door to door turned to mistrust, fanned by press stories of violent robberies and riots. The spreading of disease by the vagrants was in fact a far greater threat than violence; there were very few instances of organised protest or rioting.

Disease, rather than hunger as such, was responsible for the shockingly high mortality rates of the 1860s. The famine revealed divisions in Finland: between the south and the impoverished central and northern hinterland, and between the better-off and the poor, forced to seek work in order to receive assistance. The hastily improvised workhouses, overcrowded with starving and diseaseridden people, were particularly feared and hated. Although there was to be no recurrence of disaster on the scale of 1867–68, when famine, sickness, and disease carried off well over one hundred thousand people, the bitter memories remained. The shift from arable to dairy farming after 1870 rescued farming in Finland from crisis, but it failed to resolve the problem of rural poverty. Finland was a country of small farmers: fewer than a thousand of the overall total of 221,339 farms in 1910 exceeded one hundred hectares. Over half of the holdings were smaller than the five hectares deemed by the 1900 Senate commission on land tenure to be the minimum size for subsistence, and three-quarters of these were held on lease. Of the categories of leaseholder, the crofter (*torppari*), defined in a contemporary study as a farmer 'who has leased from the landlord a fixed area of land for a certain period, for which he performs a more or less precisely fixed annual rent, either in money, in kind or by labour', was coming under increasing pressure from landowners eager to maximise the returns from their land. Far more numerous than the crofters were the cottagers (*loiset, mäkitupalaiset*), whose tiny scrap of land was insufficient to sustain their family. Increased demand for timber did provide seasonal work in the forests and on the watercourses for those who lived on such tiny scraps of land, but it also widened the gap between those freehold farmers who profited from the sales of their timber and the rural poor. The lack of a sizeable manufacturing sector that could absorb some of the excess rural population, and, relative to neighbouring Sweden and Norway, the modest rates of emigration, ensured that there remained in the Finnish countryside a large pool of surplus labour that depended on seasonal work to eke out a meagre living.

The reforms of the 1860s and 1870s did much to free the Finnish economy and society from the tight restrictions of an earlier age. Commerce and artisanal industry were liberated from a number of controls, and legislation established the basic framework of a modern economy, enabling banks and limited liability companies to function and giving citizens the right freely to pursue whatever trade they wished, in town or in the countryside. The 1869 Church Law was the first serious breach of the monopolistic authority of the Lutheran church, although it still remained the only official religion, and freedom to worship (or not) remained restricted for several decades.

Plate 15 Otto Rissanen, with his birch-bark knapsack over his shoulder, setting off for work in the forests. Finland's forests have provided work and sustenance for centuries. The growing demands of the timber-processing industry from the 1870s onwards created opportunities for seasonal work – felling trees in the winter months, transporting them to the factories down the waterways during the spring. Living conditions in the loggers' camps were often abysmal; dozens of men had to make do with rough bunk beds, drying their sodden clothes as best they could, and subsisting on poor-quality rations. During the 1920s, large numbers of men flocked every winter to the north of Finland, where vast tracts of forest had been purchased cheaply during the war years by timber firms. Poorly paid and living in isolated, cramped conditions, they were often willing recruits to the communist cause, carried from camp to camp by party activists and

With the replacement of parish meetings by village councils in 1865, and the removal of control of education from the church to a national board in 1869, the church's secular functions were reduced, and its residual powers were to come under strong attack from liberal and dissenting circles during the 1880s. Amongst the better-educated, signs of an abandoning of religious belief had been evident from mid-century, but the rural population and urban working class remained largely unaffected by this until the end of the century. Churchgoing in the countryside was also a social occasion, enabling people living on isolated farmsteads to get together. The opening up of the countryside by improved communications, new associational activities such as youth clubs or the temperance movement, the spread of elementary schools, and the erosion of communal values and habits tended, in the long run, to work against this sociability. But if the church was no longer the all-powerful controller of local affairs from education to private morality, or a focal point of social activity, organised religion continued to occupy an important and central place in Finnish life. The church became more concerned with matters of faith, and issues of doctrine and practice were fiercely debated by clergy and laity alike. With their own estate in the Diet, and, by virtue of their continuing role as intermediaries between ruler and people, the clergy remained in the forefront of public life, figures of authority as yet unchallenged.

Poorly represented amongst the leadership of the *fennoman* movement, the clergy were nevertheless largely supportive of the Finnish-language cause, which was to dominate political debate throughout the reign of Alexander II. Although there had been significant improvements in the overall development of the language as a medium suitable for educated discourse, Finnish was

Caption for Plate 15 *(cont.)*
agitators. With his frame-saw and axe, and a birch-bark basket or knapsack containing a few provisions (salt, coffee, flour, tobacco) and maybe spare clothes, his stout boots the only solid protection against the harsh winter, Otto Rissanen from Tuovilanlahti in northern Savo was one of the thousands of impoverished small farmers who tramped to the forests every winter in search of work.

Plate 16 Centenary commemorative medal for the 'Friends of Sobriety' (*Raittiuden Ystävät*) society. Most movements have their unsung heroes, who work tirelessly in the background as organisers. Aksel August Granfelt (1846–1919), whose head is depicted on this commemorative medal, was for much of the last quarter of the nineteenth century the man at the heart of the movement to uplift and lead Finnish cultural aspirations. Son of a professor of religion and ethics, Granfelt trained as a doctor (medical men figure prominently in the national movements of Finland and Estonia) but never practised. Appointed secretary of the Society for Popular Enlightenment (*Kansanvalistusseura*) in 1878, he rescued this organisation from financial chaos and led it for almost thirty years. Many of Finland's leading authors published their first work through the society. Granfelt was also the archivist of the Finnish Literature Society from 1879 to 1896, chairman of the main temperance movement, *Raittiuden Ystävät*, from 1883 to 1902, and attended the Diet in the 1880s and 1890s as a member of the house of nobility. His children adopted the name of Kuusi during the early twentieth century, when large numbers switched from Swedish to Finnish surnames, and several members of that family have enjoyed distinguished academic careers.

still widely regarded as a peasant tongue, and claims to an ancient Finnish culture were derided by liberals such as August Sohlman, editor of Sweden's leading newspaper *Dagens Nyheter.* In Sohlman's opinion, if 'the Finnish national element in Finland [should] begin to make their own foundations in isolation from the contacts and influences of Swedish culture, then the way to barbarism and annihilation will be covered in as many decades as it took centuries for Swedish culture to lead the Finnish people, whom it had taken under its care and protection, to civilisation, self-esteem and independence'. Although resenting the cultural arrogance of this kind of discourse, a significant strand of *fennomani* acknowledged the importance of the Swedish connection. A lengthy period of research amongst the Finno-Ugrian peoples in the Russian Empire convinced August Ahlqvist of the folly of trying to create any kind of cultural bonds of kinship, and he pointedly drew a contrast on a public occasion in 1869 between a Finnish culture that had been enriched and guided by Swedish and 'our wretched kinsmen' in Russia, untouched by 'alien' influences, but left in brutish ignorance. Even his later bitter opponent, Yrjö Koskinen, hoped in the 1850s that Russia might arouse the hostility of the rest of Europe, and that Finland would be judged in consequence to stand out as an outpost of civilisation.

By the 1860s, however, Koskinen was singing a different tune, aligning himself with J. V. Snellman's position that a national spirit had first to be created and strengthened before political liberties and a state could be achieved. Snellman had himself undergone a transformation in the eyes of the authorities, from being regarded in 1848 as a dangerous communist to being appointed to the Senate in 1863. He had clearly demonstrated his loyalty to imperial Russia in his attacks on the liberals who dallied with the idea of furthering Finland's special status, and his Finnish-language programme, which aimed ultimately to eradicate all Swedish influences, also struck the right chords in high circles. The demands raised in the liberal *Helsingfors Dagblad* for the king of Sweden to propose Finnish neutrality, and for the total separation of Finnish from Russian forces, with the latter being withdrawn from the Grand Duchy, had caused alarm and irritation in the ranks of the bureaucracy. The reluctance of the university and estate of burghers to respond to the Polish crisis by sending addresses of loyalty to the emperor further annoyed the minister state-secretary for Finland, Alexander Armfelt, and he was able to find common ground with Snellman in persuading the emperor to issue a rescript on the language question, specifically in response to the petitions and requests of the 'Finnish population of the Grand Duchy', in the summer of 1863.

The language rescript was in some ways a disappointment for the Finnish-language camp, for it specifically named Swedish as the sole official language of Finland, and confined the use of Finnish only to those parts of the country where it was the dominant language. The time-frame for the implementation of the rescript was deemed too long, and there were well-founded suspicions that the Senate, entrusted with the task of preparing the necessary legislation, would seek to hinder and delay implementation. Nevertheless, the winning of recognition for Finnish as a language to be used in public documents and institutions was an important step, though in line with a process that had begun to accelerate already in the 1850s.

In the 1860s, it was the liberals who took the lead in attempting to integrate the lower orders; through such means as voluntary fire fighting corps or educational circles, the common folk could be raised up to be worthy members of the national community. The Finnish nationalist camp, of which Yrjö Koskinen became the clear leader by 1870, preferred to devote its energies to a struggle which would, in Koskinen's words, create 'a new ruling order [*herrassääty*], which would no longer be separated from the people by its language and its way of thinking – in other words, a new Finnish-language culture.'[1] Education lay at the heart of that struggle. At the local level, the nation-building ideology of Finnishness was brought into play in the battle to overcome peasant-farmer reluctance to fund the building and maintenance of elementary schools. This was important in that it helped entrench the national ideal in every parish, with the elementary schoolteachers as its standard-bearers, but it was relatively low-key, in sharp contrast to the high-profile campaigns for Finnish-language secondary schools. If the way the Senate proceeded to interpret the language rescript infuriated Finnish nationalists, who suspected with some justification that the bureaucracy was fighting tooth-and-nail to evade the implementation of its provisions, then the appointment as first director of the board of education of one of its long-serving members, Major-General Casimir von Kothen, was an even more bitter blow. Von Kothen, who had helped push through the reform of the elementary school system in the 1850s, undertook the task with much vigour, seeking to lay the foundations for a well-trained workforce and commercial middle class through a system of trade and secondary schools where practical subjects would form the core of the curriculum. At the same time, however, the downgrading or even elimination of the teaching of Finnish from the lower grades of the grammar schools that provided the classical education which was a prerequisite for entry into the university and the higher echelons of the bureaucracy was interpreted by the nationalists as a deliberate obstacle to the recruitment of young aspirants from a Finnish-speaking background. Finding themselves unable to change this through the Diet or press agitation, the Finnish nationalists appealed to the masses, raising funds to support a Finnish-language secondary school, which was opened in Helsinki in 1873.

More privately funded schools were founded in subsequent years, and by the end of the century, Finnish-language schools were even being built in coastal towns with a solidly Swedish-speaking majority, such as Kokkola (Gamlakarleby) in central Ostrobothnia, to cater for the children from the Finnish-speaking hinterland. Whereas only a quarter of secondary-school pupils at the end of the 1870s attended a Finnish-language school, that proportion had risen to over half by the end of the century, when for the first time a majority of new students enrolling at the university were Finnish speakers. It should be pointed out, however, that not a few parents chose to send their children to schools teaching in the 'other' language, and it is perhaps worth noting here that a survey of ten major Finnish towns in 1920 revealed that almost a third of the inhabitants considered themselves bilingual. The language conflict may have generated much heat in the columns of journals and newspapers, but it did not divide communities or cause the kind of violent tensions experienced in many other corners of Europe. As Yrjö Koskinen pointed out in 1869, the language question in Finland was at bottom about social change, not a quarrel between nationalities, for the ruling class was no more 'foreign' than that of many other countries, being for the most part descended either from the Finnish peasantry or from stock otherwise long since settled in the country.

The development of Finnish nationalism into a fully fledged political movement – albeit without clearly defined or definable parties – spelled the end of the period in which, as the liberal August Schauman put it in 1859, 'everyone had been more or less an enthusiastic *fennoman*'. An attempt in the early 1880s to form a liberal party proved a failure; by the end of the decade, its leading figures had mostly aligned themselves with the loose caucus of the 'Swedish party', whose members stressed the importance of defending and upholding Finland's institutions and traditions, including the linguistic and cultural legacy of the centuries-old Swedish connection. Within the Finnish nationalist camp, clear differences emerged over the years. The liberal–cultural aspirations of the Ahlqvist generation of the 1840s were challenged from the end of the 1850s by a more socially conservative *fennomani* of which the Forsman brothers, Jaakko and Yrjö (who finnicised his name to Koskinen) were the leading lights. Whereas Ahlqvist and his supporters argued in the columns of their newspaper *Suometar* for the adoption of Finnish by the elite, harmony and the preservation of western values and culture, and the defence of Finland's constitutional liberties, Yrjö Koskinen (who acquired his own mouthpiece, *Helsingin Uutiset*, in 1862) wished to create a national state by winning control of the bureaucracy. Only when Finnish-minded and Finnish-speaking men controlled the institutions and governance of the land could true enlightenment be brought to the people. Koskinen's increasingly conservative and patriarchal strand of nationalism was in turn challenged in the 1880s by a new generation of students, impatient with the cautiousness of their elders, influenced in their thinking by British liberal and utilitarian writers, and looking for social and political reform.

The gradual politicisation of public life in the Grand Duchy was tacitly acknowledged by the ruler and his advisors, interestingly enough at times of crisis within the empire. Snellman had been appointed to the Senate in 1863, as Poland was about to burst into flames; both Yrjö Koskinen and Leo Mechelin, leader of the liberal party, were appointed in 1882, shortly after the assassination of Alexander II. The real fulcrum of power however remained in the Russian, not the Finnish capital; Yrjö Koskinen proved to be as adept as Snellman in following the road to St Petersburg. He worked assiduously to persuade the governor-general, General F. L. Heiden (1881–97) to have the new emperor declare Finnish an official language in his coronation manifesto, a line of approach that alarmed the liberals and prompted the law officer (procurator) of the Senate, the liberal Robert Montgomery, to declare that Finnish could not be proclaimed an official language, since the Swedish law of 1743 specifically forbade the use of a 'foreign language' in courts of law. Montgomery was in all likelihood seeking to defend the Finnish constitutional position rather than deny the right of Finnish-speakers to use their language in legal matters, although the liberals' insistence that a Finnish legal language had first to be developed was seen by the nationalists as yet one further attempt to prevent the implementation of the provisions of the 1863 rescript.

The law which was finally approved at the end of 1883 made Finnish equal with Swedish in the courts, but higher courts were permitted to decide which language to use in all matters directly referred to them. An imperial order of 1887 decreed that the prevalent language of the region be used in the everyday business of all lower offices and courts; but Swedish still prevailed in the higher offices and institutions, and remained the language of communication between the county governors and central administration. Finnish was used only exceptionally within the departments of the Senate, and Swedish remained the language of record in all the major towns of Finland, even those with a large Finnish majority such as Viipuri and Turku. When in 1894 the ennobled baron Y. S. Yrjö-Koskinen spoke in Finnish, the first time that language had been used in the estate of nobility, he caused a furore; Viktor von Born called his behaviour unseemly and an affront to the estate, and there ensued a lengthy debate about whether or not Finnish could be regarded as an official language, only resolved by pragmatic compromise.

The language rescript issued by the emperor in 1902 marked a significant step forward, albeit in politically fraught circumstances.

It sought to make the language of local government conform to that spoken by the majority of the region, with suitable provision for bilingual areas. Higher courts and offices were obliged henceforth to deal with matters in the language which had been used initially at the lower regional level. The rapidly increasing supply of fully trained Finnish-speaking graduates (and the peculiar circumstances of the times, of which more later) made it much easier to dispense with the time-consuming use of translators. In purely Finnish-speaking regions such as Savo, Swedish soon ceased to be used. Finnish began to appear in the minutes and documents of the Senate, and from 1905, became the sole language of record for plenary sessions. It was also, overwhelmingly, the language used within the unicameral legislature that replaced the old four-estate Diet in 1907.

At the same time as Finnish was establishing itself as the principal language of the land, however, the Grand Duchy faced a challenge that threatened not only to bring to an end its constitutional autonomy, but also to make Russian the official language. All earlier attempts to disseminate a knowledge of Russian in Finland had failed, and although bureaucrats such as Alexander Armfelt and Casimir von Kothen had fully recognised the importance of Finns learning Russian and becoming familiar with the culture of Russia, they lacked the means and possibly the energy to promote and sustain effective policies. Finns were, of course, attracted to the empire, and not a few enjoyed highly successful careers as soldiers, entrepreneurs, and skilled craftsmen; but in Finland itself, the Russian presence was far less evident than in the Baltic provinces, for example. There was little or no inducement to learn Russian, and no experience of life as lived by those elsewhere in the empire (with the partial exception of Old Finland). The population as a whole was firmly loyal towards the ruler, whose mass-produced portrait adorned the walls of most peasant homes; the wilder strains of revolutionary radicalism and terrorism had never reached Finland. The poems and stories of Runeberg and Topelius had enabled the Finns to assemble a series of acceptable national images, and the arguments of the liberal-constitutionalist press made it seem as if Finland had entered almost voluntarily into a union with the emperor. Before the astonished eyes of the Russians, observed one Finnish official in 1889, the 'small embryonic state' created by Alexander I had become an autonomous state within the course of three-quarters of a century, 'a well-organised, self-governing society with thousands of schools, where, *horribile dictu*, the language of the empire is not taught, with its own industry which in part competes with their own markets, and with its own firmly secured finances and credit system in the world markets, which many richer countries might envy'. Little wonder, then, that the Senate's defence of Finland's separate status in the face of attempts to place the Finnish postal system under general imperial control provoked Alexander III to scribble, in the margins of a memorandum to the minister state-secretary for Finland, 'Does Russia belong to Finland or is it a part of it, or does the Grand Duchy of Finland belong to the Russian empire?'

A section of Russian opinion had always entertained reservations about Finland's favoured status, and one can trace a thread of despondency that Finland's good fortune would not last through the private correspondence of the Finnish ruling elite from the days of Gustav Mauritz Armfelt onwards. That elite had however been remarkably successful in warding off attempts to bring Finland closer to the rest of the empire. Nicholas I was persuaded to abandon the idea of returning to Russia the easternmost parishes of Old Finland (a proposal first made by Minister State-Secretary Robert Rehbinder, see Chapter 3) after the Senate argued that this could only happen with the consent of the estates, and he also failed to pursue the integration of the Finnish customs service into that of the empire. Although the constitutionalist claims of the Finns were never admitted by the Russians, the Swedish law code of 1734, the fundamental laws of 1772 and 1789, and Alexander I's solemn promises made at Porvoo in 1809 constituted, in Edward Thaden's words, a 'myth of contractually secured rights [which] provided ideological justification for either resisting Russificatory pressures or for reinforcing local autonomy in anticipation of what might happen in an uncertain future'.

The convening of the Finnish Diet in 1863, and the more daring demands of the liberal press for the establishment of Finnish consulates abroad and a distinctive flag that would protect Finnish merchant shipping in times of war provoked a sharp response from the journalist M. N. Katkov, but he in turn came under pressure from the Russian authorities to moderate his attacks on Finnish 'separatism'. The limits of Finnish autonomy were if anything pushed even further during the governor-generalship of General Nikolay Adlerberg (1866–81), a period in which, according to the Russian nationalist historian M. M. Borodkin, occurred all the major reforms that alienated Finland from the rest of the empire. Chief of these reforms was the military service law passed in 1878 against the advice of the minister of war, General D. A. Milyutin. This established a small conscript army, to be commanded by Finnish officers, and to be used for local defence. The imperial army command remained in charge of the coastal defence of Finland, and the Finnish units, mostly rifle battalions, were subordinated to the St Petersburg military district; but the creation of a separate force posed problems for integrated military defence planning, as Milyutin was not slow to point out.

In an age when imperial rivalries across the globe threatened to spill over into war, and when the authority of ruling orders was increasingly being challenged by radical and revolutionary movements, there was less and less room for the relatively benign and distinctly 'pre-modern' relationship between ruler and loyal subject that had hitherto prevailed in the Grand Duchy of Finland. The emergence of a powerful German empire after 1871 highlighted the need for an effective defence of Russia's western frontier; within ten years, the first comprehensive operational plan had been completed, and this was to play a crucial part in military thinking about the western borderlands. The imperatives of central co-ordination and control appealed not only to the military but also to civilian administrators looking to centralise the government of the sprawling empire, and impatient of local laws and privileges that impeded that process. And in the columns of the nationalist Russian press there were attacks on the Finnish constitutionalist claims, stories of the alienation of the Finnish bureaucrats and intellectuals from the Finnish people themselves, and of the lack of knowledge of or interest in the empire and its language amongst educated circles in Finland. The publication in 1889 of K. F. Ordin's two-volume study, bluntly entitled 'The Conquest of Finland' (see Chapter 3), initiated a pamphlet war. The Finns for their part sought to publicise their case on the international stage. Leo Mechelin's exposition of the constitutional and legal status of Finland, published in French, English, and German, was followed by J. R. Danielson's riposte to Ordin, *Finland's Union with the Russian Empire* (1891), and over the next twenty years, there appeared a series of pamphlets and articles in the major European journals on the 'Finnish question'. Where the bureaucracy in earlier decades had used their connections in the imperial capital to further and protect Finland's interests, the constitutionalist-liberals now turned to public opinion in Europe.

Access to the inner circles in St Petersburg was undeniably more difficult in the last two decades of the nineteenth century. Alexander Armfelt, son of the man who had been a confidant and adviser of two sovereigns, had unlocked many doors during his thirty-five-year tenure of the post of minister state-secretary for Finland (1841–76). Within five years of his death in office, the post went to a man from Old Finland whose career had been made in Russian service, and his immediate succesors, Casimir Ehrnrooth and Woldemar von Daehn, had both risen to the rank of general in the imperial Russian army. Although Finnish-born, these were men more familiar with the culture of autocratic Russia than of the Grand Duchy, with its own jealously guarded laws, institutions, and customs.

The atmosphere of benevolent autocracy and easy-going cosmopolitanism which had allowed loyal elites from Finland and the Baltic provinces more or less to run their own affairs for decades was now giving way to one in which the interests of the Russian empire were paramount, and the privileges of the borderlands were seen as either outmoded or downright dangerous. Alexander III's key advisors and ministers would have approved the sentiment of the polemicist Yuri Samarin, who argued that the Russians demanded to be in Russia what the French were in France and the British in the territories under British rule. And as we have seen, the emperor himself expressed his outrage when the tail seemed to be wagging the dog. The Finnish postal system was in fact merged with that of the empire by imperial edict in 1890, prompting a wave of protests in Finland. In Finnish eyes, the emperor had violated constitutional procedure by consulting neither the Senate nor the

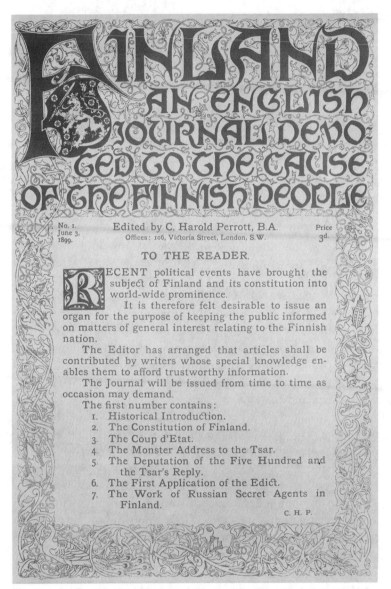

Plate 17 Finland. An English journal devoted to the cause of the Finnish people, 1899. The Finns had learnt the value of publicising their case abroad during the 1890s, having pamphlets and books outlining the Finnish constitutionalist arguments translated into French, German, and English, and writing articles on this subject for the foreign press. They were

estates. There were rumours that the Senate might refuse to pro-
mulgate the new legislation in the official gazette and from the
pulpit (new laws were read out to the congregation by the clergy).
The procurator Alexander von Weissenberg, who had earlier
aroused suspicions in St Petersburg with his attempts to codify
Finnish public law in a way deemed to give the Senate a constitutional existence, resigned in protest. Leo Mechelin also left the
Senate at the request of the governor-general, in all probability
because of his activities in publicising the Finnish case abroad.
The estates weighed into the fray at the end of 1890, voicing their
concerns in their responses to the speech from the throne that
opened the session of the Diet. The emperor subsequently issued a
rescript, assuring the estates that he had no intention of violating
the laws that governed Finland; but it was clear that the tighter
union of the Grand Duchy and the empire was now the object of
close scrutiny. Whereas the Finns had earlier sought to codify the
laws to strengthen their constitutional claims, they now resisted
determined Russian attempts to impose the framework of general
imperial legislation upon the Grand Duchy.

Unlike his predecessor, Alexander III was not honoured with a
prominent statue erected in the very centre of Helsinki, Senate
Square; and yet, in spite of his testy outbursts and lack of sympathy
with the protestations of the Senate, he was in some ways, as

Caption for Plate 17 (*cont.*)
quick off the mark in responding to the manifesto issued in February 1899
by Tsar Nicholas II. Two academics were despatched to western Europe,
where they succeeded in persuading the French newspaper *Le Temps* to
publish a pro-Finnish leader on 24 March, and the *Times* to highlight the
proposed address on behalf of Finland, to be signed by leading cultural
personalities throughout Europe. The publication illustrated above was
distributed free to the press and persons of influence. Expensive to produce,
and edited by Englishmen who were felt to be unfamiliar with Finnish
affairs, it ceased publication within the year, and was replaced with a
quarterly, *Finland Bulletin*, which appeared from 1900 to 1907. Finland's
case received a good deal of publicity abroad, attracting the interest of
public figures such as the French radical politician Clemenceau and the
British journalist W. T. Stead, who engaged in polemical debate with the
Russian minister of the interior and state-secretary for Finland,
V. K. Plehve.

Robert Schweitzer has noted, the most 'constitutional' of all the Russian monarchs who ruled over Finland. He delegated a number of important decision-making functions to the Senate, and established a working relationship with the estates that his father had never contemplated. The exceptional laws of 1881 that turned Russia into a police state were not applied to Finland, and on one occasion, Alexander censured Governor-General Heiden for having a Finnish subject arrested by the Russian police, called in to track down revolutionary sympathisers and activists in Russian units stationed in Finland. The process of integrating the western borderlands into the empire had gone much further in the Baltic provinces than in Finland, which retained intact all its administrative and judicial institutions and practices, and whose ruling elite was still able to force the emperor to abandon plans to bring Finnish tariffs and the customs service under imperial control, or to agree to changes in the Finnish criminal law code demanded by his advisors. Governor-General Heiden also managed to frustrate the efforts of the minister of war to bring the Finnish troops under closer central control, partly in defence of his own position as military district commander, but also out of concern that any meddling in Finnish affairs would only serve to alienate a loyal people.

Those pressing for change were, however, stronger than the defenders of the status quo. The aged Heiden retired from office early in 1897. Proposals drawn up in committee for the integration of the Finnish armed forces were approved by Nicholas II in June 1898; the task of pushing through this and other measures designed to bring about 'the true incorporation of Finland into the empire', in the words of the minister of war, General A. N. Kuropatkin, was entrusted to another soldier, General Nikolay Ivanovich Bobrikov. The appointment in August 1898 of Bobrikov as governor-general of Finland was part of a carefully concerted campaign to ensure the proposed reforms would be pushed through. As chief of staff of the St Petersburg military district from 1884, Bobrikov had worried about the provision made for the defences of Finland, and had become a convinced supporter of firmer Russian control over its western borderland. In the preface to the programme for Finland which he drafted in the summer of 1898, he declared bluntly that, ninety years after Finland had been conquered by

Russia, it still remained a frontier area alien to its Russian bene-
factor. The ten measures he outlined included reducing the role of
the minister state-secretary and strengthening the powers of the
governor-general, the integration of the armed forces, the abolition
of separate customs and monetary systems, and the introduction of
Russian into the Senate, civil service, and schools. Bobrikov antici-
pated opposition, and was determined not to back away from it, as
had his predecessors, but to crush it with force, if necessary.

Those in the know had more than an inkling of change in the air.
The speech from the throne that opened the session of the extraordinary Diet convened at the beginning of 1899 clearly announced
that a separate military establishment for Finland was now considered redundant and that the military service law would have to be
brought into conformity with that in force in the empire. Although
the emperor appeared to be anxious to conform as far as possible to
established practice in presenting the new legislation to the estates
for their careful consideration, it was made plain that it was now
the Finns who would have to adjust to imperial demands, rather
than be allowed to adapt imperial demands to their own peculiar
circumstances. The obfuscation and delays that had dogged
Heiden's attempts to draft basic regulations for the administration
of the Grand Duchy which would subject it to the general laws of
the empire would no longer be tolerated. A vivid example of how
Russian attitudes had hardened occurred at a reception in St
Petersburg at the end of August 1898. When the chief secretary
to the minister state-secretary for Finland tried to point out that,
for Bobrikov's appointment as governor-general to be legal, the
minister state-secretary had to countersign the imperial decree,
Kuropatkin lost his temper and shouted, 'Get this straight: His
Majesty the Emperor has by his will as ruler condescended to
institute a new order.'

In spite of these warning signals, it was the publication early in
1899 of what became known as the February manifesto that
marked in Finnish eyes the decisive departure from the path of
constitutional legality by the emperor and his advisors and the
beginning of what is still known as the 'period of oppression'.
The manifesto was significant in that it sought once and for all to
resolve the complex issue of how imperial state legislation should

be enacted in Finland by shifting the balance from Finnish to Russian institutions. By failing to define what was meant by imperial legislation, the manifesto threatened to leave Finland at the mercy of imperial ministers and the State Council, with the Senate and Diet having only the authority to make statements on the proposed legislation. But, as recent research has shown, the manifesto was in conformity with existing practice, and the claims of the Diet to be involved in the legislative process rested upon the practical experience of the previous thirty-six years, rather than upon any juridical foundation. As Tuomo Polvinen remarks, the Finns in Helsinki failed to comprehend 'that the system had worked only thanks to the tactful flexibility shown by those concerned in St Petersburg'.

The manifesto was not however such a 'bolt from the blue' as it is made out to be in much of contemporary and subsequent literature. The gloomy alarums sounded in the Finnish press, the much-used image of the fair-haired Finnish maiden clutching a weighty law book against the claws of a double-headed eagle hovering threateningly overhead, and Sibelius' symphonic poem *Finlandia* have helped preserve the images of icy times (*routa-aika*) and oppression (*sortokausi*), the standard terms used in virtually every Finnish history book for the period 1899–1905. Bobrikov's brief tenure of office was undoubtedly a political watershed, which radically affected Finnish attitudes and prospects; but what is perhaps more striking to the detached observer is that, in comparison with other borderland areas of the European empires, the Grand Duchy of Finland had managed to maintain a harmonious and beneficial relationship with the ruler for so long.

Although Snellman's followers in the Finnish nationalist camp feared that his goal of one language and one mind had not been achieved when the Russian onslaught began in earnest, there had developed in Finnish public life over the previous decades a self-confidence and sense of purpose that sustained resilience and generated resourcefulness in the bad times. Finland was a nation in the throes of consolidation, perhaps not as the language extremists would have wished, but as a body of active, participating citizens. In this process, a key role was played by associational activity in bringing people together, and in creating and disseminating a set of images of nationhood. The bringing together of people from different back-grounds and regions in pursuit of a particular goal – abstinence, education, social improvements – was an essential component in the process of nation-building. Worries about the poor standards of hygiene and housekeeping amongst the rural population on the frontier with Russia which might render the uncultured and poverty-stricken inhabitants of these frontier regions – especially the women – easy prey for the 'seductive temptations of the eastern neighbour' lay behind the founding of the immensely successful Martha association in 1899, according to its own twenty-fifth anniversary publication. In the words of the moving spirit behind the association, Lucina Hagman, the treasures of knowledge and culture had to be carried directly into Finnish homes, above all to the woman at the heart of the home, 'so that she might grow to be the stout protector of Finnish culture, a self-assured fighter for her country's rights'. In the more populous southern and western areas of the country, with good access to communications, a lively and growing provincial press competed for subscriptions; youth clubs, workers' associations, farmers' societies, choirs, and bands offered secular alternatives to church-inspired activities, and attracted sizeable memberships. A parish such as Sippola, for instance, located in the timber-processing region of the Kymi valley, had in 1915 over four hundred members of one of the earliest of the Martha associa-tions, over three hundred members of the temperance society, founded in 1886, in addition to a well-supported youth club and countryman's society, choral and theatre groups.

The promotion of the national cause was by no means confined to these cultural and social activities. Farmers' co-operatives, sav-ings banks, and insurance companies also embodied national images and ideals, not least in the names adopted from the *Kalevala* and in the architecture and decoration of the company headquar-ters. Although a sometimes mystical attachment to the countryside and rural values and a dislike of the Swedish-speaking elite that owned and ran most of the enterprises in Finland gave *fennoman* rhetoric a distinctly anti-industrial tinge – the economist O. K. Kilpi even concluded that the Finnish temperament itself was unsuited for entrepreneurial activity, and the educated classes in Finland

Plate 18 'Swedes and Finns'. A cartoon from the satirical magazine, *Fyren*, 1907. The bitter, almost savage tone of this cartoon echoes the sudden loss of status and political importance of the Swedish-speaking minority in Finland, as well as their foreboding about the future of the country in the

were more adept at collecting folk poems and artefacts than at
business – there was no shortage of young men fired with enthusiasm
for the national ideal and eager to challenge the hegemony of the old
Swedish-speaking business elite. Sons of the clergy were especially
active, founding the first 'national' bank, Kansallis-Osake-Pankki
(KOP), in 1889 and building sawmills and pulp-processing factories.
The university was not short of would-be businessmen either.
Finnish-minded professors provided the inspiration for the insurance companies Pohjola and Suomi, and the botanist A. Oswald
Kairamo, himself the son of an academic father who succeeded in
industry, was a major player in the financial and commercial world.

Those concerned to defend the position and rights of Swedish
speakers in Finland were also active in founding organisations,
which pursued the same improving and patriotic objectives as
their Finnish-language counterparts, albeit with increasing
emphasis on a distinctive Swedishness. Much heat and some division was generated by the language conflict. A leading member
of the Swedish-speaking cultural elite, C. G. Estlander, caused a
stir in 1880 when he appeared to suggest that it might now be time

Caption for Plate 18 (*cont.*)

aftermath of revolution. Rising above the gloom, with the rising sun behind
them, are those whom the Swedish-speaking nationalists believed to be the
most appropriate bearers of culture and enlightenment in Finland – army
officers, students, artists, and farmers, grouped around a flag emblazoned
with the three crowns of the Scandinavian union. Beneath them, howling
and hollering in the dark, with red banners aloft, are the agitators, villains,
and cutthroats of the socialist movement, alongside the priests representing
the Finnish nationalist movement. This bleak vision also comes through in
the poems and writings of the more intense Swedish-language nationalists,
such as Bertel Gripenberg, Artur Eklund, and Karl Robert Wikman, and in
the attribution of distinctive and separate racial (and by implication,
cultural) characteristics. Parliamentary reform in 1906 forced the Swedish-
speaking elite to reassess their position and role, and to make common
cause with the much larger rural constituency of farmers, fishermen, and
small traders along the Ostrobothnian and southern Finnish coastline. The
formation of a Swedish People's Party in 1906 helped provide a political
mouthpiece for the concerns of the Swedish-speaking population, and
ensured that it did not become isolated or shunned, as has happened to
minorities elsewhere in Europe.

for those who considered their cultural heritage to be threatened by militant nationalism to consider casting off for a distant strand (i.e., Sweden) with their Lares and Penates, their Runeberg and Kalevala, and with the bold message, *Ubi bene, ibi patria*, inscribed on their pennants. Four years earlier, Yrjö Koskinen had also aroused passions by belittling Finland's debt of gratitude towards Sweden, pointing out that Finnish culture owed far more to Russia. Yrjö Koskinen had helped push through the decision to make Finnish the only language of the Ostrobothnian student association, or 'nation'. Those who refused to accept this eventually broke with the association and formed their own, aligning themselves with the militants of the Nyland student nation and their journal *Vikingen* (the word 'Viking' was to be used by Finnish nationalists as a term of opprobrium for their opponents). The idea of a separate Swedish-Finnish nationality was pugnaciously propounded at the end of the century by members of a generation influenced by racial theories, and given distinctive characteristics – energetic, freedom-loving, individualistic, coastal-dwellers looking west across the sea for their inspiration, in contrast to the silent, dreamy Finns whose origins lay in Asia. Both sides of the language divide adopted different symbols and colours. The favoured tree of the Swedish-speakers was the pine, which stood up proud and tall in the storm, whilst Finnish writers such as Juhani Aho and Santeri Alkio found in the juniper bush qualities of survival and toughness under duress that fitted the Finnish people. Swedish-language poets such as Arvid Mörne found inspiration in the skerries and the open sea; Finnish writers looked to the forest. Aho, who wrote excitedly about the tall new buildings and boulevards that were transforming Helsinki into a truly continental city, nevertheless confessed that after a while, the heart longed for the deep country-side, and the novelist Teuvo Pakkala was highly critical of what he saw as the unnatural pretensions and alien manners of the Finnish-speaking elite in the capital. This sense of unease and alienation from the capital, the locus of wealth and luxurious living, still dominated by Swedish-speakers, frequently surfaces in the literary and political discourse of Finnishness from the end of the nineteenth century and into the first decades of Finnish independence.

The rifts and splits within the relatively small circle of educated Finns who busied themselves with associational activities and formed public opinion were however trifling in comparison with the divide that was to open up between them and much of 'the people' in whose name they claimed to speak. It was not that these activists and opinion-formers were unaware of social problems, or unsympathetic to their resolution. The land question was widely discussed and the plight of the rural poor was realistically presented to a reading public in the novels and poems of writers such as Minna Canth and Karl Tavaststjerna. The interest taken by the Russian press in the problems of the Finnish countryside and the rumours of the tsar being about to intervene in the poor peasants' favour that occasionally circulated made a solution or at least alleviation of the problems of the landless poor and of the leasehold crofters with their lack of secure rights a national necessity. The workers' associations founded in the 1880s were largely the work of middle-class reformers such as the furniture manufacturer Viktor Julius von Wright, who was inspired by the efforts of liberals in Germany and Denmark to promote workers' education. Influential social reformers such as Heikki Renvall and Wilhelm Chydenius actively propagated the right of workers to organise and to strike. Although inclined towards patriarchal arrangements, government and employers placed relatively few obstacles in the way of workers seeking to organise themselves into trade unions. For the rural population from which the workforce was largely recruited, factory work offered a better standard of living and new opportunities, especially for women. Enlightened employers such as the Nottbeck family that owned the Finlayson textile works in Tampere provided a wide range of facilities from accommodation to libraries, and were often actively involved in the running of workers' associations. In her 1903 survey of the condition of the working class in Finland, Alexandra Kollontay noted that the willingness of government, society, and the workers themselves to work together was one reason why the 'worker question' in Finland was less fraught than in other countries.

Kollontay also concluded that the workers were as yet little influenced by socialism. Yrjö Koskinen had voiced the hope that the 'weeds' of socialism would not spread to Finland in 1876, and

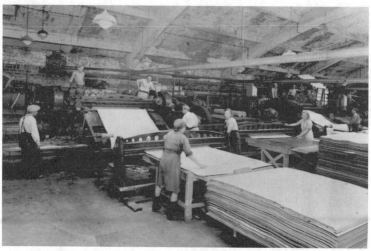

Plate 19 Workers in a veneer factory. In this photograph, taken in the 1920s, women are selecting and grading veneer at the Viiala factory in the Kymi valley. Women have always constituted a major element of the workforce in Finland (see also Plate 4). A couple of British Quakers travelling through the Finnish countryside in the middle of the nineteenth century were indeed moved to observe that the womenfolk seemed to do all the rough, hard outdoor work whilst their menfolk spent their time indoors smoking their pipes. The vast majority of workers in Finnish industry were recruits from the countryside, and for many young women, the factory offered the opportunity to escape the drudgery of farmwork and to enjoy an unwonted degree of independence. A study of working-class formation in the textile-manufacturing town of Tampere found that women working in the mills often enjoyed a modest degree of prosperity, until they married (some did not, and even bought shares in the company). They were also involved in associational activities, especially the temperance movement. A small number of middle-class women rose to prominence on the international stage, in particular, in the women's suffrage movement. They were also active in the promotion of the national cause through organisations such as the Martha association, which taught peasant women how to rear poultry, make conserves, and inculcate national values in the home. Votes for women was not a serious issue during the debates on parliamentary reform in 1906, and full and equal voting rights were given to both men and women in the Parliament Act of that year.

had advocated education and enlightenment in the national spirit as the most effective means of combating the threat. This was the underlying philosophy of the social-liberal labour movement of the 1880s; although artisans who had picked up socialist ideas during their journeyman wanderings in Scandinavia and Germany began to take over the leadership of the workers' associations from the mid-1890s, this mixture of social reformism and nationalism remained embedded in the movement.

What was different, however, was the keen sense of social injustice felt by those who took over the leadership of the associations, and the determination to be free of the patriarchal-authoritarian social order that controlled their lives. The labour movement articulated at a national level the undercurrent of hostility towards the gentry (*herraviha*) which existed amongst the rural poor and in the growing ranks of the proletariat, more often than not seasonally employed in the forests and log floats. The determination to be free of 'bourgeois guardianship' drove a wedge between the fledgling labour party, founded in 1899 (from 1903, the Social Democratic Party of Finland), and their erstwhile sympathisers now loosely organised in the constitutionalist passive resistance to russification. The editor of the main labour newspaper, *Työmies*, caused much offence by urging workers not to sign the mass address organised as a national protest against the February manifesto, and a hard core of the party leadership persisted in refusing to become involved in what they saw as a purely bourgeois conflict. As long as the movement remained numerically insignificant and politically powerless, this could be dismissed as sour grapes, and there were in any event other labour leaders, most notably in Tampere, who supported the passive resistance; but the dramatic events of 1905 were to transform the situation virtually overnight, propelling the labour movement to the forefront of Finnish politics.

The February manifesto and the measures that followed – the language manifesto of 1900, which was intended to make Russian the official language of all the highest echelons of administration and the military service law of 1901, which ended the separate existence of the Finnish army – not only split the small ruling circles, but also divided the country at large. The mood of the Senate shifted from compliance to defiance, and it took the casting vote of the vice-chairman to ensure that the manifesto would be published. Acting on Bobrikov's advice, the emperor refused to see a delegation of senators bearing a petition asking him to confirm that he had no intention of restricting Finland's constitutional rights. Delegations bearing the mass address, signed by over half a million Finns, and a petition signed by over a thousand distinguished foreign supporters of Finland's cause were also denied access to the emperor. In the summer of 1900, having failed to persuade the emperor to withdraw the language manifesto, the Senate finally split asunder, with the eight senators who had voted against publication of the law resigning.

The new Senate appointed in August was drawn largely from the ranks of the so-called 'compliance' wing of the Old Finn party, of which Yrjö Koskinen was the leading figure. A renowned polemicist, the aged Yrjö Koskinen alienated even his closest supporters by elevating the language struggle above calls for national unity. In an 'open letter to my friends', published in the Old Finns' main newspaper *Uusi Suometar* in December 1900, he expressed doubts whether the Finnish party existed any longer, since it seemed to have no programme or policy, and offered his own: all links to be severed with the 'so-called Swedish party', intransigent 'Viking' opponents of the Finnish language, support for the government that was doing its best to protect the rights of the people, and the strengthening of the Finnish language.

Yrjö Koskinen's sarcastic dismissal of 'a certain wagging Finnish tail' that followed the 'Vikings' was deeply resented by those, mostly in the Young Finn camp, who chose to make common cause with the Swedish party in resisting the assault upon what they took to be Finland's constitutional status. The leadership of this passive resistance, which took organisational form in the winter of 1900–01, was, however mostly in the hands of Swedish-speaking liberal constitutionalists such as Leo Mechelin. Government, and many of the civil service posts vacated by those sympathetic with the constitutionalist position, now passed into the hands of 'Finnish-minded' men. The language rescript of 1902, which had been carefully prepared by the new minister state-secretary for Finland, the high-ranking Russian official, V. K. Plehve, prompted Yrjö-Koskinen to declare that the Finnish people welcomed with joy and gratitude a measure which finally gave the language of the majority equal status with Swedish. In other words, the Finnish cause seemed set to make notable advances, in spite of circumstances which Yrjö Koskinen, as a firm adherent of Snellman's Hegelian determinism, regarded as an inevitable historical consequence before which small nations had to bend in order to survive.

He failed, however, to see that, in Osmo Jussila's words, 'Finnish and Swedish were competing only for the silver and bronze medals, since the gold medal had already been awarded'. And any hope that compliance might soften Bobrikov's policies were illusory. The governor-general believed that advantage had to be taken of the willingness of a certain section of the Finnish party to yield to Russian demands, 'but this has to be done exclusively for the large-scale importation of Russians into the borderland and the binding of this borderland to the empire. The Finns' compliance cannot, of course, be allowed to lead to any vital concessions to them on Russia's part.' Although unable to breach the walls of the Senate and appoint Russians, Bobrikov made progress in seeking to downgrade it to become a council led by and subordinated to the governor-general. As early as 1901, he succeeded in having a Russian appointed as governor of Uusimaa county, and the wave of resignations occasioned by the clashes over conscription in 1903 allowed him to appoint more. He ferreted into areas of Finnish life than none of his predecessors had probably even been aware of, ordering all state offices, schools, and courtrooms to display portraits of the emperor and the Russian royal family, establishing a committee to inspect Finnish school textbooks, and intervening to remove the restrictions on foreign traders after pedlars from eastern Karelia protested that Finnish officials, influenced by the rising anti-Russian mood of the populace, had been persecuting them. The governor-general also worked actively to win the hearts of the poor, promoting soup kitchens for the unemployed in the cities during the winter of 1902–03 and supporting the Senate's efforts to tackle the landless problem; but his interventions, far from providing real or lasting relief, tended if anything to arouse expectations of aid from on high which were inevitably frustrated. As in Russia, where agents of the regime were also active in promoting worker welfare as a means of combating revolutionary socialism, the policy ultimately backfired in 1905.

During his short tenure of office, Bobrikov undoubtedly made significant inroads on behalf of the empire into what he regarded as a conquered province that had somehow been allowed to detach itself, with its own national anthem and national heroes; but his efforts were also opposed and even thwarted by those in Russia who otherwise shared his basic assumptions. Personal rivalries and antipathies frequently meant that proposals were altered or even lost, and this occasionally allowed the Senate, which inherited a long tradition of being able to play the system to Finland's advantage, to frustrate the plans of the governor-general. Bobrikov also ran up against the problem of inadequate resources, especially the lack of skilled Russian-speakers with a good knowledge of the country; he was even compelled to write many of his own letters and instructions because no suitable copyists or clerks could be found. But perhaps the most serious obstacle to the fulfilment of his programme was the growing alarm in Russia that a part of the empire hitherto loyal and peaceful was now being plunged into a state of violent agitation.

That violence was largely a consequence of the introduction of a new military service law in 1901. This disbanded all units of the Finnish army save one regiment of dragoons (which Bobrikov soon had disbanded as well) and a guards battalion. The number of Finns who would actually have to perform military service was tiny; 500 of the 25,000 or so eligible for the draft in 1902, 190 in the next two years, would be selected by lot. The implementation of the law, however, brought home to the Finnish population at large the full import of Bobrikov's programme. It was also a splendid opportunity for the passive resistance to rally patriotic opposition. According to Bobrikov's own figures, fewer than half of those who received call-up papers turned up for the draft in spring 1902. In Helsinki, Cossack troops were called out to control the crowds that had gathered to jeer at the few men who did obey the summons. The image of whip-wielding Cossacks charging Finnish citizens was a rude awakening to the brutalities of political oppression long familiar elsewhere in the Russian empire. A year later, Bobrikov was given extensive powers to detain and send into exile leaders of the opposition, and to ban meetings and organisations. Many of the leaders of the passive resistance moved abroad; many more sympathisers in public service were dismissed. The larger-than-life maverick, Konni Zilliacus, one of the first journalists to suffer at the hands of Bobrikov, forged links with the Russian revolutionary movement, and helped organise the smuggling of illegal literature and weapons into Finland. A small number of Swedish-speaking students were moved to consider active resistance, and began to plot the assassination of the most hated figures of the Bobrikov regime, including the governor-general himself. A number of attempts were in fact carried out, and the procurator of the 'compliance' Senate was murdered. The most celebrated assassination was, however, that of Bobrikov himself, who was shot and fatally wounded on 16 June 1904 by Eugen Schauman, the twenty-nine-year-old son of a former senator. A few weeks later, a bomb attack in Russia carried off the minister state-secretary (from 1902, minister of the interior as well), V. K. Plehve.

Schauman acted alone, and immediately killed himself. His action was hailed as the deed of a selfless patriot by the passive resistance, but was seen as a reckless act by the beleaguered Old Finn party that still sought to keep channels to Russia open. Bobrikov's onslaught on Finland had forced many who had hitherto remained outside the narrow ambit of political decision-making to appraise their own position. Doctors, local government officials, and above all, members of the clergy found themselves in the front line. Most clergymen heeded the call of the archbishop Gustaf Johansson to obey higher authority and read out from the pulpit the new decrees, though a small minority refused to do so, and others connived with their parishioners to ensure that the words were either drowned out by a stirring hymn or unheard by the congregation, which left the church at a pre-arranged signal beforehand. The sharp decline in church attendance that set in during this period may have been coincidental, but there is no doubt that the prestige and status of the church suffered from its perceived inability to provide strong and unequivocal moral and patriotic leadership.

Bobrikov's assassination put an end to any hopes of some respite for Finland. The measures put in place to introduce the Russian language were beginning to bite; most official posts were now in the hands of men willing to comply with the new order; and the banishing of most of the constitutionalist leadership had reduced the effectiveness of the passive resistance. The suspension of the military service law could be construed as a victory for the Finns, but the Russian authorities deemed it more prudent to make the inhabitants of a strategically vulnerable borderland pay a hefty sum towards the defence of the empire than cause trouble in the ranks. Much-needed franchise and social reforms in Finland were now being delayed by the demonstrative 'go-slow' opposition of the estates, convened in December 1904 to resolve the military service question. The Diet finally agreed to vote the sum of ten million marks to be paid annually towards imperial defence in return for the suspension of the 1901 military service law, but had no time to debate thoroughly the Senate's proposals for suffrage reform, much to the anger of a labour movement demonstration outside.

The rising tide of unrest in the Russian empire during 1905 burst into open revolution at the end of October. The course of events in Finland were markedly at variance with the disorderly and often bloody clashes that occurred elsewhere in the empire. The strike which paralysed the Russian railway network was already several days' old before Finnish railwaymen working on the short stretch of line from the frontier to the Finland Station in St Petersburg joined it, on 29 October. The next day, a meeting of labour representatives in Helsinki proclaimed a general strike and elected a strike committee, but also agreed to collaborate with the constitutionalists. The impetus for the strike – which by 31 October had spread throughout most of the country – was the general desire to sweep away the measures of the Bobrikov years and to purge the Senate of 'those detestable toadies, who. . . by creeping to the Russian bureaucracy. . . have shamelessly trodden underfoot not only the law but also the people's deepest sense of justice', in the words of the 'Red' manifesto drafted by labour activists in the town of Tampere on 1 November. In that respect, it was truly a national, patriotic strike, and it passed off in relative peace and harmony. To maintain order, national guards were set up in the main cities. The Russian troops remained out of sight, though rumours of impending attacks contributed to a generally nervous atmosphere in the capital and surrounding area. Throughout the country, the old order virtually ceased to function, and many of its representatives either resigned or fled. The Senate resigned on 31 October. The constitutionalist leadership now demanded the replacement of Governor-General Ivan Obolensky and Minister State-Secretary Constantin Linder, as well as other high-ranking officials who had been appointed in place of those who had resigned or been dismissed from office for their opposition. In this, they were in full agreement with the representatives of labour and the small active resistance movement. Where they differed was on the question of suffrage reform. The constitutionalists wanted the reform to be carried out by the four-estate Diet. Labour leaders and the activists in Helsinki and other major towns demanded that constitutional reform be effected either by a convention of 'representatives of the people' or by a national assembly elected by all Finnish subjects over the age of twenty-one. A compromise suggestion by the constitutionalists on 3 November that an unofficial national assembly be elected to act as a kind of watchdog over the deliberations of the Senate and Diet on the matter of suffrage reform was rejected by the labour leaders, who had already detached themselves from collaboration with other parties. The staging in Helsinki of the election of a national provisional government the following day was essentially a futile gesture of defiance by the central strike committee, now under pressure to call the strike off. This decision was taken on 5 November.

On the surface, the strike appeared to have been a great victory for the constitutionalists. Their demands were accepted by the emperor, whose manifesto of 4 November rescinded all the offensive legislation of the Bobrikov era and authorised the Senate to prepare proposals for the freedom of the press, suffrage reform, and a constitutional decree that would recognise the right of the new national assembly (*eduskunta*) to supervise the lawfulness of the actions of the members of the government and secure the rights of speech, assembly, and association for the citizens of Finland. These proposals were to be presented to an extraordinary session of the Diet. The emperor also accepted the resignation of the old 'compliance' Senate and the appointment of a new one headed by Leo Mechelin. The only person deemed completely unacceptable to the emperor was Pehr Evind Svinhufvud, who had earned a reputation as an outspoken and very public opponent of the regime, and who was to remain a thorn in the flesh of the imperial authorities during the so-called second period of oppression. All the other members of the Senate had been principled constitutionalist opponents of the regime, including a representative of the labour movement (who was eventually disowned by an increasingly orthodox Marxist Social Democratic Party).[2] The bureaucracy was also purged of 'compliance' men.

The constitutionalists' position was however much weaker than this seeming triumph would suggest. They now occupied the position of their despised predecessors of having to work with the Russian authorities, and were identified with the preservation of the status quo ante Bobrikov at a time of change. Many distinguished scions of the great families that had ruled the affairs of the Grand Duchy since 1809, they still occupied positions of power, but could no longer expect to retain these positions by relying on deference and a reluctance to challenge their hegemony. This was as true in industry and commerce as it was in political life. The challenge to a liberal constitutionalism that was associated in the popular mind with the Swedish-speaking upper classes and city dwellers came from two interlinked directions, Finnish nationalism and the labour movement. The former, intensely agrarian in its values, more than willing to beat the populist drum against the wicked (and mostly Swedish-speaking or foreign) entrepreneurs whose supposed 'rape of the woods' aroused so much heated debate at the beginning of the century (in reality, only one-third of the timber cut was destined for industry; almost a half was purely for domestic consumption), also sought to capture the state, and to use it. The labour movement, many of whose prominent post-1905 leaders had been influenced as students by Finnish nationalism, shared these anti-Swedish prejudices, and has indeed been described as 'left-wing *fennomani*'. It was heavily dependent after 1905 on the support of the rural proletariat, and much of its rhetoric reflected the class hatred (*herraviha*) of the countryside. Collaboration with the constitutionalists during the strike week served only to reinforce suspicions and hostility towards the traditional ruling elite. The socialist newspaper *Kansan Lehti*, which had earlier supported co-operation with the passive resistance, summed up the general mood of the movement at the end of the strike, denouncing the constitutionalists as 'Vikings and their agents . . . contenders for power, a sort of clique wishing to speak and act in the name of all the people': what had begun as a patriotic demonstration against oppression had now become a class struggle.

For the organised labour movement, the strike week was a watershed. Membership of the Social Democratic Party rose from a little over sixteen thousand at the end of 1904 to 45,298 a year later, and reached a peak of almost one hundred thousand in 1906. Most of this increase occurred in rural areas; and although membership declined as the initial post-revolutionary wave of enthusiasm ebbed, the number of workers' associations continued to grow to 1,584 in 1913. The pride and joy of the workers' association was the meeting hall, usually a timber construction erected by the members themselves. By 1913, there were 841 such halls scattered throughout Finland; Finnish emigrants even carried the workers' hall culture to the iron-ore fields of northern Minnesota and the textile towns of Massachusetts. The records of the Finnish workers' associations portray a movement imbued with a sense of moral seriousness verging on puritanism, living within a Manichean world of oppressors and oppressed, socially and even culturally isolated yet also part and parcel of the mainstream of Finnish national consciousness. The Finnish labour movement grew to maturity in an atmosphere of revolution which engendered a number of myths, not least that of the workers' red guard which had broken away from the national guard at the beginning of the strike week and later became involved in underground revolutionary activities. Many of the leading figures of the party after 1905, such as Otto Ville Kuusinen, Yrjö Sirola, and Kullervo Manner (all three of whom became leading figures in the Finnish communist party in exile), grew to maturity in an atmosphere of political turmoil which not only seriously threatened the values and assumptions that had underpinned Finnish political and public life for generations, but also set Finns against each other. The events of October–November 1905 gave rise to heightened expectations of immediate and sweeping changes, and created a mood of uncompromising impatience which the new party leadership sustained by

Plate 20 Cossacks on the streets of Helsinki, 1906. The revolution of 1905 left a legacy of unrest and violence of a kind hitherto unknown in the peaceful Grand Duchy of Finland. The press contained daily reports of discoveries of caches of weapons and bomb factories, with the occasional violent bank robbery or assault thrown in. An armed workers' 'red' guard was set up during the national strike (28 October–6 November 1905) and some of their number subsequently began making contact with the Russian revolutionaries. The culmination of this collaboration occurred in summer 1906, when a rebellion broke out amongst the garrison stationed on the fortress-island of Sveaborg, outside Helsinki. Red guard units attempted to join the rebels, and pressure was put on the leadership of the Social Democratic Party to declare a general strike in Helsinki. Members of the bourgeois 'white' guards, which had also come into being as a result of the 1905 national strike, intervened when red guards tried to shut down the tramway system. Shots were exchanged, and troops and police had to be called in to restore order. The cossacks pictured here were patrolling the streets looking for red guards who were trying to link up with the rebels. Cossacks had been called out in 1902 to clear a demonstration on the Senate Square, and were much loathed and feared in the capital.

threats of renewed mass strike action if radical franchise reform was not carried through.

In private, however, the post-1905 leadership of the Social Democratic Party was distinctly uneasy about losing control of the more militant elements of the movement, and refused in 1906 to give way to red guard pressure to declare a general strike in support of a mutiny amongst the Russian garrison in the Sveaborg fortress. The Finnish socialists sedulously avoided close contact with Russian revolutionaries, preferring to emulate the German model of a disciplined, class-conscious, legally tolerated mass party. As Kuusinen himself admitted in 1917, the uncompromisingly revolutionary rhetoric of the party masked its essentially moderate character. Unfortunately, this subtle distinction was not always appreciated by the rank-and-file.

The Parliament Act of 1906 swept away the old four-estate Diet and replaced it with a single-chamber legislature (*eduskunta*) of two hundred members, elected according to the d'Hondt system of proportional representation by Finnish subjects, male and female, over the age of twenty-four. The legislation drafted by the Senate was thoroughly debated, but passed with remarkably little opposition. The house of nobility disliked the idea of a single-chamber legislature, and worried that the class which had the most experience of guiding the fortunes of the country would now be swept aside. Proportional representation and big constituencies were in part intended to calm such fears; the Senate leaders Leo Mechelin and Rabbe Wrede both claimed that large constituencies would not only sustain the solidarity of the people, but would also allow the 'more intelligent and mature' minorities to be represented.

In this assumption, they were proved right, at least insofar as the bearers of illustrious names from Finland's past were and continued to be elected to the *eduskunta* alongside the more humble representatives of the people. Most, but by no means all, were members of the Swedish People's Party, which proved to be extremely effective at bringing together the farmers and fishermen of the Swedish-speaking enclaves with the urban minorities, 'cultural aristocrats' and 'lonely Swedes' living and working in the Finnish-speaking hinterland to defend and promote what was now a minority linguistic group rather than a politically privileged class that had dominated the estates and government throughout the nineteenth century. Clergymen were also elected to the new parliament, and continued to play a not unimportant role in politics. The third prime minister of independent Finland, for example, was later to become archbishop, and the Lutheran church was able to exercise influence and control way beyond its spiritual and pastoral brief for many years after the estate of clergy disappeared.

That the twin pillars of the old order, established back in the reign of Alexander I, remained important elements in Finnish public life is in part a reflection of what might be termed the consensual conservatism of Finnish society, which valued continuity and respected established tradition, but was also prepared to embrace even radical and sudden reform in order to strengthen national solidarity. Had the revolution of 1905 freed Finland from Russia as Norway was separated at the same time from Sweden, this solidarity would in all likelihood have been strong enough to surmount the problems of poverty and landlessness which threatened social cohesion and stability. The labour movement might well have deviated to the left, as happened in Norway during the revolutionary years 1917–20, and there would undoubtedly have occurred crises that threatened to subvert the democratic order, but there was nothing in early twentieth-century Finland that is immediately identifiable as a major obstacle to the functioning of democracy, such as a reactionary and powerful landowning class, or an army with a marked predisposition to interfere in politics, whilst there was a great deal that marked the Grand Duchy out as a natural home of constitutionalist thought: the rule of law, honest government, and active citizen participation.

The fly in the ointment was that the democratic process was stalled by the autocracy, which by 1908 had begun to reassert control. What was in political terms a real revolution, propelling Finland to the front rank of modern parliamentary democratic institutions, proved abortive, or at least, premature. The renewed assault on Finland's autonomous status meant that the parliamentary system never properly functioned during the last decade of imperial rule in Finland, and many urgent reforms, such as security of tenure for leasehold farmers, could not be made. In place of practical political activity, the Finns had to make do with the politics of gesture and demonstration, which ultimately added to the frustration of those seeking amelioration in their circumstances. The revolution of 1917 seemed to offer once more a chance for reform carried forward by mass action. The privations of wartime gave an added edge to the grievances of the poor, and the aggrieved were prepared to use desperate means if necessary to secure their objectives. The social problems of Finland were by no means exceptional, but they were highlighted by the distortions of the political situation. The failure of parliamentary democracy and government meant that the new generation of Finnish politicians, especially the socialists who now occupied half of the benches of the *eduskunta*, had experienced few of the responsibilities that arise when such a system functions properly. The lack of power if anything tended to reinforce the rhetoric of the class struggle expounded by the socialists, and pushed the parties further apart. The vision of national solidarity still glimmered and was to survive even through the darkest days of revolution and civil war; but it was now deeply flawed and fissured by social and political strains.

5

The independent state, 1907–37

Seventy per cent of the electorate, 899,347 men and women in total, voted in the first elections to the new *eduskunta* in March 1907. The elections were a disappointment for the liberal-constitutionalist wing of Finnish nationalism, the Young Finns, who secured only twenty-six seats. Their Old Finn rivals managed to overcome accusations of having complied with the Bobrikov regime, winning fifty-nine seats, thanks in part to a radical programme. A newcomer to the political arena, the Agrarian Union (*Maalaisliitto*), took nine seats in northern and eastern Finland, largely at the expense of the Young Finns, from whence came most of the leadership of the new party.

It was, however, the left that fared best in the first democratic parliamentary elections in Finland. The Social Democratic Party took over one third of the votes cast, winning eighty of the two hundred seats. The real strength of the party lay in central and south-western Finland, and especially in the countryside, amongst the leasehold farmers and landless poor. It fared less well in Ostrobothnia and the north, where freehold farmers tended to dominate the local community, and in the Swedish-speaking coastal regions, where the Swedish People's Party (*Svenska folkpartiet*, SFP) scooped the pool. Social democracy continued to increase its support right up to the revolution of 1917, winning ninety seats in 1913, and an absolute majority of a hundred and three seats in the wartime elections of 1916.

The success of the left in 1907 surprised everyone, not least the socialists themselves. There was little public support for the arguments of the Young Finns for a change of government to reflect the result of the elections, and in any event, the emperor and his advisors were not minded to give way to any insistence on observing constitutionalist principles. Nicholas II chose to ignore Mechelin's request in 1908 that his government be replaced by one that had the confidence of the *eduskunta*. Instead, he dissolved the assembly, which had been publicly critical of his regime, and ordered new elections. A new government, bolstered with members of the Old Finn party, was formally announced on the day that the second *eduskunta* convened – a deliberate indication that power and authority rested with the emperor, and not with the elected representatives of the Finnish people.

The second *eduskunta* lasted only for one session. When the speaker of the house, the prominent constitutionalist Pehr Evind Svinhufvud, took issue with the manner in which Finnish affairs were being handled in his response to the speech from the throne, the assembly was once more prematurely dissolved, as were the next two. The fourth *eduskunta* was dissolved in 1910 after Svinhufvud, again elected speaker, declared that he was unable to present to the house bills that were contrary to the Finnish constitution. These bills were part of a renewed attempt to establish the principle of general imperial legislation, this time initiated by the imperial State Council and the new assembly, the State Duma, and included provision for the election by the *eduskunta* of four Finnish representatives to the Duma, and two to the State Council. The main thrust of this new offensive was to deprive the Finnish institutions of anything other than the right to voice an opinion on legislation deemed to have imperial, rather than merely local application. At the same time, a new government composed of men whose careers had been made in imperial Russian service was appointed. The governor-general, Frans Albert Seyn (1909–17), also ensured that officials loyal to the regime replaced those suspected of constitutionalist leanings, and strengthened the military presence in Finland to avoid any recurrence of unrest.

Although hailed by some Russian nationalists as the end of Finnish autonomy, and feared by the Finns as a second stage in the 'period of oppression', the main objective of these measures was the strengthening of the apparatus of law and order and an insurance of loyalty. The propensity of officialdom to get bogged down in detail meant that relatively little legislation of any significance was passed. The law of 1912 allowing other subjects of the emperor equal rights in Finland with Finnish citizens provoked resistance and led to the imprisonment of Finnish officials who refused to implement the law, but had hardly any time to have a real impact before the revolution of 1917. The *eduskunta* – which refused to elect representatives to the State Council or Duma – denounced as unconstitutional the way in which they were asked to agree to the imposition of a fixed annual payment towards imperial defence in lieu of conscription. The fact remains, however, that the costs of defence fell much more lightly upon the shoulders of the Finns than upon the emperor's other subjects. Ironically, in view of the almost universal loathing in the Grand Duchy of a Senate composed largely of superannuated admirals and soldiers, it was these very men who did much to keep the Finnish contribution to a minimum. The detailed programme of legislation published in 1914, the so-called 'russification programme' was never implemented, though it served as a grim reminder to the Finns that they could expect no concessions from imperial Russia should it emerge unscathed from the war. It was this threat, along with numerous niggling attempts to assert the Russian presence, that effectively precluded any return to the more harmonious days of the Russo-Finnish relationship.

Although the conflict between imperial interests and Finnish autonomy dominated political life in Finland after 1909, there were expectations of change that the government and *eduskunta* sought to meet in the brief window of opportunity that opened up after the revolution of 1905. Unfortunately, most of the legislative proposals placed before the assembly by the government failed to get beyond committee stage, largely as a result of political infighting, but also because the reforms proposed raised many awkward questions. The elected representatives were more willing than the government to move away from the age-old principle that the making and maintenance of roads was the responsibility of the local farmers, for instance, but were unsure as to who should pay, or whether that responsibility should be transferred entirely to the state. The cause

Plate 21 'One hundred years in captivity'. A cartoon from *Fyren,* 1908.
Karelia became a fiercely contested region – or rather, concept – during the
nineteenth century. For *fennoman* nationalists, it was the cradle of Finnish
culture, and it attracted the attention of ethnographers, artists, and writers
during the course of the nineteenth century. The activities of these Finnish
'karelianists' prompted Russian nationalists to organise in defence of
Orthodoxy, not only in the lands that had always been under some form of
Russian rule, but also across the frontier of the Grand Duchy. In 1907, an
Orthodox Karelian brotherhood was set up, with the intention of
combating Finnish influence. The brotherhood published newspapers in
Russian and Finnish, and founded Russian-language schools in Finnish

of prohibition, supported in principle by four of the five parties, almost became a symbol of the conflict between the representatives of the Finnish people and the autocracy; bills designed to prohibit the manufacture, import or sale of alcohol were passed four times between 1907 and 1914, and each time were ignored by the ruler. Prohibition finally came into effect in independent Finland in 1919, thanks to the willingness of the Russian provisional government to ratify the legislation.

It was, however, the land question that continued to cause the greatest headaches. Government enquiries and statistical surveys, a series of well-publicised evictions and rent strikes, and the willingness of the social democrats to take up the cause of the leasehold farmers thrust the crofter question into the limelight, though it was but a part of the bigger problem of rural poverty and the inability of the economy to provide an adequate and sustainable livelihood for much of Finland's population. Mostly small farmers, often obliged to move out of an old croft and create a new one on marginal land, the crofters struggled to keep up with technological and structural changes in agriculture, and with the demands on their time and labour imposed by their landlords. Almost three-quarters of the value of ground rent was paid in day labour, which might also

Caption for Plate 21 (*cont.*)
Karelia. One of its most active supporters, Archbishop Sergey, likened the union of Old Finland with the Grand Duchy to a hundred years of captivity, which had nevertheless failed to eliminate the past from the memory of the (presumably Orthodox) people, for whom Russia was not 'an alien neighbouring country, but its holy fatherland'. The Swedish-language satirical journal *Fyren* portrays the Karelian frontier as a defensive line in the fight for 'western' values of order, progress, and prosperity against the ragged Russian intruder. The conflict over Karelia was played out on many fronts, not least in commemorative statues and occasions. In 1908, a statue of the man held to be the founder of Viipuri, Tyrgils Knutsson, was finally erected in that city, after years of opposition from the Russians, and the Finnish nationalists, for whom Knutsson symbolised the 'robber knights' of Swedish domination. Three years later, the Russians erected with great ceremony a statue of Peter the Great on the hill from where he oversaw the conquest of Viipuri in 1710. The Finnish lion replaced Peter after Finland became independent; Peter was restored, and Knutsson destroyed, during Soviet times.

Plate 22 'If prohibition were to become a reality. . .' '. . . no more would Jean charm us with his divine tones.' In addition to being Finland's most renowned composer, Jean Sibelius (1865–1957) was also a well-known figure at one of Helsinki's most celebrated watering-holes. He is rumoured to have risen from the table one evening to catch the night train to St Petersburg to conduct a concert, returning two days later to find the same people sitting in exactly the same places. Then at the height of his creative powers, Sibelius had ensured his place amongst the immortals of Finnish culture with his evocative and intensely nationalistic compositions involve the use of the tenant's own horse and implements, and which the landlord invariably wanted performed at peak times of the farming year. The 1909 act, which was intended to provide a greater measure of security with minimum tenancies of fifty years, merely exacerbated the already tense relationship between tenant and landowner, for whom the even distribution of labour rent throughout the year, and the obligation to compensate tenants for clearance and construction carried out during their tenancies, were irritations and a further incentive to terminate agreements. A temporary ban on evictions appended to the 1909 act, and renewed again in 1915, merely postponed resolution of an issue widely seen as perpetuating an outmoded and unjust system.

The fact that the leaseholders and landless rallied in such massive numbers to support the socialists, and had earlier seemed more receptive to the rumours of the tsar dividing the lands than to the patriotic appeals of the passive resistance, was perceived by many contemporaries as a serious threat to the unity of the Finnish people. The mid nineteenth-century image of the loyal, obedient, god-fearing poor peasant portrayed in the writings of Runeberg and Topelius began to give way to a darker picture of a surly, brutal and vengeful rural proletariat, made bolder and more threatening by revolution and the unscrupulous agitation of the socialists. 'At

Caption for Plate 22 (*cont.*)
(*The Death of Kullervo*, 1880, *The Swan of Tuonela* and the *Karelia* suite in the 1890s, and *Finlandia* in 1899). He continued to develop as a composer, but after his Seventh Symphony (1927), he lapsed into silence for the remaining thirty years of his life. As this cartoon by Oscar Furuhjelm suggests, prohibition was not favoured by the Swedish-speaking 'cultural aristocracy'. Here, as in other aspects of life in Finland, attempts were made to attach racial or cultural proclivities to the drink problem. Finnish nationalists accused the Swedish-speaking bourgeoisie of opposing the sobering up of the Finnish people, members of the Swedish People's Party claimed the Swedes were less idealistic than the Finns, and had greater trust in the individual's capacity for self-discipline. Tempers easily frayed, and accusations flew. The socialist and veteran temperance man Väinö Wuolijoki ended a lengthy speech in a parliamentary debate of 1921 by accusing members of the Swedish People's Party of seeking to cure the 'Swedish coastal race' with alcohol, whereas 'we intend to cure the Finnish race with sobriety and the prohibition law'.

the bottom of everything, this crude, aching, centuries-old hatred of the gentry [*herraviha*], this vengeful rancour against those in this country who seem to have it too easy and who, protected by the gentry's laws, lord it over the poor', was the judgement of Ilmari Kianto, describing the impact of socialist agitation in a poverty-stricken and remote northern community in his novel *Punainen viiva* (*The Red Line*, 1909), a judgement echoed by many other writers and analysts of what went wrong between 1900 and 1918.

The general gloom and despondency of the last years of imperial rule reflected much of the uncertainty thrown up by rapid and often unexpected change – the sharp decline in religious observance, the loss of status and prestige for the clergy, and for the Swedish-speaking elite that had dominated the estates of the nobility and the burghers until the very end of the four-estate diet, the sudden rise of a verbally aggressive labour movement, and a Finnish nationalist movement no longer content simply to win control of the state apparatus, but seeking to challenge the economic hegemony of the established industrial and commercial elite. Uncertainty clouded the political future of the country. The war brought little prospect of change. Finland was not in the front line, and its young men were not required to serve in the imperial Russian army. The engineering, textile, and chemical industries enjoyed a brief boom period supplying the needs of the fighting forces, but the timber trade all but dried up as western markets became inaccessible. With the Senate and most key official posts in the hands of Governor-General Seyn's trusted nominees, and with the *eduskunta* effectively rendered impotent, political life in Finland fell into a state of virtual catalepsy.

In none of the political parties was any serious consideration given to the idea of Finland becoming an independent state; the most that was hoped for was a restoration of autonomy. An independent republic of Finland was declared to be the goal of the tiny Finnish active resistance movement in 1907, to be achieved by supporting the Russian revolutionary movement and by preparing to engage in terrorist activity should political repression return; but the momentum that had spawned activism slackened, and the movement had virtually ceased to exist by 1910. The war however provided a new opportunity. The old underground network was revived by a few survivors of the earlier phase of activism and a new generation of young men, mostly students. Contacts were made in Germany, as a result of which some two thousand young men received military training and experience on the eastern front as the 27th Royal Prussian Rifle Battalion (*Jägerbattalion*).

These activities, however, remained marginal and largely unknown. When revolution swept away the imperial regime in March 1917, the destiny of Finland seemed to lie with the political parties, given their head by a provisional Russian government willing to restore Finnish self-rule. The elections of the previous year, largely meaningless then since there was no prospect of the elected representatives meeting in session, had given the socialists an absolute majority (103 seats) in the *eduskunta*. After some hesitation, the socialists reluctantly agreed to enter into a coalition government, with the moderate trade unionist Oskari Tokoi as vice-chairman.

Within a month, it had become apparent that the restoration of Finnish autonomy was no longer adequate. Impatient at the provisional government's patent reluctance to countenance any interim readjustment of the powers of the Senate, and encouraged by their contacts with the more radical Russian revolutionaries, the Social Democratic Party openly endorsed national self-determination. The party conference in mid-June resolved to set 'against the demand of the Russian bourgeoisie for authority to subjugate the demand of the Finnish people for political independence', which would be secured by international guarantees. The Finnish socialists managed a fortnight later to secure the backing of the first all-Russian Congress of Soviets for the right to national self-determination, though the congress also insisted that the final resolution of the Finnish question should lie within the competence of the all-Russian national constituent assembly when it met. The Finnish socialists chose to ignore this important proviso, and, believing that a rising tide of radicalism in Russia favoured their cause, prepared to challenge the provisional government. A rather timid Senate bill on the exercise of authority placed before the *eduskunta* on 8 June was mauled in committee and replaced a month later by a new, radical socialist draft that effectively transferred supreme authority to that assembly. It was to convene and dissolve itself, it would decide the executive power in Finland, and appoint and dismiss ministers. The power to determine, confirm, and order the execution of all the laws of Finland was to lie solely with the *eduskunta*, which would also finally determine 'all other matters concerning Finland which formerly were decided by the emperor and grand duke in accordance with the laws then in force'. Matters of foreign policy, military legislation, and administration were, however, explicitly excluded: the socialists stopped short of proposing full sovereign independence.

The so-called law on supreme power, which secured the requisite majorities from the socialists and the growing band of activist sympathisers in the assembly on 18 July 1917, was, in fact, more an attempt to transform Finland into a parliamentary democracy than a bid for full independence, something which the rhetoric of the occasion and the circumstances in which the law was passed has tended to mask. In the final stages of the debate in the *eduskunta*, it appeared as if the provisional government had been overthrown in a radical coup. This proved not to be the case. Strengthened by the collapse of the uprising and disarray amongst the Bolsheviks, the leader of the provisional government Alexander Kerensky was in no mood to bow to Finnish pressure, and ordered the dissolution of the *eduskunta* and new elections. Their bluff called, the socialists made a couple of ineffectual protests, but in the end, meekly complied by participating in the October elections.

The main winners of those elections were the agrarians, who increased their 1916 vote by 70 per cent and won seven new seats. The socialists remained the largest single party by far with ninety-two seats, but lost their absolute majority; moreover, they now faced a more resolute and hostile bourgeois bloc, determined to make the restoration of law and order a priority. By the autumn, all the socialist representatives had withdrawn from government. The Social Democratic Party, which had earlier set its face against a revival of the red guards, now endorsed the formation of workers' units and gave its support to a series of demands drawn up by the trade unions and presented as an ultimatum to the rump government. The formation of a revolutionary council by the labour movement, the drafting of a plan for a partial seizure of power by the party's leading theoretician, Otto Ville Kuusinen, at a time when local Bolsheviks were also urging the Finnish socialists to make revolution as well, and the declaration on 13/14 November of a general strike in which public buildings were occupied and leading figures arrested by the red guards would all seem to suggest that the left in Finland was prepared to follow the Bolsheviks down the path of revolution. The evidence, however, is of uncertainty and confusion throughout. Kuusinen, who became the dominant figure of Finnish communism after 1918, later blamed the party for being seduced in November 1917 by the 'mirage of parliamentary democracy'. At the time, however, he initially argued that any seizure of power would be dangerous and that pressure should be brought to bear by other means, though he seems to have become more receptive as the strike progressed to the idea of workers' power as the only way to defend democracy.

The socialist alternative of transferring supreme authority to the *eduskunta* now faced a conservative challenge, which, drawing upon the provisions of the 1772 act of government, envisaged an elected regency council as the temporary holder of these powers. Clumsy tactics by the socialists ensured that the latter proposal won the day in the assembly on 8 November, and although the socialists did manage to combine with the agrarians to have the *eduskunta* reconfirm the law on supreme authority (omitting any reference to foreign or military affairs) on 15 November, using this as a means to push through laws on local government franchise reform and the eight-hour working day, the mood of the parliamentary majority was now swinging in favour of strong government. The disorders of the strike, compounded by the continued presence in Finland of ill-disciplined Russian troops, the absence of any effective police authority, and the threat of revolutionary chaos spreading from Russia to Finland, brought the non-socialist parties together behind the veteran of the passive resistance, Pehr Evind Svinhufvud, who promised firm measures to restore order. On 26 November, for the first and only time in Finnish history, a government, headed by Svinhufvud, was appointed by the *eduskunta*. Having toyed with, and then abandoned, the idea of a seizure of power, the left had no chance of winning majority support for the purely socialist government they proposed, and although performing useful service in Petrograd to open up the way to Soviet recognition of Finnish independence, they were effectively forced into political isolation by a government determined to enforce law and order on its own terms.

The socialists supported independence, but argued that this should be achieved through negotiation with Russia. Svinhufvud reluctantly accepted that this was a necessary precondition for recognition by foreign powers, and travelled to Petrograd at the very end of 1917 to receive confirmation from the Council of People's Commissars that it recognised the sovereign independence of the republic of Finland. The continued presence of Russian troops in Finland persuaded Svinhufvud that Germany was the best hope of safeguarding Finnish independence, and he initiated contacts that would eventually lead to agreements that brought Finland firmly within the German sphere of influence in the last year of the war. The German-trained troops of the *Jäger* battalion were expected to constitute a vital trained core of the new Finnish army, but their return was delayed, and the government had to rely on former officers of the imperial Russian army, such as General Carl Gustaf Emil Mannerheim, who on 15 January 1918 was given the job of organising the forces authorised by the *eduskunta* three days earlier. This decision was bitterly contested by the socialists, who believed it would convert the disparate units of the civil guard movement (*suojeluskunta*) into the armed force of a government intent on waging war on the working class.[1]

The Social Democratic Party had come under increasing pressure from the red guards, angered by the decision to call off the strike in November. Lacking any evident enthusiasm for revolution, but unable to break out of the political isolation ward to which they had been confined by the Svinhufvud government, the leadership drifted towards an accommodation with the guards and once more began to contemplate a seizure of power. The key player was Yrjö Sirola, who was persuaded that a revolutionary situation now existed in the country and convinced that to abandon the revolutionary masses a second time would be tantamount to moral suicide. His analysis, together with an intensification of fighting between red and white forces around Viipuri and the official proclamation on 25 January of the white guards as government troops, pushed the Social Democratic Party council into accepting the creation of a five-man revolutionary committee to co-ordinate a seizure of power.

As the left launched its bid for power in Helsinki on the night of 27–28 January, Mannerheim's troops began rounding up and disarming Russian garrisons in the vicinity of the town of Vaasa in Ostrobothnia, where a few members of the Svinhufvud government were to establish themselves.[2] There now followed a full-blown civil war, lasting some three months. The red forces controlled most of southern Finland, including the major cities of Turku, Tampere, Viipuri, and Helsinki. Although numerically superior, they were poorly trained and led (the assistance of Russian troops stationed in the country was of marginal benefit), and they lacked any clear overall objective. The strategy drawn up by the commander of the red guards at the end of January was defensive, and left a vital east–west rail connection under the control of the white forces. The socialist leadership claimed that they were fighting to defend democracy against black reaction. The Finnish People's Commissariat established on 29 January made little attempt to introduce radical social reforms, apart from proclaiming the tenant farmers free of their obligations to their landlords. The whole venture was shot through with a mood of pessimism and doubt. There is more than a grain of truth in the later accusation by one of the more radical members of the People's Commissariat that the socialists regarded it as an unfortunate episode that had to be endured without doing anything to upset the development of bourgeois democracy.

The whites had a more straightforward immediate aim, which was the crushing of rebellion and the restoration of lawful government. Mannerheim was able to create an effective fighting force, commanded by experienced ex-imperial Russian army officers and reinforced by volunteers from the Swedish military, and the *Jäger* battalion. The offensive launched in March, which resulted in the storming and capture of the industrial city of Tampere at the beginning of April, proved to be the decisive turning-point in the war, for it strengthened the whites' claim to be liberating the country just as units of German troops invited to Finland by representatives of the Vaasa government began landing on the southern coast. These troops took Helsinki in mid-April, and combined with Mannerheim's forces to eliminate the last pockets of red resistance by 5 May.

The victorious whites were however soon riven by disagreement. Mannerheim resigned shortly after leading the victory parade in Helsinki, angered by what he regarded as the government's disloyalty in discussing with the Germans the reorganisation of the Finnish army. His employment of Swedish-speaking officers and his imperial Russian army background had led to angry confrontations during the war with the *Jäger* officers. This clash of generations reached a head in 1924, when almost nine-tenths of the Finnish officer corps threatened to resign unless the government removed from the army 'all such elements whose patriotism is questionable or in whom Russian concepts, spirit and habits have taken hold'. With powerful support from the *suojeluskunta*, now the officially sanctioned paramilitary defence corps that upheld the values of white Finland during the inter-war period, the *Jäger* officers won the day, and by the end of the first decade of independence were in effective control of the army.

Mannerheim's sudden withdrawal from public life proved to be temporary. The defeat of Germany at the end of 1918 brought to an abrupt end any plans to install as king of Finland Prince Friedrich Karl of Hesse, accorded this honour by a pro-German government and a slender monarchist majority in the rump *eduskunta*. Mannerheim had already agreed to press Finland's case for recognition to the allied governments, and he was clearly marked down as the man to succeed Svinhufvud as provisional head of state, or regent, which he did on 12 December 1918 with the support of the majority of the rump *eduskunta*. Elections in March 1919 saw the return of the socialists to parliament. The creation of a new and less pro-German government fulfilled a further criterion of the victorious allied powers for recognition, which was finally accorded on 3 May 1919 by the Council of Foreign Ministers assembled in Paris for the peace conference. The continuing turmoil in Russia, however, left many unresolved issues, and, as we shall see in Chapter 6, the peace treaty between Finland and Soviet Russia in 1920 was more a final settling of the practicalities of separation than a basis for good neighbourly relations.

Mannerheim's brief tenure of the post of regent was eventful but also revealing of the continuing divisions within the country. The general was closely involved in plans being hatched by a group of

Plate 23 The ratification of the 1919 Form of Government Act by the Regent of Finland, General Mannerheim. The Form of Government Act, ratified on 17 July 1919, remained in force for eight decades, being replaced by a new constitution in 2000. During the period of autonomy, Swedish eighteenth-century fundamental laws had formed the basis of the Finnish constitutionalist case. Gustav III's 1772 Form of Government Act was used to establish a regency in 1917, and to proclaim Friedrich Karl of Hesse king of Finland in October 1918. The constitutional committee set up by the Finnish Senate in March 1917 was charged with drafting a new constitutional act. The proposals considered in October 1917 by a mixed Russo-Finnish committee envisaged the loosest of connections with Russia, with Finland having its own head of state who would exercise most of the powers hitherto held by the ruler. The Bolshevik seizure of power in November and the declaration of sovereignty issued by the Svinhufvud Senate on 4 December 1917 broke the last link with Russia. The defeat of Germany and Friedrich Karl's polite refusal of the Finnish crown in November 1918 ensured that Finland would be a republic, not a monarchy. The constitution provided for a head of state, or president, with considerable executive powers. In this respect, it differed from the constitutions adapted by the new Baltic states, or proposed by the Finnish reds in 1918, in which power firmly rested with parliament. Mannerheim, seated at the end of the table, was shortly after this occasion defeated in the first presidential election by the liberal K. J. Ståhlberg. As chairman of the constitutional committee, Ståhlberg had been largely responsible for the Form of Government Act. The regent and members of the government are

Russian *émigré* soldiers and politicians to launch an assault on Petrograd. The government, aware that the Russian *émigrés* continued to deny unconditional recognition of Finnish independence, was reluctant to commit Finnish troops to this venture. In order to force the issue, a group of activists close to Mannerheim urged him to dissolve parliament after confirming the new constitution, and to utilise the ensuing political interregnum to declare war. After some hesitation, Mannerheim chose not to follow this path. He confirmed the constitution and suffered defeat as the candidate of the right-wing minority in the election of the first president of the republic by the *eduskunta* on 25 July 1919.

Although a solid republican majority of socialists, agrarians, and progressives ensured a comfortable victory for the architect of the new Finnish constitution, Kaarlo Ståhlberg, his six-year tenure of office was anything but easy. He had to contend with open discontent within the army, and much personal abuse from embittered activists. In a manner reminiscent of another wartime military leader, General de Gaulle, Mannerheim withdrew once more to private life, but continued to pursue his own political agenda behind the scenes. He remained an iconic figure for activists such as his future biographer and close confidant Kai Donner, men frustrated by what they saw as a weak and flawed democracy that was incapable of realising their vision of a greater Finland that would liberate the Finno-Ugric peoples from the yoke of Soviet Russian rule. For other firm supporters of white Finland, however, Mannerheim was a figure from the past, isolated from the people by his poor command of Finnish, his aristocratic birth, and long years spent in imperial service. The limits of his political appeal were revealed in 1921, when an attempt by his associates to take advantage of a crisis in relations between government and defence corps to have Mannerheim appointed commander-in-chief of the *suojeluskunta* was effectively defeated by the machinations of a younger generation of activists, chief amongst them the grey

Caption for Plate 23 (*cont.*)
sitting in the plenary session chamber of the Senate building. The imperial throne at the head of the table has been removed, but the portrait of Alexander I remains in place.

eminence of right-wing student politics in the 1920s, Elmo Kaila, eager to purge the army of its imperial army officers. Having unanimously chosen Mannerheim as their candidate for the post of commander, the *suojeluskunta* delegate conference promptly backed down when President Ståhlberg let it be known that he was unlikely to approve Mannerheim, and agreed instead to the appointment of a former *Jäger* officer, Lauri Malmberg.

Elmo Kaila was one of the founders in 1922 of the Academic Karelia Society (AKS), and a leading figure in the secret society at the heart of this student body, the 'brothers of hate', which preached a virulently uncompromising hatred of all things Russian. Originally created to provide relief for refugees fleeing from eastern Karelia after a failed uprising against Bolshevik rule, the AKS became the most important forum for male student opinion for the next two decades, an elitist society, many of whose members went on to occupy high positions in Finnish public life. Ardently and at times aggressively nationalist, impatiently critical of the cautiousness and willingness to compromise of the older generation of politicians, the AKS encompassed both the elitist and authoritarian as well as the populist and radical tendencies of the Finnish nationalist tradition. From 1924 to 1928, the idea of national reconciliation was in the ascendancy. In the words of the leading AKS ideologue of the 1920s, Niilo Kärki, 'the raising of the standard of living and of culture of the lowest sections of the people can only be done by an educated class that is Finnish in language and mind, which does not regard the people with haughty contempt, but feels itself bound to them by blood ties'. To achieve this, the AKS demanded the finnicisation of the university and the establishment of common values that would end the alienation of people from the ruling elite, a divide, it was claimed, that had to a large extent led the country into civil war in 1918. This emphasis upon Finnish national integration caused a split in 1924, with those favouring national vigilance against the red menace across the frontier going off to form their own grouping, and it gave way in turn to demands to defend white Finland from its internal enemies at the end of the decade.

This shift away from an inclusive, reconciliatory nationalism that sought to establish the cultural hegemony of the Finnish-speaking people to one that threatened to reopen the wounds of civil war was in part occasioned by a growing disillusionment with party politics and the failure to open up any fruitful dialogue with either of the two parties that could claim to speak for the Finnish people at large, rather than its educated elite – the agrarians and the social democrats. The speedy return of the social democrats to parliament, and their early willingness to contemplate entry into government helped keep the balance of parliamentary politics firmly in the centre ground. On the other hand, the unwillingness of the agrarians and progressives to consider entering into a coalition with a party that sought to challenge the legitimacy of the white victory by demanding the abolition of the paramilitary *suojeluskunta* and a general amnesty for political prisoners effectively precluded the possibility of any durable majority centre-left government emerging until the late 1930s. Governments throughout the 1920s were short-lived, unstable coalitions riven by party and personal disagreements, and although a number of valuable and lasting social reforms such as the settlement of the land question were made, other issues such as the size and pay of the civil service and the perennial headache of restructuring the university in a manner that might satisfy all parties contributed to the general sense of frustration.

Ten years after the civil war, Finland was caught up in a wave of anti-communist agitation known as the Lapua movement that threatened to undermine the democratic and constitutional foundations of the young republic. That it did not may, of course, be attributed to the personal and political failings of those who sought to give direction to a movement fuelled by a crude mixture of redneck local patriotism, religious fundamentalism, and alcohol, and we shall examine this aspect in a moment. But there are many other reasons why Finland was less likely than other new states in Europe to abandon the democratic for the authoritarian path. Foremost amongst these is the resilience and strength of the basic edifice of laws, institutions, and practices that had developed and matured during the course of the nineteenth century. Here, the Finnish experience was markedly different from that of the rest of the Russian empire. Whereas in the rest of the empire, the state was seen as alien and oppressive, in Finland it was regarded as the guarantor of liberties. Although what happened in Finland during the last decade and a half of imperial rule may have dimmed that expectation, it did not destroy it. The constitution of 1919 envisaged a state in which many of the powers of the emperor were now vested in a president, elected for a term of six years by an electoral college. The constitution made a clear distinction between the president as the holder of supreme power, with extensive rights, and the government, or Council of State (*valtioneuvosto*).[3] That distinction was maintained until the end of the century, when the new constitution placed governmental power equally in the hands of the president and a Council of State whose members enjoyed the confidence of parliament. Although strong presidential leadership was a feature of post-second-world-war Finland rather than the inter-war years, and there were periods in which power was most definitely exercised by the Council of State, rather than the president, most notably during 1939–40, the quasi-monarchical nature of the office endowed it with an aura of respect and patriotic reverence which the option of parliamentary sovereignty chosen by Finland's neighbours to the south failed to provide.

The independent state, then, represented continuity rather than radical change. It was constituted within an inherited territorial framework (unlike other new states that had to be carved out of the carcasses of empires, such as Poland or Czechoslovakia), with its own infrastructure of functioning institutions, laws, currency, and with a literate, ethnically homogenous population. Although republicanism as such had little resonance amongst the Finnish people, the creation of a quasi-monarchical head of state effectively killed off any lingering hankerings after monarchy. There were divisions, certainly, which engendered sometimes bitter conflict and hostility. Those who had been on the losing side of the civil war, even their children, were, at best, on probation, under constant surveillance. But there was also recognition of an urgent need to heal the wounds of civil war. 'Cost what it may, we must as soon as possible get to a situation where, if danger threatens our country, every Finnish man will want and be able to repel it', was the unequivocal view published in the handbook for the defence corps in 1918. It was the threat of external danger, according to Risto Alapuro in his micro-historical study of the birth of independent

Finland, that constrained the white victors to accept a measure of disagreement as the price of national unity. 'Differences were feared, but this fear did not mean they were simply rejected or denied. . . It also meant they were treated with great sensitivity, in the knowledge that they had in any case to be lived with.'

There were also things that united, even if they were not always apparent until revealed by a crisis that threatened independence, as in the winter of 1939–40, or perhaps because they were so apparent – like a sense of belonging – that they did not need to be stated. This sense of belonging may perhaps be best illustrated by considering the position of the Swedish-speaking minority and those who supported the communists in Finland during the inter-war years. Both were the cause of much anger and annoyance, not least because they seemed to challenge the will of the majority – the Swedish-speaking elite by seemingly refusing to accept quietly a subordinate (and by implication, subservient) role in the cultural and economic life of the country, the communists through their uncompromising opposition to everything white Finland stood for. Both were accused of disloyalty. The use by the more outspoken advocates of a Swedish-speaking nationalism of a decidedly racist language that contrasted the bold, decisive, freedom-loving 'east Swedes' with the passive, culturally backward Finns, the agitation on the Åland islands for union with Sweden during the early years of independence, and the readiness of the Swedish press to inter-vene on behalf of the Swedish-speaking minority during the more fraught moments of the debate over the finnicisation of the uni-versity prompted Finnish nationalist hackles to rise, though never on the scale of outrage that united Finnish- and Swedish-speaking 'whites' alike in their condemnation of the impious, trea-cherous 'reds' who pledged their allegiance to the outlawed Finnish communist party in Soviet Russia. In both instances, there was undoubtedly a tendency to marginalise a minority as unpatriotic outsiders, but this never became a norm that might lead to permanent exclusion from the national community.[4]

There was within the ranks of the Swedish-speaking minority a strong determination *not* to retreat into isolation, and to participate fully in the life of the new republic, that prevailed over proposals for separate administrative provision for the linguistic minority in

the new Finnish state. The point was made forcefully by the formidable Rabbe Wrede at a meeting of the *folkting*, or assembly for
Swedish Finland, in 1919, when he declared that Swedish-speakers
in Finland were obliged for geographical and historical reasons to
live alongside Finnish-speakers:

We could say that it is Swedes who have created present-day Finland and its
culture, and the Swedish contribution to the life of Finland will, in my
opinion, remain vital in future as well. What we may not say is that it does
not concern us what happens to Finnish Finland as long as we are able to
set up as we wish a Swedish Finland for ourselves. That would be a great
mistake, for we are bound to this Finnish Finland, and its well-being is our
well-being, its misfortunes and ruin our misfortunes and ruin.

The circumstances which dictated the contours of Finnish politics
in the 1920s ensured that the Swedish People's Party had a voice and
was able to exercise influence, in government and in parliament. As a
party, it was a peculiar and at times uneasy coalition of right-wingers
who still entertained considerable reservations about parliamentary
democracy and liberals who at one stage formed their own parliamentary group; but as a pressure group dedicated to protecting the
interests of a linguistic minority, it worked well, exploiting
the divisions within the party political system to good effect.

It is more difficult to make the case for communism as a part of
the Finnish landscape. Certainly, its opponents saw it as an evil,
Russian-inspired doctrine with which the embittered exiled leadership of the failed rebellion of 1918 sought to infect the people. But
those who were drawn to communism could not so easily be dismissed as alien and unpatriotic. They were after all undeniably of
the people, a people in which Finnish nationalism had pinned its
faith for decades. The accusation levelled by Swedish-speaking
right-wingers such as the poet Bertel Gripenberg that the Finnish
people, having been inflamed for years by irresponsible nationalists
and then socialists, were especially receptive to the seductive wiles
of bolshevism, was an embarrassment for those in the Finnish
camp. Although such accusations were angrily rebuffed, there was
considerable heart-searching in the years immediately following the
civil war about the perceived immaturity and lack of culture of the
Finnish people, and no shortage of remedies to deal with this. For

the writer Volter Kilpi, the 'wild, perfidious suspiciousness and the black, base desire for revenge that seems to float in the blood of our people like a lurking beast' could only be controlled by firm, authoritative government and energetic social reforms. The socialist and strong supporter of prohibition, Väinö Voionmaa, believed that 'the immense political and societal lack of culture of our people' required 'puritanism and a bit of rough smithing', not what the Swedish-speaking elite offered, an 'aesthetic-individualist-aristocratic isolation from the plebs'. Crude, ignorant, feared and even hated by some, misguided in the eyes of others, the communist was nevertheless a Finnish reality, who could not be portrayed and demonised as of an alien race or culture; it is significant that both Kilpi and Voionmaa, for example, speak of 'our people', however unattractive elements of the people had now become.

The Finnish Communist Party was founded in Moscow by a group of exiled red leaders in August 1918. With all the fervour of the newly converted, it embraced revolution and fiercely rejected the moderate parliamentary tactics of the old labour movement, urging the Finnish proletariat to boycott the *eduskunta* elections in March 1919. This appeal was massively ignored. The revived Social Democratic Party retained the loyalty of its members and electorate. In spite of the losses suffered as a result of the civil war, party membership topped 67,000 by the end of 1919, and a third of a million voted socialist in the elections. Discontent with the moderate party leadership began to surface during the summer and autumn of 1919, at a time when the fledgling Finnish Communist Party in Russia was plunged into internecine squabbling. The final split in the Finnish labour movement was essentially over issues of immediate relevance in post-civil-war Finland; It was in no way masterminded by emissaries from Moscow, such as Otto Ville Kuusinen.

Although the left managed to gain control of a number of unions and local party organisations, they failed to capture the party. In May 1920, eighty-six delegates convened in Helsinki to form the Socialist Workers' Party (SSTP). Within three years, the SSTP could claim 23,666 members, only four thousand fewer than the Social Democratic Party, and it polled 14.8 per cent of the vote in the

1922 parliamentary elections as against 25 per cent for the socialists. In August 1923, the authorities struck, arresting the twenty-seven members of the SSTP parliamentary group and the party executive, and sequestrating the party's assets. The left continued to operate under the cover of an alliance of workers and peasants, increasing its parliamentary representation from eighteen in 1924 to twenty-three in 1929 and maintaining a strong grip over the trade union movement, but at the cost of dividing and weakening the labour movement as a whole.

The distinguishing feature of what might be called the intransigent left was its attachment to the uncompromising class-conscious revolutionary rhetoric of the old labour movement. By not adopting the title 'communist', it avoided immediate repression, but the SSTP at least was far from being, or even understanding how to be, a Bolshevik-style party. The split established a deep cleavage within the labour movement, that lasted for decades. Much of the 'red' heartland, that had suffered the worst losses as a result of the civil war, remained loyal to the Social Democratic Party, though there were communist strongholds in and around Turku and Helsinki and in certain southern areas with a concentration of industry. It was, however, in the north and north-east, where the old labour movement had not established the kind of strong presence that it had in the south, that the intransigent left succeeded in pushing aside the social democrats, capturing most of the workers' associations and the votes. In a sense, 'backwoods' communism was almost like the last wave of the radical labour movement, sustained by poverty and resentment. Often living on isolated, impoverished farmsteads, having regularly to seek work in the forests in the winter, embittered by the raw exploitation of their labour, the rural proletariat of northern Finland were far removed from the disciplined, party-conscious model of the communist favoured by Moscow. A common theme in the many police reports covering this vast and vulnerable region is indeed the poverty and ignorance of the people, the lack of schools, reading material – other than the local communist newspaper – or anything that might serve to inculcate patriotic values. The general conclusion was that there was an overriding need to win the hearts and minds of these people, rather than rely simply on brutal repression.

Similar anxieties informed the discussions of schoolteachers, clergymen, and officials. The sobering experience of civil war muted anti-church attitudes, which had been prevalent amongst the intelligentsia during the first decade of the twentieth century. In his 1918 assessment of the future, the leading Nietzschean Volter Kilpi argued strongly for Lutheranism as a spiritual foundation for the new state, and another prominent pre-war cultural radical, L. Onerva, admitted in May 1918 that the people now needed 'the sound elementary school of the church'. Church leaders such as Lauri Ingman declared that the constant denigration of the Christian faith and its values had played a major part in fomenting rebellion. Younger church activists sought to promote the church as the moral backbone of the fatherland, and were willing to engage in active politicking, as in the run-up to the 1922 elections, when a successful national campaign was mounted to ensure that denominational religious education should remain a compulsory subject in schools. A small minority of the clergy, inspired by foreign examples such as the docklands settlement movement in Britain, attempted to build bridges to the working class; but the great majority retained a suspicion and hostility of the labour movement and a profound desire for strong leadership (the clergy were the most ardent supporters of monarchy in 1918) and strict moral and legal controls of private as well as public life.

Teachers and school inspectors were rather more cautious in their public statements, and preferred to concentrate on practical issues, such as the need to attract properly qualified staff to remote (and politically vulnerable) regions. The more optimistic pinned their faith on compulsory education, introduced in 1921, as the way to heal wounds. But all were uncomfortably aware, as one teacher put it at a meeting of elementary schoolteachers in the Tampere district in 1921, that:

The father or relative of many a child bears the name of traitor to his country, and this has left behind a legacy of bitterness which has also affected the children. In these instances, it is certainly wise to be silent, but there are times when this is not enough. Where the wound remains infected, the stinging medicine of truth has to be administered, remembering only that we do this in love, for truth is our support, the truth that our fight has been Finland's greatest fight for liberty. . . Looked at in terms of our present social circumstances, the prospects for nurturing love of our fatherland are not good, since the majority of elementary school pupils belong to the working class, a very motley group living in wretched conditions. This is the group we ought to try and influence, but how?

Those on the defeated side of the civil war not unnaturally experienced and saw things rather differently. The deep sense of exclusion and injustice that had found expression in the records of the pre-1918 movement was now reinforced by the bitter memories of the white terror and the triumphalist images of white Finland. The sand and gravel pits where red prisoners had been shot, and the denial of requests to erect memorials to the dead were in stark contrast to the adulation accorded to the victors and the public monuments extolling the patriotic heroism of the white soldiers. However much national solidarity was desired, there were many barriers to full working-class participation. The defence corps remained off-limits to socialists, employers refused to treat unions as serious negotiating partners, and labour activities were subject to close police surveillance. The left continued to develop its own particular form of Finnish identity in the workers' halls and the sports movement. Of *proletkult*, the *Volksbühne*, the 'new' woman (or man), the Finnish labour movement remained largely ignorant, preferring innocent recitals of poetry or song, country-cousin plays, and much the same sort of sports as favoured by its bourgeois counterparts.

Change, more than anything else, caused the scars of civil war to fade. The land reforms of the early 1920s, gradually improving standards of living, the development of a market economy and its impact on even the small farmer, and the emergence of a popular mass culture which united the nation across language and class divides, all served by 1938 to make the experience of twenty years ago less immediately relevant in daily life (even if it took that long before the first hesitant steps were made to bring workers and bourgeoisie together on the sports field).

Memories were, however, still very much alive ten years earlier, and were painfully revived by the Lapua movement, which threatened at one stage to destroy parliamentary democracy in Finland. Lapua is a small town in southern Ostrobothnia, a region with a strong sense of bloody-minded independence stretching back to

Plate 24 The white hero immortalised in stone: the memorial to the fallen, Lapua. Memorials to the fallen are rarely neutral. Those who fell on the white side in the 'war of liberation' (*Vapaussota/Frihetskriget*) of 1918 were honoured with handsome 'heroes' graves', usually adorned with a suitable text. This memorial in the town of Lapua, in the white heartland, hails the fallen as the guardians of 'our homes, our faith', who prevented the people falling into slavery by their heroic deeds. The defeated reds were denied the opportunity to erect memorials for their dead, many of whom were shot out of hand in the immediate aftermath of what the left saw as a class war. In an intensely rural society, where everyone is known, the bitter memories of a war in which large numbers of men were actively involved hung heavily for many years. Finland during the inter-war years was in many respects a divided society. Those whose loyalties were on the left had their own newspapers, entertainments, and sports clubs; those who broke ranks – joining a 'bourgeois' club, or, even worse, acting as a strike-breaker – were ostracised as class traitors.

the rebellions of the late sixteenth century, and reinforced by the recent experience of the civil war. The freehold peasant farmers of Ostrobothnia were exalted as the upholders of the true spirit of Finnishness, a role they were more than happy to fulfil. When a misguided bunch of young communists who had planned a rally in Lapua at the end of November 1929 was attacked and beaten up by the locals, this was widely hailed across the non-socialist spectrum as the righteous response of outraged patriots. The demands for the suppression of all communist activities issued by the 'men of Lapua' also won wide approval. White Finland seemed threatened by an upsurge of communism. Elections in the summer had returned twenty-three communists to parliament. Communists were also active in the unions, whose membership had risen from 50,472 in 1925 to 90,231 in 1928, and were being urged to intensify the class struggle in preparation for the forthcoming revolution envisaged by the Communist International. The edgy political relationship between the new state and its eastern neighbour coloured two protracted industrial disputes; the Crichton-Vulcan shipbuilding works hit by a seven-month strike at the end of 1927 had orders to build submarines for the Finnish government, and the national dock strike of 1928–29 affected Finnish timber exports at a time when the USSR was flooding the market with cheap wood in order to help finance the five-year plan for industrialisation. White opinion was also outraged by continuous reports of 'workplace terrorism' against loyal workers, and the threatening tone of communist-inspired demonstrations.

Communism was, however, much weaker than its activities seemed to suggest. The police had managed to penetrate and break up the underground organisation in 1928. The strikes had stretched the resources of the unions to breaking point, whilst the aggressive campaign against the social democrats had effectively split the central organisation. The unions faced a powerful enemy, the strike-breaking *Vientirauha* (export peace), founded in 1920, and specifically intended to fight the threat of communism. Able to draw upon a membership of over thirty thousand – mostly farmers or their sons, schoolboys and students, and refugees from Karelia or Ingria – this secretive organisation, supported by leading industrialists and led by the former activist Lauri Pihkala, was a seedbed for the anti-communist movement that acquired national notoriety in 1930.

The government had begun preparing measures to curb communist activities before the Lapua incident, and secured parliamentary approval at the beginning of December to authorise the minister of the interior to ban temporarily any association deemed to have contravened public order. An attempt to stiffen press controls failed to obtain the requisite majority in March 1930. The leaders of the Lapua movement responded by smashing the presses of the communist newspaper in Vaasa. The government's inability to deal firmly with the lawbreakers or the riots that occurred at their trial in June encouraged Lapua to go further and unleash a wave of kidnappings and beatings of suspected communists. Finding the prime minister, the agrarian Kyösti Kallio, unwilling to bend to their demands, the movement called for a new government and parliament, and planned a march on the capital. The situation in mid-June was tense, with rumours of an impending coup. Secret soundings in the army found that there were so many officers who would refuse to move against Lapua that giving such an order would be out of the question. On 1 July, the government placed before parliament a protection of the republic act, and a series of measures designed to prevent individuals belonging to parties which sought the violent overthrow of the Finnish state standing for public office, extending banning orders on publications deemed criminal or immoral from three months to a year, and making the spreading of derogatory statements about government, parliament, officials, or the lawful social order a criminal offence carrying a prison sentence. Although receiving the necessary vote of confidence, Kallio offered his resignation to make way for the one man thought to have the confidence of the Lapua movement, the white hero of 1918, Pehr Evind Svinhufvud. Svinhufvud had in fact been in contact with the Lapua leaders in June, and offered posts in his government to two of them, the farmer Vihtori Kosola and the clergyman Kauko Kares, an offer turned down at the last minute.

The new government took immediate action against the twenty-three communist members of parliament, ordering their arrest on charges of treason. The trade union central organisation was shut down, the socialist and small farmers' electoral organisation which had fronted the political activity of the communists was broken up, and some five hundred left-wing activists were taken into custody. The government failed, however, to secure the necessary five-sixths majority for the immediate promulgation of the anti-communist legislation, which meant new elections.

Lapua did not put up its own candidates, claiming to stand as the moral conscience of the nation, above party. Its activists did, however, try to have communists removed from the electoral register and harassed socialist candidates and voters, in addition to ejecting the few remaining communists from local councils. On the eve of the elections, Lapua activists seized the former president of the republic and hate figure of the right, Kaarlo Ståhlberg and his wife, abandoning them somewhat shamefacedly in the eastern town of Joensuu. With the communists out of the picture, the social democrats were able to attract over a hundred thousand more voters than in 1929, but with sixty-six seats, they fell one short of the number that would block legislation requiring amendment of the constitution. This enabled them to maintain their principled opposition to the measures aimed at outlawing communism, whilst allowing the government to secure the two-thirds majority it required.

Communism was a broken reed in Finland, and the purges in the Soviet Union from 1935 onwards all but wiped it out as a serious political force. The real threat to the established order in Finland after 1930 came from the right. Although less than satisfied with Svinhufvud's insistence on observing legal niceties, the right managed in February 1931 to ensure his election as president, by the narrowest of margins, over the hated Ståhlberg, the candidate favoured by the socialists and progressives in the electoral college. Pressure was brought to bear on members of the agrarian electoral bloc by the head of the defence corps and other influential figures. The last waverer was apparently persuaded to change his mind when told that armed Lapua supporters were on the way to the capital and were ready to unleash a bloodbath if Ståhlberg were elected.

Svinhufvud's election as president and the passing of further legislation to choke subversive left-wing activities seemed to take some of the steam out of a movement that was already beginning to exhaust itself with internecine wrangling and personal intrigues, but the threat from the extra-parliamentary right was not dead. Rumours of a possible coup began to circulate yet again in the autumn of 1931. Trouble which had been brewing over the winter in the commune of Mäntsälä, some fifty kilometres north of Helsinki, burst into an open conflict in February 1932, when a group of armed men attempting to break up a socialist meeting found themselves in confrontation with the police. Ignoring demands to disperse, the rebels managed to secure the backing of the Lapua leadership, now directed by a former army officer, Major-General Kurt Wallenius. The leadership of the defence corps waited on events, though it also took up the call for a change of government which was made by the governing council of the Lapua movement. Assured by the army commander of the loyalty of the troops, the government stood firm. Svinhufvud's radio appeal to the rebels persuaded most to give up, though defence corps troops staged brief acts of defiance in Jyväskylä and Seinäjoki, where they took over the railway station, in the town of Pori, and elsewhere in Satakunta and south-west Finland. Certain army officers sympathetic to the rebels were also prepared to hinder the progress of units called into action to go to Mäntsälä, but failed to secure clear directions from Wallenius. Wallenius himself claimed that the leadership of Lapua had only done what white Finland was demanding in calling for a change of government, and that he had done his uttermost to avoid violence. The week-long crisis degenerated into farce, with Wallenius getting drunk with the head of the defence corps, Lauri Malmberg, on the back seat of the car taking him for further questioning in Helsinki. Malmberg, whose role during the crisis was at best equivocal, was allowed to remain head of an armed force officially under state control; ten of the leading rebels received light prison sentences, the remainder were allowed to return home. The minister of the interior and governor of Uusimaa county, whose firm actions had in large measure stifled the revolt, were virtually hounded out of office. If the Mäntsälä incident had revealed the pitiful inability of the right to stage a coup, its aftermath also showed how easy it was to undermine or destroy those who were brave enough to stand up for legality against intimidation. Ståhlberg's decision not to stand for re-election as president in

1925, and his reluctance to stand against Svinhufvud in 1931, the character assassination of the minister of war and the suicide of the man asked by the government to sort out the crisis within the defence corps in 1921, and the murder in 1922 of the progressive minister of the interior by a disgruntled activist, may all be attributed to this pressure from the right. Others, such as Lauri Relander, president between 1925 and 1931, even Prime Minister Kallio, simply gave way to the pressure.

In the summer of 1930, it did seem as if the 'law of Lapua' had supplanted the law of the land. The authorities appeared powerless or unwilling to prevent the spate of assaults and involuntary car-rides to the border, where the unfortunate victims were dumped. Kallio was himself in breach of the constitution when he ordered county governors to prevent the publication of communist news-papers, and there were a number of dubious features in the process by which a new government was formed by Svinhufvud. The largest party in the *eduskunta*, the most resolute defender of legality and the constitutional system, was kept at arm's length, even when its members and property came under attack. Parallels were drawn with the march on Rome when a peasant-farmers' march was planned, and the words of Artturi Leinonen, the editor of the main agrarian newspaper in Ostrobothnia, 'where is the man, or men?' continued to resonate uncomfortably around the still unfinished walls of the new parliament building.

Beneath the braggadocio and bombast, however, lay serious weaknesses. 'Movement' is too orderly a description of the Lapua phenomenon; it was more a rolling, rambling assemblage of personalities, each with his or her own particular motives and agenda.[5] The farmer Vihtori Kosola may have been flattered by those who saw him as the Finnish Mussolini, but his addiction to the bottle at times of stress and his breathtaking political naivety (he is reported to have asked, in his cups, 'Hey, tell me, what is a dictator, really? Is he the sort of chap who doesn't have to obey the law?') ruled him out as a serious contender for the 'strong man' job. Kosola and his associates were, however, a force to be reckoned with in Ostrobothnia, where they saw off attempts by the local agrarian party bosses to control them. In the longer term, however, the excesses and unpredictability of the Lapua leadership pushed the agrarians into the ranks of the defenders of the constitution and democracy. Lapua's demand for the powers of parliament to be curbed, with the right to vote restricted to those who had paid direct state tax for two previous years and their spouses, majority elections, the reduction of the *eduskunta* to 150 members, and a shortening of the session to two months of the year, also threatened to curtail the rights and interests of the small farmers who supported the agrarian party. Lapua might be a handy stick with which to beat leftist troublemakers, but it was to the agrarians the farmers turned at election time, despite their suspicions that the rural ideals of the party's founder, Santeri Alkio, had been abandoned by place-seeking, smart-suited politicians.

Lapua also failed to take advantage of the economic crisis, which hit small farmers struggling with debt particularly hard. It had less success than the communists in establishing a base amongst the various protest movements that sprang up around the country in response to threats of eviction and foreclosure, and it made no inroads at all into the working class. For industrialists anxious to beat down the unions and patriots who affected to see in Lapua the resurgent spirit of the white Finland of 1918, it served a useful purpose. With the crushing of communism, Lapua lost much of its appeal for many of its erstwhile backers, alarmed and embarrassed by continued lawlessness which threatened to damage Finland's reputation in Britain, a country vital to the Finnish export trade. The emergence of Svinhufvud as the man of the hour in all likelihood sealed the political fate of Lapua, for he had a reputation as the stern defender of the law to maintain. Although more willing to align himself publicly with the ethos of Lapua than to heed the wishes of the electorate, the great majority of whom voted in the presidential election for candidates or a party opposed to Lapua, Svinhufvud was quite prepared to stand firm when the Lapua council seemed poised to push the country into civil war.

Activist conspirators who still hankered after a renewal of the war of liberation against Russia were probably more of a nuisance than a serious threat to the stability of the political order. These were people who, in the words of the head of the secret police, 'were never in government, but nevertheless followed events closely seeing for some reason the responsibility for the fortunes of the whole country resting upon their shoulders'. Working through informal networks, they sought to exercise influence behind the scenes. The most inveterate conspirator of them all, Kai Donner, had the ear of the most powerful in the land, though he was not always heard. In the run-up to the autumn 1930 elections, he played a devious game, negotiating on behalf of Lapua with the government, pressing for manipulation of the elections to ensure a bourgeois victory, but looking primarily for a war, which would justify tough action being taken. Svinhufvud managed to talk down demands for known communist sympathisers to be deprived of the right to vote, and the majority of the council of the Lapua movement voted down Donner's idea of manipulating elections. Donner also failed to achieve his long-desired aim of propelling Mannerheim to power, largely because caution overrode any lingering inclinations the great man might have had to resume the leadership of the affairs of state. Mannerheim preferred to allow his associates and confidants to sound out the ground for him, and confined himself to oracular pronouncements and little demonstrative actions calculated to put a distance between himself and those at the front line. Addressing the farmers' march in July 1930, he endorsed the aims of what he believed to be a 'disinterested popular patriotic movement', and his continued presence in the capital encouraged rumours that he was awaiting the call to assume power. His appointment as chairman of the defence council by Svinhufvud in 1931 quelled most of these rumours, though he still retained links with organised groups of veterans of the war of liberation who were widely suspected of planning a coup, and he declined to give his full support for firm action against the rebels during the Mäntsälä crisis.

Mannerheim was, in the end, too aloof, perhaps too fastidious to be the leader of a raw-boned populist movement. He was also, like a number of industrialists and businessmen who gave their backing to Lapua, a member of the old ruling elite. Lapua's willingness to embrace all who opposed communism, irrespective of language, caused discord in the ranks of the Finnish nationalists, and although most were prepared to let the language issue take second place to the fight against communism, a minority, including the young Urho Kekkonen, broke with their former colleagues in the

Kokoomuksen puoluekokouksesta on alkanut kiertää sellaisia jälkijuttuja, että
siellä sittenkin on edustajiston enemmistö aidannut kokoomuksen ja iikooällät
eri karsinaansa, vaikka Paavo Virkkunen puhuikin kauniisti mustien karitsojen
puolesta, ettei niitä jätettäisi "laillisuusrintaman" raadeltaviksi. — Maltilliset
kokoomuslaiset, joita lienee jo ollut puoluekokouksessa enemmistö, katsoivat
kuitenkin, että jos vieroittamista ei jo nyt viimeinkin toimiteta, ei emästä ole
kohta jäljellä muuta kuin luut ja nahka.

Plate 25 Separating the black sheep from the white. The guarded attitude
of the liberal-progressive newspaper *Helsingin Sanomat* towards the Lapua
movement turned to open hostility towards its successor, the increasingly
fascist IKL. This cartoon was drawn during the time when moderate
elements in the conservative National Coalition (*Kokoomus*) were urging
the party to break with the IKL. Two of the moderates, Pennanen and
Haataja, are here guarding the white sheep in the *Kokoomus* pen, whilst
their fellow party-member, Paavo Virkkunen, still wishes to take care of the
black sheep in the IKL pen. Having lost over half its seats in the 1933
elections, which it contested in an unwise electoral alliance with IKL, the
National Coalition gradually drew away from its flirtation with anti-
democratic politics, and under the guidance of the former Old Finn senator
J. K. Paasikivi, followed a more moderate course. The IKL and National
Coalition drew support largely from the same constituency – the educated
Finnish-speakers fired with the vision of a greater Finland and fuelled
with a visceral loathing of all things Russian. Measured against the other

AKS and gravitated towards the agrarians. The authoritarian-nationalist strand had been in the ascendancy in the AKS from 1928 onwards, and was to take many into the more openly fascist party formed after the demise of Lapua in 1932, the Patriotic People's Movement (IKL). The populist-democratic mantle of Finnish nationalism was taken up by the agrarians, who made much of the running in the long drawn-out campaign to finnicise the university.

The university in Helsinki was, by the 1930s, not the only institute of higher education in the land. A Swedish-speaking institute, Åbo Akademi, and a Finnish university had both been founded by private initiative in the town of Turku in the early years of independence, and there was extensive provision for vocational training. The university of Helsinki was, however, of immense symbolic importance as the cradle of the nation's intellectual life as well as the traditional educator of those who constituted the ruling elite. The law finally approved by the *eduskunta* in 1923 attempted to establish that the language of instruction should be in proportion to the given numbers of Finnish- and Swedish-speaking students. It was a compromise that satisfied nobody. The Swedish-speaking professors felt constantly under threat. Ardent Finnish nationalists thought it intolerable that students were still expected to listen to lectures in Swedish at the national university. For those on the populist wing of the 'pure' Finnish movement, such as Kekkonen, the finnicisation of the university was an essential condition for the advancement of democracy. Declining job prospects for graduates, and the loneliness of living in a city where Swedish was still very much the language of service and snobbish society, were powerful incentives for the student from the Finnish-speaking hinterland to rally behind the demands of the AKS and other societies such as the Helsinki 'pure' Finnish club, which declared its aim to be the elevation of the Finnish-speaking majority to become the rightful master of the house in their own country in all areas of public life.

Caption for Plate 25 (*cont.*)
fascistoid parties that sprang up in Europe in the inter-war years, the IKL seems to have been appropriately depicted in this bucolic cartoon, bleating rather than baying.

Although these clubs and societies claimed to stand above politics, their single-minded pursuit of the language question had major
political repercussions. It helped sustain what in Finnish nationalist
eyes was an unholy alliance of the social democrats and the Swedish
People's Party, it placed fragile government coalitions under pressure, and it attracted the attention of the Swedish press and politicians. Swedish intervention in what was already a highly charged
debate did the Swedish-language cause few favours, but it did alarm
Finnish politicians anxious not to alienate a potentially crucial ally
in times of need. Pure Finnish nationalism had a clear upper hand in
the conservative National Coalition and the Agrarian Union during
the 1930s, and even began to attract some support amongst the
social democrats, but it failed to achieve its goal of a purely Finnish
university in Helsinki, largely because each party or faction had its
own particular remedy. The agrarians made most of the running in
1932, but demands made within the party for a one-language state
and the abolition of dual-language facilities in the *eduskunta*
seemed to threaten social stability and persuaded a significant
minority of the National Coalition parliamentary group to join
the progressives, social democrats, and Swedish People's Party in
defeating an agrarian bill for the finnicisation of the university. The
parties most outspokenly in favour of pursuing the finnicisation
programme suffered losses in the 1933 elections, but this did not
lessen the pressure for reform. The university question came to a
head in 1935, with massive demonstrations and meetings organised
by the students' organisations, but the government failed to secure
the necessary majority for its bill. A resolution of this bitter conflict
was finally achieved in 1937 by the centre-left government of
A. K. Cajander. Finnish was henceforth to be the administrative
language of the university, and all Swedish-speakers, including
the fifteen occupying chairs specifically designated to the linguistic minority, had to show ability to teach and direct research in
Finnish. All Finnish-speaking teachers had to demonstrate a competence in Swedish, and Swedish-speaking students had the right
to use their mother tongue in exams and course work.

The gradual decline of Swedish, now (in 2005) spoken by only
5.6 per cent of the population, as against 14.3 per cent in 1880, and
other more arresting symptoms of this decline, such as the influence

of Finnish upon the language itself (especially slang) and its virtual disappearance from advertising hoardings, can in retrospect be interpreted as vindicating the more moderate approach to the language question that was initiated with the constitution of 1919, which declared Finnish and Swedish to be the two official languages of the country, and which in subsequent legislation has sought to ensure the rights of the minority in a state in which Finnish is incontrovertibly the dominant language.[6] This would, however, be to underestimate the force and vehemence of the Finnish nationalist drive for hegemony in the first two decades of independence, and to forget that, although a minority, Swedish-speakers were, or were perceived to be, still dominant in many areas of public life. Over a third, for example, lived in towns, and three-quarters of these were to be found in the capital, Finland's second city Turku, and the Ostrobothnian towns of Vaasa and Pietarsaari. In the two southern towns especially, Swedish-speakers were more likely to hold better jobs and enjoy higher social status. The higher echelons of officialdom still had large numbers of Swedish-speakers – almost three-quarters of the staff of the Bank of Finland and 60 per cent of the administration of customs and excise in 1933, according to the pure Finnish camp – and they were also well represented not only in business and industry, but also in skilled trades and certain professions. Finnish-speakers up from the countryside often had lower skill levels and expectations, and were unable to take advantage of the kind of informal networks available to the urban Swedish-speaker. The percentage of Swedish-speaking children in secondary education, was also disproportionately higher, although declining from 28 per cent in 1920–21 to under 20 per cent a decade later. And beneath the surface, petty snobbery played maliciously upon the perceived cultural deficiencies of the peasant people which Finnish nationalism was otherwise proud to parade as the 'true' nation (and provided rich material for film-makers and novelists).

An overweening obsession with the cultural connotations of the language question meant that many new cultural directions elsewhere either passed Finland by or were regarded with suspicion. Modernism had more resonance amongst writers in Swedish, such as Hagar Olsson and Elmer Diktonius, but as Diktonius himself observed, Swedish-speakers were more concerned with preserving their cultural inheritance than with issues of the day.[7]

Peasantist images dominated much of the literature of the period, partly as a reaction to the civil war, but also in response to the land reforms which firmly established the new republic of small farmers. The number of landowners more than doubled between 1910 and 1940, although the great majority farmed less than ten hectares. Most farms still produced the food they consumed, but, thanks to a well-developed co-operative system, were able to buy seed, fertilisers and other necessities at advantageous terms, and market their produce. Milk output almost doubled between 1920 and 1939, there was a threefold increase in potato production, and – significantly in a land where rye had for centuries been the main staple item of diet – there was almost a tenfold increase in the output of wheat in the 1930s. Most of the work was still performed by manual and animal labour. There were only 6,000 tractors in the whole country at end of the 1930s, milking machines were virtually unknown, and the trees that were felled mainly by saw and axe in the winter months were hauled out of the woods by horses. The wood-processing industry made rapid strides during the inter-war years, although there was a sharp fall in production of sawn timber during the depression, and stiff competition from other producers in northern Europe, not least Soviet Russia. The pulp and paper industry, which before independence had relied heavily on the Russian market, managed successfully to find new markets in Britain and western Europe; Finland was the only producer to be able to increase output year by year during the period. But, with virtually the entire Finnish export trade consisting of foodstuffs and raw or processed natural products, the country's economy was overwhelmingly reliant on the land and the generally ill-rewarded labour of those who tilled the fields, tended the beasts, or felled the timber.

In comparison with their counterparts in other new states of eastern Europe, with their harsh history of serfdom and oppression, Finnish peasant farmers had long enjoyed the benefits of free and active institutions, from the peasants' estate down to the local farmers' society, the support and encouragement of the better placed in society, such as the clergy, and, it has been argued, had been drawn into the market economy well before independence. They were literate, active citizens in a democracy that placed them squarely in the foreground of the national self-portrait; and although there undoubtedly remained a suspicion of the 'gentry', that epithet applied more to city folk who devised taxes and regulations to torment the farmer than to members of a former and oppressive ruling class of landowners, as was the case in Latvia or Poland, for example.

A 30 per cent increase in the volume of cultivated land between 1920 and the outbreak of war in 1939 is indicative of the fierce determination to preserve farming as the main livelihood in Finland for the foreseeable future, but it was also a powerful reminder of the continuing struggle to extend the frontiers of human settlement in a cold and largely infertile northern land. Pioneers in earlier centuries had ventured beyond the historic regions of Finland – to the uplands of Sweden, the north coast of Norway, the White Sea coasts of Russia. Although more Finns migrated and settled in more populous parts of the world, such as St Petersburg in the nineteenth century and non-European destinations such as the United States and Canada in the twentieth century, they tended to become assimilated into their new environment.[8] Finnish-speaking settlers in the sparsely populated far north could and did leave a distinctive mark, which did not pass unobserved.

The existence of these communities on the other side of the official frontiers of the republic of Finland provided ardent nationalists with plenty of ammunition to fire at the Swedish and Norwegian governments for their alleged discrimination against Finnish-speakers in Norrbotten or Finnmark. All governments, in fact, that attempted to establish or enforce national norms and conditions north of the Arctic Circle ran up against communities with very different notions of territory, and which drew sustenance from a rich and transnational mixture of cultures. Settlers pushing northward may have decisively reshaped the culture of the indigenous Sami population, but had in their turn been deeply influenced in what they ate, how they dressed, how they spoke. It was not just the reindeer herders who moved across frontiers. The far north was the cradle of one of the most enduring of the religious revivalist movements of the nineteenth century, that associated with the

Plate 26 The bus service comes to the village. One of the great unsung projects of nation-building was the creation of a comprehensive network of communications that would link even the remotest village with the rest of the country. This work has continued right up to the present, though many of the schools and other public buildings erected in the countryside in the post-war years are no longer in use. Roads and telephone lines allowed rural communities easier access to the wider world. In common with other parts of the world where great distances separate communities (Sweden, North America), the Finns were quick to adopt the telephone (and seem in recent times to have graduated effortlessly to the mobile phone). Entrepreneurs were also quick to start operating bus services; the rather solid vehicle pictured here with members of the Tsokkinen family ran between Suojärvi, right on the Russian border, and Värtsilä (both now in Russia).

preacher Lars Leevi Laestadius (1800–61). Laestadius worked in Swedish Lapland, but his message easily transcended frontiers and created a community of believers that was largely indifferent, or even hostile, to the secular world. The ruthless exploitation of the forests in the twenties and thirties, which attracted large numbers of migrant workers, also helped foster a peculiar brand of far northern communism – or more accurately, anarcho-syndicalism. Finnish communist exiles pinned their hopes on the region as a base from which to launch a new offensive – there was actually an abortive raid on the isolated north-eastern Finnish commune of Kuolajärvi in 1922 – and had visions of a Scandinavian federation stretching from the Atlantic to the White Sea.

Those charged with upholding law and order and the inculcation of Finnish national values in the remote and vast northern hinterland of Oulu county (a separate administrative county of Lapland was not created until 1938) in the 1920s were acutely aware of the problems they faced. Improvements made by neighbouring states, such as the building of roads and the extension of the telephone network undertaken by the Norwegian government in Finnmark, prompted a spate of criticism of the Finnish state in communities such as Utsjoki, already heavily dependent on Norway for food supplies and other essentials. The high hopes for the economic development and integration of Lapland raised by the acquisition of an ice-free port at Petsamo in the 1920 peace treaty with Russia were not realised, though it did serve to direct more attention to the region as a whole. The development of a distinctive northern regional identity however probably owed more to the upswing in the timber industry and the growth of Rovaniemi and Kemi as industrial and cultural centres from which to organise associational activities and to promote a specifically 'northern' or 'Lapland' message through the local press. The image of Lapland that was constructed during the early decades of Finnish independence was very much that of the coloniser at the edge of civilisation, battling with a hostile natural environment. Writers of the period showed little understanding of Sami culture, and some, such as Major-General Kurt Wallenius, were openly contemptuous of people they considered racially inferior. With six distinct language sub-groups and significant cultural differences determined by the natural environment, not state boundaries, few in number, and living in scattered settlements from the central highlands of Sweden and Norway to the extreme eastern tip of the Kola peninsula, the Sami were especially ill-equipped to survive in an age dominated by the all-powerful nation state. By drawing upon the one incontrovertible advantage that an indigenous people have over incomers, a comfortable physical as well as mental awareness and understanding of time, space, and place, pioneer writers such as Pedar Jalvi and Hans

Aslak Guttorm were able to present a self-image with which the Sami could identify, and which, in a more tolerant age, the dominant national culture would be willing to support and encourage.

Worried about security in vulnerable frontier regions and driven by nationalist ideals, the representatives of the new Finnish state had little sympathy for peoples who cared little for frontiers and had only the haziest of notions of national loyalty. The decision of the League of Nations in 1921, supporting the legitimacy of the Finnish claim to the Åland islands, finally dashed the hopes of those islanders who wanted sovereignty transferred to Sweden, but the secret police continued to monitor closely separatist sentiment. The police were inclined to play down political conviction in favour of self-interest, an interpretation they applied on the eastern frontier as well. A police report at the end of 1919, for example, confessed that:

It is difficult to say whether the frontier district is red or white. There are relatively few socialists. But all along the frontier there are a number of villages inhabited by poor crofters and equally poor farmers, for whom farming is unprofitable, who think of nothing else but the opportunity of making easy and good pickings from the dodgy dealings they have been accustomed to doing for years. These people are at the present time just as willing to offer their services to the Bolsheviks as to the Russians in former times.

Pedlars, the large gangs of men tramping the country in search of work, the prevalence of weapons (especially the large sheath-knife, or *puukko*, which, one county governor believed, virtually every male from under-age boys upwards carried), and the deleterious effects of prohibition were all matters for concern for the police and the upholders of law and order. Enforcing prohibition was a particular headache for the authorities, since it involved extensive surveillance in a generally futile effort to catch smugglers or catch those who purveyed liquor. From 1921 to the ending of prohibition in 1932, almost three-quarters of all recorded crimes in Finland were breaches of the prohibition act or were drink related. In the face of all the evidence that prohibition was patently not working, politicians across the political spectrum, with the exception of a few brave souls in the Swedish People's Party, continued to insist that it was a necessary civilising measure.

Plate 27 The bootlegger thwarted: a pile of canisters confiscated by the police. The introduction of prohibition in 1919 inaugurated a golden age for the purveyors of illicit liquor. Smugglers made use of routes used in earlier times to carry underground literature into Russia, or to spirit revolutionaries out of the country (Lenin made use of one such route in the winter of 1907). According to a contemporary survey of those convicted of breaches of the prohibition law, sailors, chauffeurs, and widows were most likely to find themselves in court, the first two for carrying the booze, the last for selling it. The big fish, the *pirtutrokarit* (bootleggers), were less often caught, though the police did occasionally capture a clutch of stills, or – as in this instance – a pile of the canisters used for retail purposes.

The high costs of policing prohibition and the pressing need of the state to raise additional revenue at a time of economic depression was decisive, but because none of the politicians wished to take the responsibility for ending the experiment, a referendum was held at the end of 1931. With a comfortable majority of 70 per cent in favour of repeal, the politicians bowed to popular opinion and the law was repealed by 120 votes to 45 in February 1932. Control was henceforth to be enforced by a state alcohol monopoly 'in such a way that, at the same time as the illicit trade is hindered, the use of strong drink is reduced as much as possible and drunkenness and its destructive consequences is prevented', as the law put it. The state monopoly Oy Alko Ab sought to restrict consumption, especially to working class patrons, by limiting the number of outlets and opening times, making them distinctly unwelcoming, and limiting the amount served. Three classes of restaurant were created, effectively mirroring social classes; the countryside remained dry.

Refugees from eastern Karelia were another problem for the hard-pressed authorities. Between 1918 and 1920, a bewildering array of armies tussled rather ineffectually for control in the region. An allied expeditionary force under British command, based in Murmansk and Archangel, supported anti-Bolshevik Russian forces, but also recruited Finnish red exiles to fight against the incursions of white Finnish forces, thought to be acting in the German interest. Finnish efforts to secure all or part of eastern Karelia through military action came to nothing. In order to obtain the ice-free port of Petsamo (promised to the Grand Duchy by Alexander II, but never officially placed under Finnish jurisdiction) in the peace agreement reached with Russia in 1920, the Finnish government had to withdraw troops occupying two Karelian border parishes. Finnish negotiators managed to insert into the peace treaty a passage referring to the Karelians' right to self-determination, but the Soviet side insisted this had in fact been realised with the creation of the Karelian workers' commune, some weeks before the treaty was finally initialled in Tartu. To Finnish activists, the treaty was a 'shameful peace', a betrayal not only of the Karelian people, but also of the full realisation of Finnish national statehood. The fact that the Karelian workers' commune was inspired and led by the exiled leaders of the red uprising in 1918 was even more galling. Karelia, romanticised and lauded as the cradle of Finnish culture, was now inaccessible beyond the frontier, and in the hands of the enemy. But in fact, as recent studies have shown, the Finns who were responsible for running what was from 1923 an Autonomous Soviet Socialist Republic in Karelia were mentally and emotionally much closer to Finnish nationalism than to Soviet communism. They saw themselves as bringing Finnish culture and enlightenment to the less favoured inhabitants of Karelia's backwoods, and they visualised Karelia as the vital first step towards the creation of a Finnish-Karelian-Scandinavian

Plate 28 Väinö Tanner. Seated at his desk at home, cigar in hand, the fifty-year-old Väinö Tanner exudes firmness and resolution, the undisputed leader of his party at a time of deep crisis. Tanner had made his name in the workers' co-operative movement, and it was this experience that brought him into the coalition Senate of 1917 as the man charged with alleviating a serious food shortage in Finland. A moderate who stood outside the inner circles of the party, Tanner sat out the civil war on his farm outside Helsinki, but took up the reins of leadership when the Social Democratic Party began to revive at the end of 1918. Tanner was that rare thing in Finnish politics, a man who liked power and who was not afraid to take responsibility. His authority in the Social Democratic Party was frequently challenged, but he remained in charge right up to the end of the war in 1944. Tanner showed personal courage in standing up to the threats of the Lapua movement, but there was also a strong streak of obstinacy underneath his braveness. Convicted in 1946 on charges of having conspired to take Finland to war alongside Germany in 1941, Tanner returned to active politics in 1957 as a leading opponent of President Kekkonen's foreign policy. Already demonised in Moscow, his reappearance on the political stage threatened to drive his party into the political wilderness. Since 1990, his reputation and memory have been rehabilitated in the general process of reassessing Finland's recent past.

federation. Their policies for the 'karelianisation' of the republic, which in practice meant the teaching of Finnish and promotion of Finnish culture aroused resentment, especially in the more populous southern half of the republic (Olonets Karelia), where the Russian language and culture was strongly established. Increasingly isolated, they were easy targets for their opponents when the policy of encouraging the growth of national identity was replaced in the 1930s with an emphasis on loyalty to the Soviet state.

As the exiled Finnish communist leadership was being scythed down by Stalin's purges, Finnish social democracy was beginning to emerge from the long shadows cast by the Lapua years. The social democrats had in fact held office for a year in 1927 as a minority government, but the experience had neither convinced their opponents of the feasibility of working in coalition with the left, nor overcome the considerable ideological reservations within the party about going into government at all. The Lapua threat helped unite the party, and strengthened the personal authority of its leader, Väinö Tanner. Although the electoral popularity of a few high-profile left-wingers and secret communist sympathisers remained high, the moderates were now firmly in control. Success in the elections of 1936, which gave the social democrats five more seats, encouraged the party to begin serious discussions with the agrarians over forming a government. President Svinhufvud's opposition brought these plans to nothing, and the agrarians finally formed a minority government. In the presidential elections of 1937, however, the socialists learned from their tactical error in the electoral college in 1931, which had allowed Svinhufvud to win. Their agreement to switch their support from Ståhlberg after the first ballot to the agrarian candidate Kyösti Kallio on the second, should Ståhlberg not secure victory, was respected by the agrarians, who rejected attempts to persuade them to vote in the second ballot for the still-popular Svinhufvud. In the end, Kallio won comfortably, and the way was now clear for a majority coalition. Like so many other governments of the inter-war years, the post of prime minister was held by a representative of the Progressive Party, the smallest of the five main parties in parliament (holding a mere seven seats after the 1936 elections, four fewer than in 1933).

The Cajander government remained in office until dramatic circumstances intervened in December 1939. Its two principal partners, the agrarians and social democrats, both increased their mandates in the elections of 1939. The IKL (Patriotic People's

Movement), having managed to persuade the courts to overturn a temporary banning order in 1938, slumped from fourteen to eight seats. The achievements of the centre-left government were modest in comparison with those of the socialist-led government in Sweden, but Finland's problems were of a different magnitude, and the real significance of the coming together of agrarians and socialists is the implicit acknowledgement that the scars of the civil war were beginning to heal. The prospect of hosting the Olympic games in 1940 helped draw together a people whose middle-distance runners had won renown and glory around the world. Increasing consumption of wheat, eggs, and meat were a good indicator of modestly rising living standards, sustained by an impressive average annual growth rate for industry of 8 per cent and greatly improved yields per hectare in farming. Finnish standards of health care and education were high; infant mortality rates fell by half between 1900 and 1939. A threefold increase in the number of buses and radio licences in the 1930s helped further the bringing together of the people that had been so earnestly desired by the radical-populist nationalists of the 1920s. Finland at the end of the 1930s was still an overwhelmingly agrarian country, and Helsinki remained remote and alien to many country dwellers; but its architects and designers were at the cutting-edge of the modern movement, and their work was amply displayed by the wide variety of newspapers and magazines, for which a literate public had a voracious appetite. If Finnish culture during the first two decades of independence was an occasionally discordant amalgam of traditional and modern, rather like a *kantele* (a traditional stringed instrument) hanging on the wall of a functionalist building, to employ the striking phrase of the social commentator Matti Kurjensaari, it was never overburdened with nostalgia for a forgotten past, nor did it lend itself easily to exploitation by repressive or reactionary authoritarian movements. There were, nevertheless, a number of vital questions underlying the assumptions of the national state that had yet to be resolved, questions of loyalty and solidarity, and of the actual territorial identity of the state, for which the experiences of the 1940s were to prove the decisive test.

6

War and peace, 1939–56

On 2 December 1939, a new Finnish state came into existence. Declaring that the time had now come to realise the perennial hopes of the Finnish people for a reunion with their close relations, the Karelians, to form a united nation, and to settle the frontier question in a manner satisfactory to both sides, the government of the democratic republic of Finland announced that it had agreed to conclude a mutual assistance treaty with the Soviet Union. The first of the seven articles of the treaty transferred to Finland 70,000 sq. km. of Soviet Karelia, with Finland in turn ceding an area of 3,970 sq. km. in the Karelian isthmus. Finland also agreed to lease for thirty years to the Soviet Union a naval base on the Hanko peninsula, west of Helsinki, and to sell a number of small islands guarding the approaches to Leningrad plus a sliver of land on the Arctic coast.

How had the Finns managed to resolve their differences with their eastern neighbour in such a felicitous manner, at a time when the clouds of war were rolling over Europe? The clue to understanding this document lies in the opening statement, which confidently predicts the speedy liquidation through the heroic fight of the Finnish people and the efforts of the Soviet Red Army of 'that regular hotbed of war which the former plutocratic government in Finland had created for the benefit of the imperialist powers on the frontiers of the Soviet Union'. The people's government of the democratic republic of Finland had in fact been created in Moscow, and was installed in the Finnish frontier town of Terijoki, occupied on 1 December, one day after Soviet troops and bombers had attacked Finland. The Soviet attack was launched some three weeks after the final breakdown of negotiations in Moscow over territorial adjustments and base facilities demanded by the Soviet Union. Headed by the one surviving Finnish communist of any significance, Otto Ville Kuusinen, but otherwise stuffed with un-known nonentities who had also managed to escape the purges, the Terijoki government, as it was commonly known, was at one level a ploy to justify to the Soviet people the invasion of Finland. It was very much in line with the policy adopted in the early years of the revolution of setting up workers' communes (for example, for Estonia in 1918–19 and Karelia in 1920) prior to the Red Army 'liberating' their territory: the pious intention to broaden the government with the inclusion of other democratic and peace-loving elements, and the sedulous avoidance of terms like 'soviet' and 'socialist' looked forward to the policy that was to be pursued in eastern Europe, beginning in the Baltic states less than a year later.

The attack came as a huge shock to the Finnish government and people, lulled into believing that nothing would happen after talks in Moscow finally broke down in mid-November. The creation of a new government in Terijoki and the invasion of Finland, ostensibly at the request of that government, also struck at the very foundations upon which the independent state had been built, for it openly challenged the verdict of 1918. Had Kuusinen's government been installed as victors in Helsinki, the proclamation issued on 1 December 1939 would indubitably have become the official interpretation of Finland's history, expunging from the textbooks the white version, which regarded 1918 as the year in which the fatherland was liberated from the grip of barbarous bolshevism and misguided traitors. The red version, spelled out in the proclamation, saw 1918 as the year in which 'the reactionary, greedy plutocracy . . . with the help of foreign imperialist troops drowned in streams of blood the democratic liberty of the working people of Finland'. The war now being pursued was thus one of liberation, a freeing of the working people of Finland from the capitalist clique that had squandered the benefits of independence with their constant intriguing with imperialist forces against the Soviet Union, 'the great friend of the Finnish people'.

The war fought between Finland and the Soviet Union during one of the coldest winters of the twentieth century and its portentous sequel, known in Finnish historiography as the 'continuation war', was very much a clash between sharply differing ideologies that had existed ever since the revolution of 1917 had torn the old imperial order asunder. The very granting of Finnish independence by the new Soviet regime was an ideologically motivated act, very much in line with Lenin's belief that conceding the right of nations to self-determination would help intensify the class struggle in the newly independent states, which in turn would hasten the revolution and eventual reunification of the victorious socialist republics. The seeming inability of the Finnish socialists to seize their opportunity and make revolution clearly irritated Lenin, and his later pronouncements tended to portray the granting of independence to a bourgeois state as necessitated by circumstance. The commissar for nationality affairs, J.V.Stalin, took a much narrower view of the rights of nations to self-determination, holding that proletarian interests – which were upheld by Russia, the first workers' state – should always take precedence over bourgeois nationalism. There is an interesting and early insight into Stalin's views in a conversation recorded by a Finnish official at the end of November 1917. Although not unreceptive to the idea of granting Finland independence, Stalin nevertheless felt that 'most of the small peoples living on Russian territory, having acquired complete political autonomy, will surely come to see that it is in their interests to remain with Russia (in a federation) and he thought that Finland in this respect would hardly be an exception, when the alternative might well be that it was unable to preserve and safeguard its independence, which would thus become nothing but a fictitious independence'.

Independence was nonetheless freely conceded by the Soviet regime. This was something its white Russian opponents were never quite prepared to do, even as the price for securing Finnish assistance in toppling the Bolsheviks. White Finland's association with Germany in 1918 also threatened to follow Stalin's prophecy that the country's independence might well become seriously compromised. In their anxiety to secure German military assistance to restore law and order in Finland, the Finnish representatives in Berlin failed adequately to consult their government, and entered into agreements carefully designed by the Germans to bring Finland firmly within their economic and military control. The terms of the secret treaty were in some respects even more severe than those proposed by the Soviet Union in the negotiations of 1939, not only placing the Finnish pilot service at the disposal of the imperial German navy and allowing the Germans the right to set up naval bases wherever they chose on Finnish territory, but also giving Germany full powers of control over Finnish imports and exports.

The one thing Germany did not demand was territory; and the white government was willing to accept German military and economic hegemony, and even closer political ties in the form of a German monarch, in return for support for the Finnish demands on east Karelia. The acquisition of Karelia was, according to Svinhufvud, vital for Finland not only for national reasons, but as an area for settlement. Its vast reserves of timber also attracted the attention of Finnish businessmen, something of which the Karelian proponents of autonomy were watchfully aware. The Germans were, however, unwilling to support the Finnish claims, and the allied powers who emerged victorious in the war at the end of 1918 were to be even less encouraging.

Karelia remained a highly sensitive issue for independent Finland. The government was aware that the likely diplomatic and political consequences meant that they could not afford to be seen officially and fully endorsing the kind of full-blown military intervention in Karelia advocated by the activists, and experience showed them that little could be expected either from a policy of active diplomacy to press Finland's claim to the region. Efforts to use the Germans to bring pressure to bear on the Russians in 1918, to persuade the Allies in 1919 to support a plan for a plebiscite in Karelia or to get the Russians in 1920 to agree to an article in the peace treaty between the two countries that would guarantee the Karelians the right to self-government, all failed. But no Finnish government could afford to ignore the issue. Karelia may not have been burnt into the heart of every Finnish patriot as were the purported 'lost lands' of other more demonstrative peoples of Europe, but it was very much kept alive by nationalist organisations such as the AKS and

KARJALAN POULESTA.

„Somap' on sotahan kuolla,
Kaunis miekan kalskehesen."
Kalevala.

Valok. O. A. Väisänen.

HONKIEN HOIVISSA
Uhtuan - Jyskyjärven matkalta kesällä 1918. Monet kuvassa näkyvistä suomalaisista vapaaehtoisista saivat itäisimpinä vartioina uhrata henkensä „Karjalan puolesta", mihin kirjoitus heidän valkoisissa käsivarsinauhoissaan heitä velvoitti.

Plate 29 'For Karelia'. This postcard, issued by the Academic Karelia Society to raise funds for Karelian refugees, shows Finnish volunteers on the road between the eastern Karelian villages of Uhtua and Jyskyjärvi in the summer of 1918. A plan to occupy the northern regions of Karelia was worked up at Mannerheim's headquarters in March, whilst the civil war was still raging in Finland. The idea of Karelian autonomy won some support in the northern half of the region, which lay within the administrative district of Archangel, but there was also resistance to the idea of union with Finland. The white Finnish forces that invaded the area in spring 1918 were soon repulsed by a much larger force of Karelians and Finnish reds. For ardent Finnish nationalists, the liberation of Karelia became a holy mission. Although government hesitated to commit itself officially to supporting military action, it could not afford to ignore the kith-and-kin argument, explicitly enunciated in the third verse of Heikki Nurmio's 1917 *Jäger March*: 'Häme, Karelia, its White Sea shores and land, one great Finnish state'. General Mannerheim's order of the day, issued on 23 February 1918, in which he swore in the name of the Finnish peasant army not to sheath his sword before 'Lenin's last soldier and hooligan is driven not only from Finland but from Archangel Karelia as well', was also to prove an embarrassment for Finnish governments in the future.

numerous 'kith-and-kin' societies. It had faded somewhat as an issue by the late 1930s, and the Finnish minister to Moscow was probably right in his view that the Soviet leadership did not consider the advocates of a greater Finland a serious threat; but, given the opportunity in 1941, the sacred mission of the Finnish nation to rescue their kinsfolk from the clutches of Bolshevik barbarity could and did burst into life again.

The vision of a greater Finland carved largely out of Soviet territory was augmented by a strongly anti-Russian sentiment, which seriously affected the official relationship between the two countries. Members of the first Russian legation to be established in Finland after the signing of the peace treaty in 1920 were subjected to public insults and were kept at arm's length by representatives of the state from the president downwards. Virtually all the pre-independence ties were severed. Trade with Russia dwindled to a fraction of what it had been before independence. Finns no longer travelled openly and legally to seek fame or fortune in Russian service, and those who went illegally – and thousands did so in search of work during hard times – ran the risk of ending up in a prison camp or worse. The few Finns who did rise in the service of the new Soviet state, such as Major-General Akseli Anttila, minister of defence in the Terijoki government or the Red Army commander Toivo Antikainen, faced the prospect of a long term of imprisonment in Finland (as happened to Antikainen, apprehended in 1934) as well as running the risk of ending up before a firing squad in Stalin's Russia.

Soviet Russia was not the only country with which the new Finnish state was on bad terms. Finnish nationalist agitation on behalf of Finnish-speakers in Finnmark caused some ill feeling in Norway, and relations with Sweden were damaged by the dispute over the Åland islands, and were also affected by the language question; but these differences were never allowed decisively to shape or direct official policy. Furthermore, there were many informal and semi-official links – between trade unions, co-operative movements, cultural organisations, or even at a personal level – that facilitated Finland's alignment with the other Scandinavian countries from 1935.

The informal connections that had been cleverly used by the Finnish elite that ran the affairs of the Grand Duchy were severed by revolution and the separation of Finland from Russia. No longer able to tread the 'path to St Petersburg' as had their predecessors, the members of the Finnish government were simply unable to fathom or appreciate the intentions of the new rulers, now located in Moscow. Some did try, though with very limited success. As foreign minister, Aarne Yrjö-Koskinen concluded a non-aggression treaty with Russia in 1932, and as minister in Moscow, worked hard to foster better relations. He was obliged, however, to conclude that the extreme suspiciousness that pervaded Soviet foreign policy thinking made the task virtually impossible. Mannerheim's unofficial visit to Germany in 1935 in response to an invitation to join Hermann Goering on a hunting trip was interpreted by Soviet intelligence as paving the way for a secret agreement or pact. The visit to Helsinki in August 1937 of a German U-boat squadron was enough to provoke howls of protest about Finnish–German military collusion in the Soviet press, and it effectively undermined the first halting steps towards a more secure relationship undertaken by Rudolf Holsti, who had paid the first visit by a Finnish foreign minister to Moscow in 1937. Lacking any clear insight into or understanding of the mental world of an increasingly paranoid Soviet leadership, the Finns were unable or unwilling to see that visits by German military personnel or units were highly likely to be construed as collusion with the Third Reich against the Soviet Union; and even when the Soviet leadership appeared to have been persuaded by Holsti that Finland would in fact not allow its territory to be used by a foreign power intent on attacking the Soviet Union, it remained to be convinced that Finland actually had the military capacity successfully to repel any such threat.

At virtually no time did Finnish and Soviet security and foreign policy interests coincide. Finland was unwilling to be a part of the Soviet plan of collective security for eastern Europe put forward in 1933, and came increasingly to be placed by Soviet Russia alongside Poland and Nazi Germany as potential aggressors. Finnish confidence in the League of Nations cooled in the 1930s, just as Soviet Russia joined the League. In 1936, Finland signed the Oslo declaration whereby the small northern European states absolved themselves of their obligations under Article 16 of the League covenant to provide military assistance to fellow-members deemed to be victims of aggression. The *eduskunta* had the year before approved a government resolution declaring Finnish solidarity with Scandinavian neutrality. Finnish governments had earlier fought shy of using the term 'neutral', which they felt was inconsistent with their commitment to collective security through the auspices of the League of Nations. They were also wary of a neutrality that could be construed as serving Soviet security interests, which was one reason why the non-aggression treaty of 1932, although renewed for ten years in 1934, failed to provide a sound basis for a more durable relationship. Neutrality for Finland after 1935 meant avoiding conflict with Russia, though not through the kind of active bridge-building policy which was the hallmark of President Urho Kekkonen's foreign policy in the 1960s and 1970s.

The inter-war Finnish political leadership was not so naive as to believe that neutrality would be respected, and it did take seriously the defence of the country, even if the military complained of inadequate provision; but if Finland's leaders hoped that by aligning their country with the Scandinavian neutrals, it might secure military support in an hour of need, they were to be disappointed. Clear differences emerged between Finland and Sweden in their discussions concerning the fortification and defence of the Åland islands, which had been demilitarised in 1921 as part of the League of Nations settlement. Sweden was primarily interested in protecting itself from Germany, and insisted on seeking Soviet consent, even though Russia had not been a signatory of the 1921 demilitarisation treaty. When the new Soviet commissar for foreign affairs, V. M. Molotov, flatly refused to give his country's consent in May 1939, the Swedes hastily withdrew from the project.

It was as these discussions got under way in 1938 that another and more unwelcome initiative was put before the Finnish government by a junior Soviet diplomat, Boris Yartsev. Yartsev, who was also an officer of the NKVD, or secret police, had in fact been entrusted with this mission by Stalin himself. It seems that Stalin was sceptical of the chances of securing a mutual assistance agreement with Finland as recommended by his advisers, but approved the plan, emphasising it was essential to declare that the USSR had no intention of interfering in Finland's internal affairs. The Finnish side rejected any idea of a mutual assistance agreement, offering instead a written assurance that Finland would not allow its territory to be used in any attack against the Soviet Union. This was initially rejected as inadequate by Yartsev, but at a later stage of the discussions, the Soviet side seemed willing to accept this and the fortification of the Åland islands, provided that it was also allowed to participate. In return, however, the Soviet Union sought leave to build an air and sea defence base on the Finnish island of Suursaari, which commanded the approaches to Leningrad. This the Finns turned down as incompatible with the policy of neutrality Finland and its Scandinavian neighbours had adopted, as well as a violation of Finnish sovereignty. Yartsev was nothing if not persistent, and the sending of a delegation from Finland to Moscow at the end of the year to discuss trade seems to have been interpreted as a sign of a greater willingness by the Finnish government to accommodate Soviet security demands. Finland was at all events removed from the list of the potential enemies on the western borders of the Soviet Union, only to be returned to the list in June 1939, after a further round of talks had ended in failure.

In the autumn of 1939, the Soviet Union was in a far more favourable position than it had been in the spring of 1938, when Yartsev made his first approach to the Finnish government. In order to deal with Poland, Hitler had bought Soviet neutrality through the infamous non-aggression pact concluded by his foreign minister Joachim von Ribbentrop at the end of August 1939. Having failed to persuade any of his western neighbours to enter into a security system primarily designed to protect the Soviet Union, Stalin now had the secret consent of his hitherto arch-enemy to make what arrangements he could with them. The Baltic states were first in line. All three were hurried into signing mutual assistance treaties that allowed the Soviet Union access to military bases on their territory. Finland was treated rather differently. Its negotiators were not subjected to the kind of bully-boy tactics employed against the hapless Estonians and Latvians. Molotov quickly abandoned the idea of a mutual assistance treaty, and the Soviet side appeared willing to consider alternatives that might equally well ensure their security demands were met. The talks stretched over a month, giving the Finnish political and military leadership plenty of time to consider the options.

These options were in truth few, but enough to divide the inner circle of men who guided Finland through these crucial weeks. Firmly believing that right was on Finland's side, and convinced that the Soviet Union was bluffing and would back down in the face of determined resistance to its demands, the foreign minister, Eljas Erkko, allowed his negotiators little scope for manoeuvre in Moscow. The minister of defence, Juho Niukkanen, presented to government and the political parties a more optimistic view of Finland's defence capabilities than did Mannerheim, appointed commander-in-chief of the armed forces on presidential authority on 17 October 1939. Mannerheim, who had long been critical of the politicians for failing to provide adequate resources, urged the government to avoid a war that would be disastrous for Finland, and added his voice to that of the chief Finnish negotiator, J. K. Paasikivi, in pressing for concessions to Soviet demands. The principal sticking-point was the demand of the Soviet Union for the leasing of a naval base on the Hanko peninsula, to the west of Helsinki. Mannerheim and Paasikivi favoured offering an island base as an alternative, and when Stalin seemed disposed to consider this option during the final round of talks in early November, Paasikivi tried to secure government approval for authority to make the offer; this was refused, and the talks came to an abrupt end on 9 November.

In later life, as the man who was to steer Finland through the tricky early years of a new relationship with the Soviet Union, Paasikivi publicly criticised pre-war Finnish foreign policy for its lack of realism and understanding of great power politics. There is some substance in this accusation. Little had been done over the years to lessen the Soviet suspicion that Finland was pro-German. Alignment with the Scandinavian states in the end failed to give Finland any sort of assurance. Close collaboration between the Swedish and Finnish armed forces may have encouraged some to think that Sweden would come to Finland's assistance in the event of a Soviet attack, but the Swedish prime minister warned Erkko at the meeting of Nordic heads of state and foreign ministers in mid-October that Finland should not count on any military assistance from Sweden, and this was repeated at the end of the month in a message to the Finnish government. Erkko's advice to Paasikivi to forget that the Soviet Union was a great power was at best ill-judged, and his own unwillingness to heed the advice of others or to reveal the full picture to the government and parliament places a great deal of responsibility for the breakdown of talks in November 1939 upon his shoulders.

Paasikivi's criticism, rooted in his own experience as an Old Finn member of government during the last years of imperial Russia, does, however, skate over the all-important question of how far Stalin's Russia could be trusted to honour any agreement arrived at by negotiation. It also fails to show how making concessions to Russian security concerns could be reconciled with Finland's own interests, given that the one major threat to Finland's continued existence as an independent state was generally assumed to be from the Soviet Union. And although Paasikivi clearly recognised the powerful strains of the interests of state that permeated the pro-tracted talks, he seems never to have fully grasped the fact that the Soviet state was also an ideological construction, and Stalin was at one and the same time a creator and a product of that ideology. He could no more escape from it than could the Finnish politicians separate themselves from their belief in and commitment to the existence and destiny of the Finnish nation. The war that erupted on the western frontiers of the Soviet state in September 1939 was in Soviet eyes a new and more dangerous episode in a deeply ideological conflict. Resolving security issues through frontier adjustments or even mutual assistance pacts in the autumn of 1939 would have been no more than a breathing-space, a prepara-tion for the final political conflict. Mannerheim may well have been right on military grounds in urging the Finnish negotiators in Moscow to make concessions, but the foreign minister, Eljas Erkko, was also justified on ideological grounds in urging the negotiators not to make concessions that would mean the end of a free Finland.

Stalin's ideological world-view was, however, of the narrowly purist variety; he had no faith in revolutionary fraternalism. The failure of the Finnish people to rise up and welcome their supposed liberators may have been a bitter blow to Kuusinen, the head of the puppet government installed in Terijoki, but in all likelihood was less of a surprise to Stalin than was the demonstration of their capacity to resist successfully the might of the Red Army. Stalin's decision to go for a military solution of the Finnish problem in November 1939 probably owed more to Soviet intelligence reports of Mannerheim's deeply pessimistic assessment of the capacity of the Finnish armed forces to resist for more than a fortnight than it did to a belief that the working people of Finland were yearning for liberation from the yoke of bourgeois oppression. Stalin does, however, appear to have underestimated the task of defeating Finland militarily, dismissing the proposals of the chief of general staff for a lengthy campaign involving up to fifty divisions, and setting in July 1939 a time limit of two weeks for operations with a significantly reduced force.

The final breakdown of talks on 9 November compelled the Soviet leadership to go for a military resolution of the crisis. Plans for a massive assault were finally approved in mid-November, at the same time as Kuusinen was being summoned to Moscow to form his people's government. The Finnish armed forces had been mobilised in mid-October, but the strain and cost of having so many men in arms was beginning to tell, and the minister of defence had to fight hard to prevent almost two-thirds of these men being demobilised on 20 November. Had the Russians delayed their assault for a further two or three weeks, Finnish unanimity and resolve might well have begun to crack. As it was, the attack found the Finnish army well-trained and prepared, albeit woefully under-equipped in artillery and aircraft, and a nation united in its determination to resist.

The Soviet attack was launched on 30 November, after a frontier incident had been fabricated on 26 November as an excuse to renounce the 1932 non-aggression treaty and to portray Finland as the aggressor to the Soviet people. The Soviet plan envisaged the complete occupation of Finland within a month. The main thrust of the attack was in the Karelian isthmus, with the objective of seizing Helsinki within two weeks. The first week of war did not go as expected: instead of the rapid advance envisaged, the Red Army progressed at no more than three to five kilometres a day, with huge columns of vehicles clogging the narrow roads. But Mannerheim was also worried that his subordinates were not doing enough to

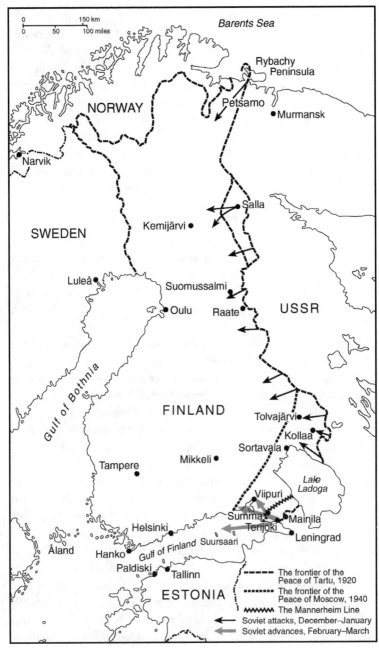

Map 3 The Winter War, 1939–40.

hinder the enemy's advance. He shared their deep unease at the army's woeful lack of resources in the face of a force superior in numbers and equipment, and urged the government to do all it could to reopen negotiations with Moscow. By the end of the first week, the advancing Red Army had reached the prepared defensive position which was to become known as the Mannerheim line, and had begun to threaten important strategic positions further north. A series of defensive actions by the Finnish forces from mid-December to the beginning of January stemmed these advances, boosting Finnish morale and arousing the admiration of the rest of the world. The smashing of two Russian divisions at Suomussalmi and Raate was particularly important, for it prevented the realisation of the plan to cut Finland in half by an advance on Oulu, but there were equally spectacular successes at Tolvajärvi (north of lake Ladoga) and at Summa on the isthmus.

Although outnumbered, the Finns possessed a number of advantages over their opponents. They had a far superior knowledge of the difficult terrain in which the battles were fought, and they were better equipped to fight in winter conditions. They were most effective in small units, especially in launching surprise guerrilla attacks upon an enemy whose unpreparedness for winter combat all too often allowed it to become dangerously exposed. They were good marksmen, making their meagre rounds count, and they soon learnt a number of techniques for disabling tanks. Lack of experience in fighting large staged battles meant, however, that counter-offensives were often poorly prepared and badly executed. The Red Army suffered from poor planning, confusion, and a general inexperience of fighting in winter conditions. Voroshilov's letter to Stalin on 21 December is revealing: 'the roads are choked, the infantry does not function at the front as an organised force, but drifts hither and thither more or less out of control, and at the first volley of shots, breaks up in disorder, rushing off into the forest'.

The Finns' dogged resistance shattered any illusions in Moscow of an easy victory, and led to hurried and radical changes of command and tactics. By January, some forty-five divisions, or around six hundred thousand soldiers, had been deployed for a fresh assault on Finland. Against such overwhelming numbers, Mannerheim's forces, their reserves seriously depleted, stood little chance in the long run. Finland had thus only two serious options: either to obtain significant military assistance from elsewhere, or to make peace, relying on its record of valorous resistance so far to persuade the Soviet Union to negotiate and to agree to moderate terms. Moscow began in fact to drop hints from the beginning of January that it was willing to negotiate with the government in Helsinki, though it would appear that the Soviet leadership had also resolved to launch a major offensive to take the city of Viipuri and then force the Helsinki government to negotiate. On 29 January, Moscow let it be known through the Swedish foreign ministry that it was not averse in principle to negotiations with the Finnish government, though it declared ominously that its terms would not be the same as those presented in the autumn. This was a major breakthrough, for the Soviet Union had resolutely refused to accept the legitimacy of the broad-based government headed by the former governor of the Bank of Finland, Risto Ryti, that had replaced the Cajander coalition on the first day of war. The Kuusinen government remained in being as part of the Soviet armoury of threats; but the way was now open for the Ryti government to pursue the option of a negotiated peace with the Soviet Union.

The road to peace was, however, bestrewn with obstacles, not least the aggressive and uncompromising tone adopted by the Soviet leaders. Although the inner circle of government and the military command were at one in making peace Finland's highest priority, they were also aware that the public mood, buoyed by success on the battlefield, would find a harsh peace extremely difficult to swallow. There was considerable opposition in wider circles of government to peace negotiations, especially once the extent of the Soviet demands became known, and even Mannerheim and the foreign minister Väinö Tanner wavered in their belief that a negotiated end to the war was the only realistic option.

The alternative that flickered like a will-o'-the-wisp through the dark days of the massive Soviet assault on the isthmus in February was the prospect of allied Franco-British military intervention on Finland's behalf. The idea of sending an expeditionary force, supposedly in response to the League of Nations' appeal for assistance to Finland, but in reality intended to cut German access to Swedish supplies of iron ore, took shape in allied circles during December

Plate 30 Children in Helsinki preparing for evacuation, 1939. Some seventy thousand children, mostly between the ages of three and seven, were evacuated from Finland during the war. Most were sent to Sweden, though some went to Norway and Denmark. Many remained in Sweden for the entire war; some ten thousand stayed there permanently. The war placed heavy demands on all sections of the population; children were called upon to take part in farm work, collect wild fruit and mushrooms, and were drafted into the defence corps and Lotta Svärd auxiliaries to help on the home front.

1939. The 'big plan' that envisaged the dispatch of up to one hundred thousand French, British, and Polish troops to Scandinavia by mid-April was finally approved by the supreme allied war council on 5 February. The great majority of these troops would, in fact, be used to occupy the northern Swedish iron-ore fields and vital coastal areas; a maximum of fifteen thousand would be sent to the northern front in Finland. To give the plan a sheen of legitimacy, the Finns would have officially to request assistance, and the Scandinavian governments grant transit permission. There was little prospect of either Norway or Sweden risking a German invasion by allowing allied forces onto their soil, and the Finnish leadership was sceptical from the start about the ability of the allies to deliver the assistance promised. However, as the Soviet attack in the isthmus forced the Finns to withdraw from the western section of the Mannerheim line on 15 February, and a fortnight later, to a position defending the approaches to the city of Viipuri, the hope of allied assistance was something that they could not afford entirely to ignore. Mannerheim, although well aware that any allied assistance would be too little and too late, did not finally abandon the idea until 9 March. He gave little comfort to the ministers who visited him at his headquarters at the end of February, seeking, as one of them admitted, to have him take responsibility for a humiliating peace which the politicians would have a hard task persuading the people to accept. Mannerheim cannily pushed the responsibility back on to the politicians, declaring 'I have explained the military situation. It is your business, gentlemen, to make the political decisions, not mine.'

The Soviet terms were revealed in the third week of February to the Finnish government via the Swedish foreign ministry, acting as official intermediary. Not only did the Soviet Union demand the lease of a naval base at Hanko, but it also wanted the entire Karelian isthmus, including the towns of Viipuri and Sortavala. The government hesitated between swallowing the Soviet terms and hanging on to see if allied aid would really materialise. Sweden's firm refusal to allow the transit of troops or to provide military assistance to Finland had to be balanced against the possibility of losing all hope of allied support and having to face alone an irresistible Soviet advance on Helsinki. Red Army units crossed the ice-covered Bay of Viipuri and established a bridgehead in preparation for that advance in the first days of March; Viipuri itself was threatened. Having agreed at the end of February to accept the Soviet terms as the basis for negotiations, the Finnish government was momentarily encouraged by a hasty but fundamentally deceitful promise by the French prime minister, Daladier, to send fifty thousand men and a hundred bombers to Finland by the end of March to press the allies for further clarification of their intentions. The admission by the British envoy that no more than six thousand men were likely to arrive by April at the earliest persuaded Tanner that there was no alternative to negotiations with Moscow, although Ryti was still prepared to play the intervention card as a means of forcing the Russians to moderate their demands. On 3 March, it was decided to accept the Soviet terms as a basis for peace talks, but in the event of Moscow refusing, then allied assistance would be requested. The allies were prepared to extend until 12 March their deadline for a request for assistance. Moscow was willing to start talks, but rejected any idea of a truce; the army would advance and continue to put pressure on the Finns to make peace. The Finnish government bowed to the inevitable on 5 March, and a delegation headed by the prime minister set off a day later for Moscow via Stockholm. Here, they found that the Soviet demands were even more onerous than they had earlier been led to believe. The news from the front offered no comfort. The Finnish army was now defending a much longer line in the isthmus, the troops were worn out, and the reserves were seriously depleted. Finnish losses in less than two weeks mounted to almost two-fifths of the total for the entire war. Mannerheim reported on 9 March the opinion of his commanders that the situation was untenable unless allied aid could be obtained immediately. The two ministers who had fought most tenaciously against negotiations, both members of the agrarian party which had strong roots in the Karelian isthmus, still insisted that the allies be asked for assistance, but were overridden by Tanner, acting as head of government in Ryti's stead. The delegation was authorised to accept the peace terms; having tried in vain to soften the terms or obtain some measure of financial compensation for the territory to be surrendered, the Finns finally signed the peace treaty in the small hours of 13 March 1940.

The peace terms were onerous for Finland; but having to conclude peace with a government it had dismissed as a renegade band of imperialist stooges was also a blow to Soviet prestige. Although the threat of allied intervention cannot be entirely discounted as a reason for Stalin's willingness to make peace, it is far more likely that he was persuaded by a desire to disengage from a costly war, particularly as the Finnish government now seemed willing to accept terms more advantageous to the Soviet Union than those it had proposed in the autumn of 1939. Strengthening the security of Leningrad was presented to the Soviet public as the main benefit of the peace. The awkward fact that tiny Finland had not been defeated was explained away by claiming that the Finns had enjoyed the support of Britain, France, Sweden, and Italy, and had constructed with their assistance the mighty Mannerheim line. The breaching of that line was proclaimed a heroic victory, which had forced the Finns to the negotiating table. On 14 March, the final issue of the newspaper put out by the Kuusinen government, expressing its regrets that the oppressed workers of Finland had been prevented from rising by the nationalistic agitation and repression of the ruling class, declared that the treaty with the Soviet Union was now rescinded at the request of the people's government, which now was in the process of dissolving itself. A fortnight later, by order of the supreme soviet of the USSR, the Karelian–Finnish Soviet Socialist Republic was established; the newly acquired Finnish territories were included within its boundaries. Elections were held in the new republic on 16 June 1940, at the same time as Red Army tanks rumbled into the three Baltic republics and plans were being laid to stage the allegedly 'popular' revolutions in these countries that would bring about regime change and requests to be admitted into the Union of Soviet Socialist Republics. The leadership of the Karelian–Finnish SSR was drawn from those who had manned the people's government and the Finnish people's army: a consolation prize for Kuusinen and his crew, perhaps, but clearly an indication that the idea of imposing on Finland a regime that would comply with Moscow's wishes had not been abandoned.

The Treaty of Moscow gave to Russia Suursaari and the neighbouring islands, the Salla enclave in northern Finland and the Finnish part of the Rybachy peninsula on the Arctic. The most grievous territorial loss was, however, in the south, where the frontier was redrawn to the west of lake Ladoga and the bay of Viipuri. The Hanko peninsula was also to be leased for thirty years as a naval base. Finland lost almost a tenth of its territory and around 13 per cent of the national wealth, including valuable timber stocks, factories and refineries, the city of Viipuri, and the Saimaa canal that had linked the port of that city to the eastern Finnish hinterland. The treaty came as a terrible blow to a people largely ignorant of the critical state of the country's defences, and the uneasy peace that followed severely tested how far the wartime sense of common purpose and determination to repel the invader would survive.

The Winter War has generally been seen as the time when the nation came together, and the wounds of civil war were finally healed. The fact that the Social Democratic Party had been in government since 1937, and had adopted a positive attitude towards national defence, undoubtedly helped pave the way, though it would seem that the party leadership was at times more zealous in its advocacy of reconciliation than the rank-and-file. Relatively few socialists seemed to have joined the *suojeluskunta*, in spite of party exhortations, and the leadership's decision to have dealings with this paramilitary body that embodied all the bitter memories of 1918 was much criticised. The much-trumpeted 'January engagement' of 1940 was in fact no more than an agreement between the employers' federation and the trade unions to try and improve industrial relations in future through negotiation, a statement of symbolic significance that did nothing to alleviate the everyday hardships that workers and their families faced. The speed and energy with which government and parliament responded to the problem of coping with over four hundred thousand refugees – the rapid resettlement act of June 1940 aimed to create up to thirty thousand small farms from state and purchased private land – was exemplary, but the influx of so many people, with their own very distinctive dialect and customs, caused friction as well as contributing to the general mood of uncertainty about the future.

The months immediately following the signing of the peace in Moscow saw the whole of western Europe from the North Cape to the Pyrenees fall under German control, whilst the Soviet Union absorbed the Baltic states. Any hopes that Finland might be able to conclude a defence alliance with Sweden were torpedoed by the Soviet Union. The Finns had to give way to Moscow's demands for the demolition of fortifications built during the war on the Åland

Plate 31 Sewing tracksuits for sportsmen. The Lotta Svärd organisation was the female equivalent of the defence corps, set up in 1918 and acquiring a national organisation in 1921. With an active membership of well over one hundred thousand, it was able to provide a wide range of services in peacetime and during the war. The tracksuits which the women are making are for the SVUL, the Finnish gymnastics and athletics union, which was also closely associated with the ideals of White Finland. The workers' athletics union (TUL) was formed in 1919 by those clubs and individuals expelled from SVUL for having participated on the red side in the civil war. The Finnish athletes who competed in the Antwerp, Paris, and Amsterdam Olympics in the 1920s were in the eyes of committed leftists running for White Finland; the true socialist participated only in the Red Olympics. The shared experience of war helped blur the sharper edges of class antagonism, though the politically conscious working class still retained a suspicion of 'white' organisations. The defence corps and the Lotta Svärd auxiliaries were included amongst the 'pro-Hitler' and anti-Soviet organisations to be immediately dissolved according to the terms of the 1944 armistice, and were disbanded soon after.

islands and for the use of Finnish railways for troop transits to and from the Hanko base, though they were able to stall on the Soviet demand for exclusive nickel-mining rights in the Petsamo region by referring to the existing licence agreement with the Mond Nickel Company and alluding to possible German interests. Rumours of a renewed attack reached such a pitch by August that Mannerheim demanded partial mobilisation, which the government refused to sanction for fear of further provoking their eastern neighbour. The government also sacrificed Väinö Tanner, already demoted from the post of foreign minister in the reshuffle after the peace was signed.

The demonisation of Tanner was part of the long-running ideological battle waged by the communists against the social democrats. In the summer of 1940, it assumed a new dimension with the formation of the Society for Peace and Friendship between Finland and the USSR (SNS). What one writer has characterised as the most turbulent period of left-wing activity since the revolutionary year of 1917 is an indication that the experience of the Winter War did not entirely obliterate the memory of the civil war of 1918. For many on the left, the Soviet Union had not ceased to be a workers' state, and it was now in a position to bring pressure to bear on the bourgeois government of Finland. The formation of new governments in the Baltic states in June 1940 was welcomed by the SNS, which also called for the formation of a government in Finland that would 'sincerely promote the development of economic, political and cultural relations between Finland and the USSR'.

In spite of Soviet protests, the government took a tough line on the activities of SNS, with the police breaking up demonstrations and arresting ringleaders. The Social Democratic Party leadership also expelled a group of dissidents associated with SNS, and actively backed the creation of a new association, *Suomen aseveljien liitto*, which was intended to bring together 'brothers-in-arms', socialist and non-socialist, who had fought side-by-side in the defence of Finland. It was also a response to efforts by a group of young working-class radicals who had fought on the front in the Winter War to form their own organisation (*työläisrintamamiehet*) independent of any ties with the bourgeoisie. From the ranks of the 'brothers-in-arms' generation of socialists emerged many of the post-war leaders of social democracy, fiercely patriotic, and more than ready to take on the communists. Former front-line soldiers such as the stonecutter Aarne Saarinen and the glazier Erkki Salomaa, both active in the *työläisrintamamiehet* movement which managed to get off the ground in spite of obstacles placed in the way by officialdom and the reservations of the communist party leadership, were also to play a leading role in post-war Finnish communism, becoming the leading proponents of a distinctively 'national' line during the mid-1960s.

The evidence would suggest that a re-evaluation of policy towards Finland occurred in Moscow during August 1940, with new plans for military operations and instructions to the NKVD to set up its own network in Finland. At the same time, however, Germany began to show a more positive interest in Finland. One of the first consequences of Hitler's momentous order at the end of July to make plans for an attack on the Soviet Union was an indication that Germany was now willing to supply arms to Finland. The agent chosen to deliver this message dropped strong hints that Hitler was not prepared to allow the USSR to attack Finland. The willingness of Mannerheim and Prime Minister Ryti to agree to the transit of German troops through Finland to northern Norway sent a clear signal to Berlin that the Finns were eager to secure the protection of the Führer's umbrella, to borrow the phrase used by State-Secretary Weizsäcker of the German foreign office. Although Hitler acknowledged in talks with the Soviet commissar for foreign affairs, V. M. Molotov, in Berlin on 12–13 November that Finland was still within the Soviet sphere of interest as defined by the secret protocol of the non-aggression pact of August 1939, and hinted that Germany would have no objections to the USSR proceeding at some time in the future to settle the Finnish question much as Molotov had envisaged, 'on the same scale' as in Bessarabia and the Baltic states, he was adamant that Germany would not countenance at this juncture a renewed Soviet attack on Finland that would plunge the Baltic region into conflict.

The Finnish political leadership was undoubtedly encouraged by the more positive messages coming out of Berlin, though the Germans also made it very clear that they would not countenance anything that might lessen the Finns' willingness to play along with plans for the invasion of Russia. Hitler was able, for instance, to use Soviet opposition to plans for a union of Sweden and Finland that had gathered momentum in Sweden during the summer and autumn of 1940 to advise abandonment of an idea which, if realised, might have made the united states less amenable to German pressure. The Germans also encouraged the Finns to resist renewed Soviet bullying over the Petsamo nickel mines. Paasikivi, who had tried hard to find a compromise solution to this complex question, resigned as Finland's envoy to Moscow in protest at being kept in the dark about the extent of his government's involvement with Germany. Although he regarded Germany as the only power that could save Finland from falling completely at the mercy of the Soviet Union, Paasikivi had learnt by bitter experience during his time as prime minister in 1918 that the interests of the Reich overrode everything else, and he feared the present Finnish government was allowing itself too willingly to be led by a new German regime.

Paasikivi was the only experienced Finnish politician in whom Moscow expressed confidence as a possible successor to the ailing President Kallio, who had been persuaded to resign at the end of November 1940. Four other possible candidates – Svinhufvud, Tanner, Mannerheim, and T. M. Kivimäki, now Finland's envoy to Berlin – were effectively blackballed by Moscow; Ribbentrop made it plain that Germany did not favour Mannerheim. The electoral college of 1937 had to be resuscitated by special legislation in December 1940 to choose someone to see out Kallio's term of office. Its choice was the prime minister and acting president, Risto Ryti. Ryti was the only serious candidate to whom none of the major belligerents objected, but he had also effectively led the country through its most severe wartime crisis. As president (re-elected without opposition by the 1937 electoral college in 1943), he provided Finland with the kind of vigorous leadership that Kallio had been conspicuously unable to offer. He was, however, very much in the traditional mould of Finnish political leaders, preferring to work with a small inner circle that included Mannerheim, and the great man's confidant, the minister of defence Rudolf Walden, bypassing or ignoring completely the rest of the government and parliament. Although he later denied it, Ryti as prime minister gave his consent to the transit agreement with Germany without consulting the president, and he was also reluctant to divulge information even to those who needed to know, such as the minister of the interior and local officials who were taken completely by surprise when German transport ships docked in Vaasa and Oulu on 22 September. This secretiveness was to cause further confusion and disarray as Finland was drawn into a further round of hostilities with the Soviet Union, this time alongside Germany.

Ryti's reluctance to divulge information or to state openly his objectives mirrored the way in which the German high command drew the Finnish military and political leadership into its ambit. High-ranking Finnish officers who visited Germany on a regular basis from the end of 1940 were drip-fed information about the invasion of the Soviet Union, code-named Operation Barbarossa and given Hitler's official sanction on 18 December. It was assumed that Finnish troops would play a role in this, and the Finnish military never challenged or questioned this assumption. Talks and meetings during the spring of 1941 resembled nothing so much as a polite game of poker, which neither side seemed willing to bring to a conclusion. The Finns were invited on 20 May to discuss co-ordination of military measures against possible Soviet aggression; they learnt five days later that Germany was contemplating an aggressive war, or crusade against bolshevism, in which Finland might wish to take part; and in further discussions between 3 and 6 June in Helsinki, the details of military co-operation were worked out. Although it was agreed that the Finnish army should begin mobilisation on 15 June, the Germans did not reveal the date for the invasion of Russia to the Finnish GHQ until the day before, 21 June. The Finnish government, which had been largely kept in the dark about these negotiations, was told on 9 June by Ryti that, in view of the escalating tension between Germany and Russia, Mannerheim had requested the mobilisation of reservists. Ryti's expressed wish that Finland would be able to remain outside any conflict between Russia and Germany concealed the extent to which Finnish forces were committed to the German war plans; the foreign minister Rolf Witting was rather more frank in virtually admitting to the foreign affairs committee of the *eduskunta* four days later that German policy would now direct Finland's fate.

Like Sweden, Finland had to adapt to the reality of German domination in Europe; strict neutrality was not an option. Unlike Sweden, however, Finland had already been involved in war, and had had to accept harsh terms which few were prepared to accept as the final verdict. The bullying behaviour of the Russians in the months following the signing of the peace of Moscow was hardly designed to lay the foundations of a more secure relationship between the two countries. The military plans drawn up in August 1940 and the demands made by Molotov during his talks with Ribbentrop and Hitler in November indicate that the Soviet Union was still seeking a final solution of the Finnish question. The softer approach towards Finland adopted in 1941 came too late: the Finns were now confident of Hitler's protection and were no longer prepared to engage in meaningful dialogue with their eastern neighbour.

At one level, the absence of any political agreement or clearly defined military alliance between Finland and Germany suited Finland's wartime leaders, for it allowed them to claim that Finland was in fact fighting a separate and defensive war, provoked by a Soviet air attack on Finnish cities on 25 June, three days after Germany had launched its invasion of Russia. This was primarily intended to reassure public opinion at home rather than abroad, where it was generally assumed that Finland had slipped into the German camp. Although there was some disquiet amongst socialist members of the government and of parliament, this was caused more by the failure of the inner circle to keep them informed; with the presumption that, in a dangerous situation, Finland should take all possible measures to defend itself, they had no argument. The successful campaign waged by Finnish forces, now enjoying numerical and firepower superiority over their opponents, regained virtually all the territory ceded in 1940 by early September and did much to overcome initial reservations. So too did Mannerheim's insistence on remaining commander of the Finnish forces rather than assuming supreme command of all forces operating on Finnish territory, which would have placed him under the German high command, and the willingness of the Germans to go along with the Finnish claim to be fighting a separate war. But once the old frontiers had been regained and crossed, doubts began to surface.

The regaining of the old frontiers had been achieved at enormous cost, with some 16 per cent of Finland's population on active service in the forces or civil defence. Mannerheim was indeed able to use the argument that Finland had strained its resources

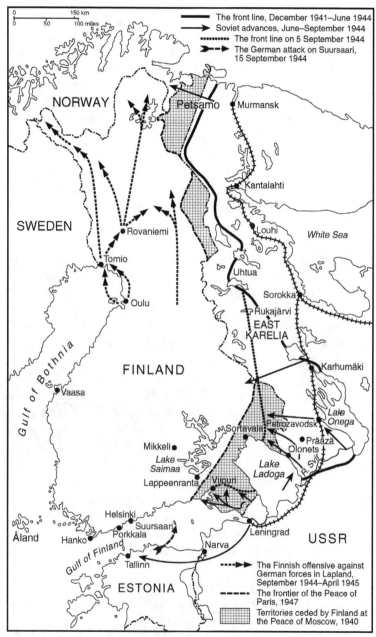

Map 4 Finland at war, 1941–45.

to the limit and could not therefore commit troops to the siege of Leningrad, as the Germans wanted, but this merely highlighted the awkward question of how long Finland could afford to maintain the fiction that it was fighting a separate war. The Germans were remarkably tolerant towards their co-belligerent, but there was no guarantee that Finland would continue to enjoy such latitude. There was also no indication of how and on what terms Finland might disengage from its war with Russia, a question that became pressing from early 1943 onwards.

The astonishing advances of the main German forces deep into Russia during the first weeks of the campaign created in Finland a sense of euphoria and a strong belief that the Soviet Union was on the verge of defeat. Without doubt this emboldened the Finnish leadership to advance the case for a new 'short' frontier running via easily defensible waterways from the White Sea to the Gulf of Finland, and to press ahead with plans already drawn up for a civil administration under military direction for east Karelia. This aroused misgivings abroad. Witting was obliged as early as July to reassure the American minister to Helsinki that the government was unaware of the contents of Mannerheim's order of the day of 10 July, in which he repeated his 1918 pledge to liberate Karelia, and to deny that Finland sought to annex east Karelia. Continued American and British pressure on Finland to halt the advance prompted the social democratic parliamentary group to demand a statement of war aims from the government. In its response to parliament, the government announced that those areas ceded to Russia in 1940 would be reincorporated into Finland. It justified the occupation of east Karelia on security and humanitarian grounds, but it gave no indication of a desire to claim the occupied territory. With the mood of confidence still high, it is likely that the majority would have backed annexation; only a few left-wing socialists and members of the Swedish people's party expressed reservations.

Although they were aware that Finland was in no position to dictate its own peace terms, but was in the end dependent upon the outcome of the conflict between the great powers, the annexation of east Karelia was nevertheless a clear aim of the wartime leadership. As early as April 1940, President Ryti authorised the geographer

Väinö Auer and the historian Eino Jutikkala to prepare the case for east Karelia belonging to Finland: their efforts were published in the autumn with the suggestive title of *Finnlands Lebensraum*. Instructions issued on the eve of the war to recruit refugees from east Karelia into combat units were clearly designed to give the invasion something of the character of a war of liberation (in much the same way the Russians recruited Finnish exiles into special units of the Red Army in 1939). Mannerheim's 10 July order of the day in fact spoke gleefully of Karelia rising, with its own battalions marching in the ranks of the Finnish army. A meeting convened on 20 July in the first big east Karelian settlement to fall into Finnish hands was intended to demonstrate the Karelians' wish to be united with Finland, but was in fact stage-managed by the intelligence section of army headquarters. What the military usually referred to as the conquest of east Karelia provided the ideal opportunity for the enthusiasts for a greater Finland, and there was no shortage of those in the echelons of administration set up to prepare the region for eventual incorporation into Finland.

Most of the population had been evacuated before the advancing Finnish forces, leaving behind some eighty-five thousand people, mostly the elderly, women, and children. Of these, fewer than half were Karelians. In the early stages of the occupation, the Finnish administration pursued a policy of what can only be described as ethnic cleansing. Even before occupation, plans had been set in motion to move the Russian population out of the area once the war was over, and replace them with other Finno-Ugric peoples. Those deemed 'non-national' were rounded up and placed in concentration camps as the first stage of the process of expulsion. By early 1942, some twenty-four thousand were being held in these camps. A poor harvest and disruptions in the procurement and distribution of foodstuffs during the winter of 1941–42 caused hardship amongst the Finnish urban population, but proved disastrous for those interned, already on grossly inadequate rations. Over three thousand of those interned in the concentration camps, and ten thousand Soviet prisoners-of-war held in Finland are known to have died as a result of famine. Conditions were subsequently improved, partly in reaction to the bad image created abroad; unfavourable allied press comment seems, for example, to have persuaded Mannerheim to order an end to ethnic discrimination in wage levels and food rations in 1943.

Notwithstanding the enthusiasm and devotion to the cause of greater Finland of those who worked in the institutions set up to finnicise the 'nationals', the hearts and minds of the Karelians were not won over. The much-vaunted land redistribution schemes remained for the most part on paper, and such parcelling out of collective farm land that did take place was done unsystematically. Education was intended to be the cornerstone of finnicisation. Over a hundred elementary schools were set up, with folk high schools and a grammar school in Olonets. The language of instruction was Finnish, and the teachers, volunteers from Finland, placed heavy emphasis on religious and patriotic values. Great efforts were also made to persuade the local population to join a religious congregation, although this caused much rivalry and friction between Orthodox and Lutheran pastors working in the field. Surveys conducted by the Finnish army indicated that the local population in general welcomed these activities, but they also noted that the purpose of these activities, the inculcation of Finnish values, had failed to evoke a positive response.

The commitment to the cause of securing for Finland a region regarded in nationalist circles as the cradle of Finnish culture was less evident in the case of the Ingrians evacuated to Finland from the German-occupied area around Leningrad. Stalin's deportation of Ingrians in the 1930s had provoked a storm of protest in Finland about the treatment of a kindred people; but Finnish officialdom took some time to be persuaded to accept evacuation, and never got round to considering whether or not the evacuees should be offered permanent residency, let alone citizenship. The evacuees were gradually released from quarantine to supplement the agricultural labour force. Of the sixty-three thousand Ingrians in Finland at the signing of the armistice in autumn 1944, over five-sixths eventually opted to return to the Soviet Union, four thousand fleeing to Sweden and almost four thousand remaining in Finland.

The aggressively nationalistic tone adopted by those in charge of the finnicisation of east Karelia, which denied any place for Finland's other official language in the school curriculum, for example, was one reason why members of the Swedish–Finnish minority felt uneasy, but many were also worried that Finland was rapidly losing the sympathy and support of neutral Sweden and the allies. As the tide of war began to turn against Germany, this became an important matter. Public opinion surveys revealed a growing mood of doubt and uncertainty from the autumn of 1942 onwards. As the remnants of the German sixth army were surrendering in the ruins of Stalingrad in the early weeks of 1943, Finland's political and military leaders agreed that Finland should seek to disengage itself from the war at the earliest opportunity. Initial soundings through the good offices of the United States in the spring of 1943 proved abortive. The Americans considered that the Finns would not accept the Soviet demands, which included not only the restitution of the 1940 frontier and the payment of war reparations, but also other conditions that placed a question-mark against Moscow's avowed wish to preserve Finnish independence. Finnish hopes that the Germans would understand their wish to withdraw from the war were cruelly dashed in March, when the Finnish foreign minister was brusquely told to break off all contacts with Russia forthwith. The Finns managed to hold off a demand for a pact that would tie them irrevocably to the German side, but the temporary reduction of grain supplies was a not too subtle reminder that Berlin had the means to force its hard-pressed partner to comply.

The new government installed after Ryti was re-elected president in March 1943 was intended to appear more acceptable to the Russians as a negotiating partner. The fascist IKL no longer held any portfolios, and Witting, considered pro-German, was replaced as foreign minister by a businessman with many contacts in Britain and America, Henrik Ramsay. The new prime minister, Edwin Linkomies, was more prepared to stand up to Mannerheim and Ryti than his rather ineffectual predecessor, Jukka Rangell, but in a crisis, his stubbornness could be an impediment to extricating Finland from the war. Decisions continued to be made or not made by an inner circle; but by the summer of 1943, disquiet about the conduct of the war had brought together a number of politicians, mostly from the social democratic and Swedish people's parties, into the so-called 'peace opposition'. The main concern of this

group was that Finland appeared to be drifting away from the one
remaining power that might help it get out of the war, the United
States, and into the arms of Germany. It was as unwilling as the
government to grapple with the unpalatable fact that, since the
allies of the Soviet Union had effectively given Stalin a free hand
to deal with Finland at the Teheran conference at the end of 1943,
peace would have to be made on Moscow's terms. This much had
been grasped by Paasikivi and, more surprisingly in view of his bitter

Plate 32 President Ryti, Prime Minister Rangell, and Marshal
Mannerheim. This photograph was taken on one of the many visits paid by
Finland's political leaders to Mannerheim's headquarters in the eastern
Finnish town of Mikkeli. Carl Gustaf Emil Mannerheim (left, in uniform)
had thirty years of service in the imperial Russian army behind him when
he assumed command of the fledgling Finnish army in January 1918. An
aristocrat who never learnt to speak Finnish fluently, his world-view and
attitudes shaped in a world of service and loyalty to the ruler that was
swept away in 1917, Mannerheim acquired in his lifetime a mythical status
as the saviour of the fatherland, and his popularity remains undiminished.
Risto Ryti (right, wearing the white hat) and Jukka Rangell (centre) fared
less well. Both were amongst the group of politicians tried in 1946 for their
part in leading Finland into war (Mannerheim feared that he would be
included in this group, but this seems not to have been desired by the Soviet
Union). Ryti's memory has been rehabilitated since 1990, but Rangell has
disappeared into obscurity.

opposition to the signing of peace in 1940, by Urho Kekkonen. They were, however, isolated voices: the 'greater Finland' ideals propagated by societies such as the AKS remained deeply rooted within the generation that had passed through higher education during the inter-war years, and these were the people at the forefront of the war effort – army officers, clergymen, planners, and administrators in east Karelia, the state information department, the writers and commentators who moulded public opinion.

The problem with the policy of the Finnish wartime leadership was that it tried to face two ways at once, as Albin Wickman of the Swedish People's Party observed in September 1943: 'for the chauvinists amongst our people, we present a picture of a people which is successfully carrying out a war of conquest: facing outwards, we project ourselves as an especially sober and restrained people fighting only to safeguard our historical frontiers and our ancient Nordic freedom'. Trapped as it was between the growing pressure from Russia and its allies to sue for peace, which its own military advisers considered the only realistic option, and the uncompromising mood of large sections of the public, which refused to contemplate anything less than the restoration of the 1939 frontiers, the government now faced the unpleasant consequences of this policy. Renewed contacts at the end of 1943, this time through Sweden, showed that the Finns still hoped to retain the 1939 frontiers, albeit with some adjustments made in the interests of Soviet security concerns. The lifting by the Germans of the siege of Leningrad in January 1944 and the advances being made by the main Soviet armies meant that it was only a matter of time before the Finnish forces had to face a massive onslaught, and this persuaded the inner circle that Finland would have to accept the 1940 frontier. Negotiations conducted by Paasikivi in Stockholm and Moscow revealed, however, that the Soviet Union insisted upon the internment or expulsion of German troops stationed in Finland and reparations in the form of goods to the value of six hundred million dollars, to be delivered within a period of five years. These terms were unacceptable to government and to parliament, and were officially rejected on 15 April. The Finnish historian Olli Vehviläinen concludes that the government chose what at the time seemed the lesser of two evils; it was not prepared to risk the wrath of Germany or to split the country by accepting terms that would seriously threaten Finland's continued independence.

In the end, the issue was to be resolved by force of arms, and the Finns would be forced to accept these conditions. Anxious to knock out Finland before launching the planned major offensive against Germany, the Russians mounted a carefully planned offensive on the Karelian isthmus on 9–10 June 1944. The Finnish troops there were ill-prepared for the massive onslaught from a force many times superior in numbers and firepower, and were forced to retreat. Reinforcements from east Karelia and supplies of aircraft and anti-tank weapons from Germany helped prevent the retreat turning into a rout, though Viipuri fell on 20 June. The withdrawal from east Karelia ordered by Mannerheim also managed to tie down large numbers of Soviet troops that might otherwise have been used to deliver a knockout blow in southern Finland.

Taken by surprise by this rapid turn of events, the politicians in Helsinki strove desperately to find a way out. As in previous crises, they turned to Mannerheim, who turned down the offer of the premiership on 14 June and the offer of the presidency two days later. Mannerheim's own position shifted according to his assessment of the military situation: initially in favour of a new government, he swung against this as the front appeared to hold in the third week of June, and he put pressure on Ryti to commit Finland to Germany rather than capitulate to the Soviet demand that Finland should surrender and sue for peace. On 22 June, the German foreign minister, von Ribbentrop, had flown to Helsinki, promising substantial military assistance. In return, Ryti, in a letter to Hitler, agreed as president of Finland that neither he nor 'any government of Finland or persons appointed by me shall enter into ceasefire or peace negotiations or discussions to that end without the consent of the government of the German Reich'.

The Ryti–Ribbentrop agreement almost split the government, with the social democrats coming within an ace of resigning. It pushed the Americans into breaking off diplomatic relations, and convinced much of the Swedish press that Finland had now finally fallen completely under German domination. For Ryti himself, it was an act of political suicide, but his resignation from office a month later allowed his successor to declare himself not bound by a personal assurance made in a letter to Hitler. That successor was the seventy-seven-year-old Mannerheim, whose assumption of office demanded considerable skill behind the scenes to ensure that the notoriously touchy old soldier did not back out at the last minute, including the passing of exceptional legislation by the *eduskunta*. Mannerheim's prestige, which had taken something of a battering during the early chaotic days of the Soviet onslaught on the isthmus, had been enhanced by the successful defensive action fought at Tali and Ihantala between 25 June and 10 July. Not only had this prevented a potentially devastating Soviet breakthrough into southern Finland, it had also persuaded the Soviet high command to break off the offensive and withdraw troops to the Byelorussian front. His elevation to an office which he had been denied by the parliamentarians a quarter of a century earlier may have afforded the marshal some grim satisfaction, and it was certainly a sad reflection of the inability of those politicians who had led Finland into war to produce a man of equal stature and authority; but at the hour of crisis, it made sense that a military leader who had undoubtedly played a major role in shaping Finland's wartime policy should finally set aside his reservations and assume responsibility for that which he had hitherto always claimed was the duty of the politicians. His cautious, phlegmatic temperament and the high respect in which he was held in German military and political circles – Hitler had indeed flown to Finland specially to honour the marshal's seventy-fifth birthday – helped ease Finland out of the war without incurring massive retaliation from Germany. The terms of the armistice finally agreed on 19 September 1944 were harsh. That other aged war-horse who was still to play a vital role in guiding his country's affairs, J. K. Paasikivi, was filled with dread at the prospect of unending Soviet interference and control; the Swedish government believed that Finland had effectively become a Soviet vassal state. In the light of evidence from Soviet archives, however, these terms were probably a good deal better than the fate which might well have befallen Finland had its leaders agreed to surrender and sue for peace in June. Had the terms of surrender for Finland drafted by marshal Voroshilov's committee been enforced, Finland would have been reduced to a virtual satrapy of Moscow, its army disarmed, much of its territory under Red Army occupation, its economy and administration under Soviet control.

As it was, Finland had to accept the 1940 frontier, surrender Petsamo, its foothold on the Arctic Ocean, and lease a base at Porkkala, a short distance to the west of the Finnish capital. The Soviet side agreed to halve the demand for reparations of six hundred million dollars' worth of goods, though they insisted on payment at 1938 prices. The German troops were to be disarmed and the Finnish forces demobilised within two and a half months. The Soviet high command was given *carte blanche* to indicate which airfields it might wish to use in the war against Germany, and the Finnish government had to make available all routes deemed necessary for access to these airfields. No Finnish vessel or aircraft, civil or military, was permitted to leave its port or base without permission. Until the final withdrawal of German troops from Finland, there was to be no communication abroad allowed for the diplomatic missions located in Finland, a matter of great concern for the Swedish government. Finland had to agree to co-operate with the allied powers in arresting and trying those persons suspected of having committed war crimes, and to close down all 'pro-Hitler' and anti-Soviet organisations. Some four hundred organisations were placed on the proscribed list by government action within days of the signing of the armistice, including the fascist IKL and the AKS. More were added to the list after the allied control commission set up to oversee implementation of the armistice had taken up its quarters in the Hotel Torni in Helsinki in October.

The chairman of the commission was Andrey Zhdanov. As the communist party boss in the Leningrad region in the 1930s, Zhdanov had made a number of threatening pronouncements about Finland, and he had also masterminded the Soviet incorporation of Estonia in 1940, so the Finns had good reason to fear him. He quickly saw through the attempts of the Finnish high command to hide its demobilised troops in the ranks of the *suojeluskunta*, which he demanded should be banned as a 'Hitlerite' organisation, and insisted that the Finnish army be scaled down to its January 1939 level of thirty-seven thousand men, not the sixty-eight thousand of the interim peace period which the Finnish generals wanted. Zhdanov and his deputy

Savonenkov also complained that the Finnish high command was pursuing delaying tactics against the German forces in Lapland. This obliged the Finns to break their gentleman's agreement over a phased withdrawal with their former comrades-in-arms. By the end of the year, Lapland had been almost entirely cleared, though not before considerable destruction had been wrought by the retreating Germans.

The demobilisation of the Finnish army in accordance with Soviet wishes, the removal of any lingering threat from German forces in the country, and other signs that the main terms of the armistice were being met allowed Zhdanov to return to more pressing duties in Moscow, leaving the running of affairs to his deputy. The impression gleaned by the experienced American journalist John Scott from his interviews with members of the control commission in October 1944 was that the Russians wanted an independent but a friendly Finland. A less optimistic conclusion was drawn by the British journalist Paul Winterton, who felt that Finland was independent only in quotation marks, and would have no alternative in future but to obey any instruction the Kremlin might care to issue. The British members of the allied control commission occupied a subordinate role, generally deferring to their Soviet colleagues. The Americans, who had never declared war on Finland, were able to pursue a more independent policy which resulted in the formal restoration of diplomatic relations in September 1945, and the approval of a thirty-five-million-dollar credit by the Export-Import Bank in December 1945.

As the split between the wartime allies widened, the United States continued to regard Finland as part of the western world, in spite of its dependence on the Soviet Union. The evidence that Finland was significantly different from other former co-belligerents of Germany was noted and commented on by American observers and diplomats throughout the remaining months of the world war, and this reinforced the image of Finland as an honest and gallant democracy that repaid its debts. The Soviet Union had used its military facilities in Finland sparingly; the country was not occupied, as was the case with Romania and Bulgaria, and its institutions and media responded to the discreet pressures of the Finnish government, rather than the commission. The man who did his utmost to ensure that this was the way things happened was J. K. Paasikivi, summoned to form a government in November 1944, and continuously at the helm of the Finnish state for the next twelve years. Paasikivi enjoyed the confidence and respect of the Soviet leadership, but was also highly regarded by the British and Americans. He set the tone for Finland's new policy in numerous public speeches and addresses, and did not hesitate to lecture and give orders to those he believed were placing the country's fragile position in danger by their words and actions. Compromised politicians were urged to withdraw from public life; although Paasikivi fought tenaciously to avoid having to bring Finland's wartime leaders to trial, as the control commission demanded, he did not hesitate to do this once he saw he had no option, or to advise the members of the tribunal to rethink their sentences in line with the demands of the control commission. The sentences passed on those accused of taking Finland to war in 1941 – which included Ryti, Tanner, and the two wartime prime ministers Rangell and Linkomies – were seen by the Finnish public as unjust, but in Paasikivi's eyes, they were a political necessity. From the Finnish point of view, it was important that the men had been tried by a domestic tribunal set up for the purpose by legislation; there were no executions, and all were released before their sentences had expired. The one absentee from the dock was Mannerheim, in spite of the evidence collected by the lawyer charged with investigating the circumstances that led Finland into war in 1941, and it would seem that the Soviet leadership preferred to avoid unrest in Finland that would in all likelihood have followed had the man dubbed a major war criminal in Soviet wartime propaganda been charged. Sick and ailing, Mannerheim was allowed to resign with honour the office of president at the beginning of March 1946. Paasikivi, who had in all but name exercised the office since the previous March, was elected president by parliament, thus continuing the run of emergency legislation needed to provide Finland with a head of state that was ended only in 1950, when Paasikivi comfortably won the presidential election.

Paasikivi had included in his first government in November 1944 a man who until recently had spent much of his time avoiding arrest, the communist leader Yrjö Leino. Of the two dozen or so people who met in a tailor's workshop in a Helsinki suburb on 14 October 1944 to establish the communist party as a legal organisation in Finland, Leino was unusual not only in that he still remained free, but also because he had not spent time in the Soviet Union. Born mostly around the turn of the century, these were the people who had come to political maturity in the 1920s 'whom the turn of events associated with Lapua had thrust outside normal society, into training in the Soviet Union and prison in Finland', in the words of their historian, Kimmo Rentola. Rigidly obedient to the call of Moscow (and unsure how to proceed when that call was contradictory or silent), locked into their own curiously constructed world and deeply distrustful of anything that might be thought to challenge it, these men and women from the ranks of the Finnish proletariat, with the addition of a few exiles from the Soviet Union (but not Otto Ville Kuusinen, who was denied that opportunity), were to lead Finnish communism for the next two decades. Their decision to found the Finnish People's Democratic Union (SKDL) at the end of October 1944 was in line with Moscow policy and helped bring over a sizeable proportion of the dissidents from the Social Democratic Party, allowing the new party to scoop nearly a quarter of the votes cast in the March 1945 elections, giving it forty-nine seats, one fewer than the social democrats, in the *eduskunta*.

Leino's inclusion in the first Paasikivi government owed more to the insistence of the agrarian politicians Kaarlo Hillilä and Urho Kekkonen, anxious to bring the communists into the fold and thus minimise the risk of Russian intervention in the event of unrest, than to any desire of the communists. By the spring of 1945, they had grown more confident, although they had to be pushed by Moscow into demanding the post of minister of the interior in the second Paasikivi government, formed after the elections. The 'big three' coalition of social democrats, agrarians, and the SKDL governed Finland for the next three years. On Paasikivi's election to the presidency in 1946, the ex-social democrat Mauno Pekkala, now a member of the SKDL, became prime minister. Leino occupied the post of minister of the interior, and the communists were able to gain control of the security police, which carried out a number of investigations as part of the programme of purging Finland of

Plate 33 President Paasikivi and the 'Big Three' government, 1946. Juho Kusti Paasikivi first sat in this room, the plenary session chamber of the Senate, in 1909, as an Old Finn senator. Portraits of Finnish heads of state have replaced those of the emperors (see Plate 23). A painting of his immediate predecessor as president, Marshal Mannerheim, hangs directly behind Paasikivi. Rather like another famous statesmen, Paasikivi was out of office during the inter-war years; but whereas Winston Churchill was called upon to lead his country to victory in war, Paasikivi was called upon to lead his country out of defeat. He inherited the Old Finn tradition of trying to find a workable accommodation with the Russians, which at one and the same time recognised the realities of power but also sought through engagement to preserve and strengthen the Finnish national state. As the first prime minister of Finland after the civil war of 1918, he could never have imagined that he would be called upon a quarter of a century later to form a government that included sworn enemies of White Finland. Upon his elevation to the presidency in March 1946, the post of prime minister passed to the former social democrat Mauno Pekkala, who had shifted his allegiance to the communist-dominated Finnish People's Democratic Union (SKDL). Four of the six SKDL members of the government were members of the Finnish Communist Party, including the minister of the interior, Yrjö Leino. Leino is the third man from the president's left, sitting on the right of Pekkala and the non-party foreign minister, Carl Enckell. The bespectacled man on the president's immediate right is the minister of justice, Urho Kekkonen.

anti-democratic elements the communists were sworn to carry out. The communists also made significant inroads into the trade unions, and were able to secure more votes than the social democrats in the local elections of 1945. With Zhdanov at hand to offer advice and give directions, Finland seemed set to follow the countries of eastern Europe. Leino felt confident enough to assure his party comrades in April 1945 that 'we are proceeding with brisk steps towards democracy'; his wife Hertta, daughter of Otto Ville Kuusinen, described the 'big three' coalition as a 'democratic people's government'; even her ultra-cautious father felt that there were grounds for satisfaction at the pace of democratic change.

By the end of 1946, however, the communist leadership were openly expressing their frustration at having achieved so little. The hoped-for emasculation of their social democratic rivals had not occurred; the new 'brothers-in-arms' generation had taken a firm grip of the party machine, and were preparing a vigorous onslaught against the communists. Zhdanov had made it plain that security was the main priority for the Soviet Union, and as long as Paasikivi could deliver that, the communists would have to work out their own way to power. In the first flush of success in 1945, the communists had ignored the well-known Finnish maxim that the bear had to be shot before it could be skinned. They deluded themselves into believing that, by obeying Moscow's demands for those deemed enemies of the Soviet Union to be driven from public life, they were truly embarking on the path to power they saw being followed in Hungary or Czechoslovakia. In truth, their ambit of control was pitifully small, and it crumbled away to nothing once their partners in government became aware that the Soviet Union was unlikely to intervene as long as Finland adhered to the terms of the peace treaty which came into force in September 1947 and was willing to accommodate Soviet security interests. The fate of Yrjö Leino is instructive. His stock had already begun to slide within his own party and in Moscow by 1948; in May of that year, a motion censuring him for allowing Finnish citizens to be included amongst a group dispatched to the Soviet Union in 1945 as suspected war criminals received majority support in the *eduskunta*. The conservatives responsible for the motion attempted in vain to reassure President Paasikivi that they did not wish Leino to resign. Paasikivi, however, stuck faithfully to the constitution, whilst privately raging at the stupidity of the conservatives in provoking trouble a mere five weeks from the elections. Leino refused to resign and was sacked; the party faithful demanded mass demonstrations, and for a while, it did seem as if the long-awaited revolutionary upsurge was about to take place. But the communists, having lost control of the trade unions to the social democrats, reluctant to back a man already on his way out but desperate to remain within government, meekly accepted a compromise reshuffle which shifted the ministry of the interior from their grasp.

A month earlier, President Paasikivi had ordered a state of alert to deal with a rumoured communist coup that failed to materialise, and he was prepared if necessary to replace the coalition with a minority social democratic government – as in fact occurred after the elections, which saw the SKDL slip back to thirty-eight seats as its partners in government both increased their mandate. In eastern Europe, the communists were able to dominate the weaker socialist and peasant parties, squeezing them into a compliant bloc. In Finland, this never happened. The social democrats and agrarians proved themselves to be every bit as tough and wily as the communists. In the end, the communists, 'both prisoner and warder', in Osmo Jussila's phrase, needed their partners in government more than they needed the communists.

In retrospect, the strikes and demonstrations of 1947–48 seem to highlight the communists' frustration and impotence, though they were undoubtedly worrying at the time to those who did not wish to follow the Czechoslovak road which Hertta Kuusinen declared to be the right way for Finland. It was as tension was at its height, following the proclamation by Zhdanov at the founding conference of the Cominform in September 1947 of the doctrine that the world was now divided into two irreconcilable camps and the communist seizure of power in Prague in February 1948, that Stalin raised the idea of a mutual assistance treaty between Finland and the Soviet Union. With the exception of the communists, who welcomed the idea, and a few socialists and agrarians, who were willing to enter into negotiations, politicians and the public were resolutely opposed. Army officers unofficially sounded out their colleagues in Norway and discreetly approached the Americans for promises of assistance should the crisis erupt into conflict, and the veteran activist Lauri Pihkala informed the American military attaché of the existence of an underground resistance movement ready to fight the Russians. These approaches clearly showed that three years of communist-led 'democratisation' had done little to quench the anti-Soviet resolve of sections of the armed forces and public. The Americans promised to support the Finns if they took their case to the United Nations. This if anything made the Russians increase pressure on Finland, obliging Paasikivi to give way and agree to talks in Moscow.

The idea of a mutual assistance treaty had been on and off the agenda since 1945. Mannerheim had in fact drafted an outline agreement in January 1945, in which mutual respect of each other's independence and non-interference in each other's internal affairs was tacked onto the first article, which bound the two contracting parties to assist each other, with all the forces at their disposal, in the event of aggression directed against Finland, or the Soviet Union via Finland, or against the two simultaneously. The Finns therefore had had time to think and prepare their position, and in the event, were able in the negotiations that took place in Moscow in the spring of 1948 to persuade Stalin to abandon the eastern European mutual assistance treaty model and accept their own proposals.

The treaty of friendship, co-operation, and mutual assistance (FCMA) concluded in Moscow on 6 April 1948 bound Finland to repel an armed attack by Germany or its allies directed at Finland or the Soviet Union through Finnish territory. It was to do so 'within the frontiers of Finland and in accordance with obligations defined in the present treaty and, if necessary, with the assistance of, or jointly with, the Soviet Union' (article one). Article two of the treaty decreed that the contracting parties should confer with each other if it were established that the threat of an armed attack as described in article one existed. The vagueness of this provision left the door ajar for the Soviet Union to claim that such a threat did actually exist; but otherwise, the treaty did offer Finland some assurance. It would only be called upon to defend its territorial integrity, and any Soviet assistance was to be subject to mutual agreement. The treaty was to remain in force for ten years after its ratification, renewable thereafter for five-year periods if neither party signalled in advance its desire to terminate the agreement.

The mood of despondency, which in certain quarters had bordered on panic, took some time to subside. Finland's decision not to participate in the Marshall aid programme was widely interpreted as a further sign of the country's subjugation to the will of Moscow. There were persistent rumours of secret clauses to the agreement reached in Moscow. The Americans threatened to withhold credits if the treaty were ratified by the *eduskunta*, but quickly changed direction a month later when news leaked out that the Russians were about to reduce Finland's reparations payments. The flow of credit and exports from the west increased significantly after the communists were defeated in the July elections and eliminated from government. Although the Americans continued to harbour doubts about Finland's future, they were willing to concede that it was a special case, and were prepared to offer economic and discreet political assistance. The last reparations payment was delivered in the autumn of 1952. The staging of the Olympic games in Helsinki that year was a further boost to Finnish self-confidence and an affirmation of national survival (Finland was to have hosted the games in 1940).

By the autumn of 1955, the tension of the last years of Stalin's rule had noticeably abated. Talks in Moscow to discuss extending the FCMA treaty were conducted in a friendly and relaxed atmosphere. Although the Finns found the Russians unwilling to consider any readjustment to the Karelian frontier, and they had to accept a twenty-year extension to the 1948 treaty instead of their preferred ten years, they obtained the return of the Porkkala base, and the green light for entry into the Nordic Council and the United Nations. Fears, worries, and suspicions still dogged the relationship. Paasikivi suspected that the American military attaché was behind stories published on the eve of the Moscow talks in the Dutch press of former officers of the Finnish army plotting a coup which would take Finland into NATO; Moscow worried that Väinö Tanner would be a candidate in the forthcoming presidential elections, and urged Paasikivi to remain in office; the Americans suspected that behind the Soviet concessions lay a hidden agenda, which sought to use Finland to promote Moscow's 'peace-loving'

Plate 34 The Olympic games in Helsinki, 1952. Helsinki was originally scheduled to stage the Olympic games in 1940, and the main stadium pictured here was in fact completed in 1938. One of the finest and most enduring buildings of the functionalist era of architecture, it was designed by Yrjö Lindegren (1900–52) and Toivo Jäntti (1900–75). Finnish architecture and design began to acquire an international reputation in the twenties and thirties. One of the foremost architects working in the late *art nouveau* style, known in Finland as *Jugend*, Eliel Saarinen (1873–50) began turning towards rationalism with the design for the main railway station in Helsinki (1914–19). Saarinen later worked mainly in the United States. The greatest proponent of functionalism in Finland was Alvar Aalto (1898–1976). Aalto was always very careful to work with nature, rather than against it. The starkly functional lines of the Paimio sanatorium are designed to bring maximum light and air to the patients, and sit easily in a wooded landscape. The bentwood chairs designed by Aalto and his wife Aino (1894–1949) for the sanatorium have become classics in their own right.

designs within the Nordic Council. But Paasikivi was right to claim, as he did on several public occasions during the last six months of his presidency, that the relationship had significantly improved, and had not hindered the forging of strong economic and cultural contacts with other countries.

How Finland survived the turmoil of three wars, an uneasy armistice, and the looming threat of a possible Soviet take-over has exercised the thoughts of many commentators ever since the 1940s. The opening up of the archives in the 1990s allowed a fuller picture of the motives and objectives of the Soviet leaders to emerge, though it is arguable whether this has substantially altered the verdict delivered over thirty years ago by Anthony Upton, that as long as Stalin had Paasikivi, he did not need the Finnish communists. Finland was undoubtedly fortunate in that it was of lesser strategic or political importance than, say, Poland, or even the Baltic states in the conflict between Russia and Germany. This to a large extent explains why neither Hitler nor Stalin was willing in the last analysis to commit large numbers of troops for the subjugation of Finland in the summer of 1944; both men had more important fish to fry. Both appear to have respected the Finns' ability to fight, and were in general respectful and moderate in their language and treatment of those Finns with whom they had to deal. No Finnish political leader had to endure the kind of systematic bullying meted out to the hapless Estonians, Latvians, or Lithuanians in 1939 and 1940, not to mention those in eastern Europe imprisoned or executed in the years after 1945. Both Germany and the Soviet Union manipulated the Finns mercilessly to suit their own ends; the more prescient Finnish politicians such as Paasikivi, brought up on the pessimistic *obiter dicta* of Snellman and Yrjö Koskinen about the helplessness of small nations in the face of great power interests, accepted this as the way of the world and sought to make the best accommodation they could, again drawing on the experience of the past. Those such as Ryti, who appealed to justice and morality, were fated to be amongst the losers.

Germany made little or no attempt to undermine the social and political order of Finland by building up its own faction. Ribbentrop's hopes of being able to stage some sort of coup in Finland during the critical days of June 1944 were immediately quashed by the German envoy, who told him firmly that there existed no pro-Nazi group in Finland that might even be considered to carry out such an act. The Russians certainly did contemplate the idea of a communist Finland that might become part of the Soviet Union, though they seem to have had little faith in the ability of the Finnish communists themselves to carry this out. When Leino told Zhdanov in May 1945 that the general aim of the Finnish communists was union with the Soviet Union, he may well have been telling his master what he thought he wanted to hear, but in any event, he was guilty of being more papist than the pope. Zhdanov gave no indication that that was what the Soviet Union wanted, but he made it perfectly clear in his dealings with Finnish leaders, communist and non-communist, that the recognition of the security interests of the Soviet Union had to be at the heart of any future relationship between the two countries. Advice there was in plenty for the communists, but it was up to them to make the decisive moves. Jussila has suggested that what Kuusinen in 1918 condemned as the 'illusion of parliamentarianism' that had led the old social democratic party off the revolutionary path in November 1917 still exercised a powerful influence over the communist leadership, and that they played the game according to the balance of forces within parliament. This may explain their patent inability to establish the kind of ruthless hegemony achieved by the Czech or Hungarian communists; but it also points out the essential differences between the Finnish and the eastern European cases. Political institutions and parties had not been smashed up by dictators, native or foreign, in Finland. The parties with which the communists had to contend had strong roots and were certainly not willing meekly to accept a subordinate role in the forging of a people's democracy (nor were they ever so coerced by the control commission, even though the Russians would dearly have loved to see the destruction of the party of their arch-demon, Väinö Tanner). And, in the end, the Finnish communist party was the child, albeit an orphan fostered in a strange land, of the old pre-1917 labour movement. Its leaders may have rejected many of the un-Leninist illusions of that movement, but they never disavowed it. Although they denounced Scandinavian social democracy as a cat's paw of western imperialism and did their best to emulate the eastern European model of socialism, they were in their history, traditions, and temperament much closer to their counterparts west of the Gulf of Bothnia than they were to those south of the Gulf of Finland. 'New faces' on the political scene they may have been, declaring themselves to be in the vanguard which would bring about the transformation of Finnish society, but they were in their own way quite as attached to the past as those they denounced as reactionaries.

7

The Kekkonen era, 1956–81

Life in Finland during the second half of the twentieth century was dominated and shaped by two things: a rapid transition from agrarian to post-industrial society and the country's relationship with the outside world, above all, with the Soviet Union. It was also dominated by one man, Urho Kalevi Kekkonen, president of the republic from 1956 until 1981, a controversial figure in his own lifetime and still the subject of intense debate some two decades or more after his death. The limited opening of the archives in Moscow following the collapse of the Soviet Union has revealed a degree of collusion between the Finnish and Soviet political leadership that has tarnished the reputation of Kekkonen and those closely associated with his policies. 'Finlandisation', a term first used by politicians and commentators *outside* Finland to warn of the dangers of a certain model of Soviet control being applied elsewhere has now been appropriated by the Finns themselves, and seems set to be added to the other descriptive epithets of Finnish history. Whereas for the 'finlandisers' of the 1970s, such as the right-wing West German politician Franz-Josef Strauss or the political commentator Walter Laqueur, the villain of the piece was the Soviet Union, which used a variety of manipulative practices to ensure control over a small and weak neighbour, already bound to it by treaty, 'finlandisation' as interpreted by Finnish writers since 1991 has focused directly on the Finns' own culpability for this state of affairs. Although a final verdict is far from being reached, it has to be said that most of the blame so far has been heaped on Kekkonen's shoulders.

To a large extent, this can be attributed to the fact that Kekkonen was an exceptionally energetic politician, who engaged actively in all major aspects of public life for well over four decades, and who was elevated to the status of principal architect and guide of the nation's post-war political destiny. Kekkonen's tenure of office should, however, be viewed in the light in which the exercise of power and authority have evolved over time in Finland, and within the context of the pressures for national consensus and unanimity that were a feature of Finnish public life from at least the 1880s onwards. The immediate legacy of the 1940s is also important. The war and its outcome forced Finland to embark upon a new and different relationship with its eastern neighbour and former ruler. At one level, this was a profoundly conservative accommodation that allowed the Finnish political leadership to manage affairs with their eastern neighbour much as their nineteenth-century predecessors had done, and to use this as an instrument of control within Finland itself. Maintaining good relations with the Soviet Union became an overriding priority, even an obsession. Conforming to the official foreign policy line became from the mid-1960s a precondition for any political party or individual wishing to taste the fruits of office. Avoidance of acts or pronouncements that might be construed in Moscow as hostile, discreet self-censorship, and a tendency to elevate the Paasikivi–Kekkonen foreign policy doctrine to the status of an official liturgy were all part of what Finnish writers now refer to as the 'finlandisation' of their country, a period in which the 'nation was on its belly', to quote the title of one of the first books that delved into such matters.

Criticism of features of the Kekkonen era now held to have been demeaning to the nation may, however, lead to some of the more worthy aspects being undervalued. A relationship in which both parties had a strong vested interest in stability and continuity could and did create a sense of security. More subtly, perhaps, the Soviet–Finnish relationship allowed the two nations to coexist with the minimum of intercourse. There was none of the casual intermingling of peoples that occurred in much of western Europe as mass tourism developed from the 1960s onwards. Finnish visitors to the Soviet Union were rather dismissively regarded as 'vodka tourists', and were in any case carefully confined to specific areas. There was little in the way of an active or free exchange of ideas in spite of the many officially sponsored contacts and visits. The relationship did little to challenge either the intellectual assumptions and emotional attachments underpinning Finnish national identity or the new currents and ideas that reached Finland from the west, but it did allow the Finnish people to get on with their own lives without any evident hindrances. Economically, socially, and culturally, Finland followed more or less the same trajectory towards affluence, consumerism, and welfare-state security as other western European nations. A small minority of citizens may have clung to the view that Finland's rightful place was amongst the people's democracies of eastern Europe, but they were never in a position to persuade or coerce the majority to follow that path. Kekkonen presented himself to the public as the man whom the Soviet leaders could trust, and did so with some degree of success; opinion polls in the 1970s recorded a high level of satisfaction with the conduct of Finnish foreign policy, and a firm belief that Finland was a safe country to live in.

Beneath the assurances of the politicians, however, there was always a sharp edge of anxiety, which if anything grew more intense during the final years of Kekkonen's presidency. The relationship was always affected by international tension, particularly in Europe, and by the strategic and technical twists and turns of the arms race. Much has been made of the way in which it influenced Finland's internal affairs, but it also played a part in the power struggles within the Communist Party of the Soviet Union (CPSU), particularly in the immediate post-Stalin years. Consorting with known agents of the KGB and of the international department of the CPSU was a risky game to play, but it was also a way in which Finnish leaders could have access to the decision-makers in Moscow; they simply could not afford to rely solely on the conventional diplomatic channels, since power did not reside in the Soviet foreign ministry. The leading Soviet agents were experts in Finnish affairs, fluent in the language, and with a wide range of contacts built up over many years of service in Finland. They appear to have won the trust and confidence of the president and a number of leading politicians (so much so that the Finns used them on occasion as official interpreters in confidential discussions), though they have undoubtedly exaggerated their own importance and influence in their subsequent memoirs. To see them as puppet-masters, manipulating Finnish politicians and public figures according to the directions of the politburo of the CPSU, would, however, be to ignore the confusions and cross-currents of Soviet policy-making, and the ability of the Finns to fight their own corner. Notwithstanding its more reprehensible ramifications, which have left a bitter aftertaste, this was never a one-sided relationship, imposed by a ruthless, determined power upon a weak and supine small neighbour.

In contrast to his immediate predecessors in the presidential office, Kekkonen had grown to maturity in an independent Finnish state. Born in a remote parish in north-eastern Finland in 1900, he was brought up within the social-radical traditions of Finnish nationalism, and the desire to bring about a transformation of Finnish society that featured in his writings and activities as a student politician in the 1920s and early 1930s never entirely faded away in later life. The young Kekkonen was drawn to the socially inclusive policies preached within the Academic Karelia Society by Niilo Kärki. Kekkonen himself conceived of nationality as the desire of a particular linguistic group to civilise and develop itself. He saw it above all as an ethical principle, a search for justice that would guide the people to the future, not anchor them in the past, as the conservative strand of Finnish nationalism sought to do. He showed himself to be a political animal to his marrow from an early stage, leading a successful attack to wrest control of the League of Finnishness (*Suomalaisuuden liitto*) from the hands of an older generation in 1927, engaging in fierce polemics in the student and national press, and later directing the affairs of the national sports association. As the minister of the interior in the Cajander government, he tried unsuccessfully in 1938 to have the fascist IKL banned, and he showed himself willing to take on difficult and controversial tasks in the immediate post-war years, fighting within his own Agrarian Union for a radical change of foreign policy and playing a leading role in the process of staging the 'war-guilt' trials in 1946.

By the end of the 1940s, foreign observers were singling him out as a leading contender for high political office in Finland, although he had also acquired a reputation as an intriguer. The British minister to Helsinki described him, at the end of 1949, as a man whose 'ability has never been questioned, but his sardonic, mordant wit has earned him many enemies and his various flirtations with the communists have not added to his reputation for "reliability" in right-wing circles'. Those right-wing circles, not least within his own party, were more than happy to feed rumours of such flirtations to the British and Americans, and the latter, in particular, entertained deep suspicions of Kekkonen throughout the fifties. His visit to Moscow during his first premiership in 1950 for the signing of a five-year trade treaty – the first concluded by the Soviet Union with a non-socialist country – boosted his status and position at home, and offered significant advantages to Finnish industry. The American and British ministers to Helsinki, however, saw the invitation merely as evidence of how Moscow sought to draw Finland into its orbit, and they suspected that pressure had been brought to bear on the new prime minister to make him more dependent on the support of the Finnish communists. The evidence of the five governments of which Kekkonen was prime minister between 1950 and 1956 would seem to undermine any notion of collusion or agreement with the communists, who proved to be the fiercest opponents of attempts to keep inflation in check through strict wage controls. The communists also routinely accused Kekkonen of being in league with western business interests, which casts an interesting light on another aspect of post-war Finnish foreign policy, namely, the necessity of maintaining vital trading links with western markets. The degree to which Kekkonen may have colluded with the KGB and the international department of the Communist Party of the Soviet Union, and his possible motives, remains a matter of controversy, but no one has yet seriously challenged his determination to ensure that Finland was not excluded from the process of economic integration taking place in post-war western Europe.

Kekkonen had stood for the presidency as the candidate of the Agrarian Union in 1950, but came a poor third to Paasikivi. Uncertainty about the outcome of the presidential election scheduled for 1956 seems to have persuaded Foreign Minister Vyacheslav Molotov, then engaged in a final struggle for power in Moscow, that the octogenarian Paasikivi should continue in office. The Finnish communists backed this as a tactic to dish the social democrats. Paasikivi seemed not disinclined to accept the honour, if invited to do so by all the major parties. Kekkonen had not been idle, however, in promoting his own cause, not least in Moscow. He had already shown on previous face-to-face encounters with the Soviet leadership a willingness to make initiatives, the fulfilment of which would be likely to redound to his credit; and he was either fortunate or perspicacious enough to realise that concessions were in the offing as part of the general relaxation of tension that led to the four-power summit in Geneva in the summer of 1955. Having already pushed through the Austrian state treaty in the teeth of opposition from the old guard, the first secretary of the CPSU, Nikita Khrushchev, was able in August 1955 to persuade the party central committee to support the return of the Porkkala base to Finland. The minutes recorded that this 'would without doubt have a favourable influence on the outcome of the presidential elections in Finland at the beginning of 1956', which some have seen as a tacit endorsement of Kekkonen's candidature. The extent to which he had already become Khrushchev's choice for the presidency is however questionable. Khrushchev's own position was by no means secure at the time, and there was no guarantee that Kekkonen would actually manage to swim against the tide to return Paasikivi or to secure sufficient support to win a majority of the votes in the electoral college. The outcome was uncertain right up to the final stages. The Finnish communists remained firm in their resolution to support Paasikivi in the electoral college, should he be willing, and the Soviet foreign ministry at least was convinced that their preferred candidate would in fact be returned by a coalition of conservatives, communists, and the social democrats, who would eventually abandon their candidate Fagerholm to ensure Kekkonen's defeat. On the eve of the electoral college convening, the communists received orders from Moscow to ensure Paasikivi's elimination by splitting their votes between Kekkonen and Fagerholm on the second round of balloting. Kekkonen won by the narrowest of margins on the third round, thanks to the votes of a handful of delegates from the small bourgeois parties who were persuaded to join the agrarians and communists.

Kekkonen's immediate predecessors had become head of state in exceptional circumstances, when national unanimity and solidarity was at a premium. The circumstances of his victory, the labile state of Finnish party politics, and a seemingly permanent prices-and-incomes crisis that exploded into a general strike and the withholding of dairy products by the farmers' organisation as the new president assumed office, meant that Kekkonen would have to fight to assert his authority and win the kind of consensual respect that Paasikivi had enjoyed. His first term of office was particularly difficult. The president had little success in persuading the main political parties to support his foreign policy. He relied heavily on the assistance of a small coterie of allies, such as the secretary of the Agrarian Union, Arvo Korsimo, his former private secretary during his time as prime minister, Ahti Karjalainen, and professor Kustaa Vilkuna, the wartime head of the censorship and surveillance bureau, and the solicitous attentions of 'a sincere friend of ours' (as Karjalainen described him in a note to the president in June 1958), Viktor Vladimirov, the principal KGB man at the Soviet embassy. The Soviet press and political leadership continued to complain about what they took to be the hostile and malevolent tone of Finnish articles and publications, and worried about the return to public life of Väinö Tanner and the activities of right-wing socialists such as the party secretary, Väinö Leskinen. The controversial election of Tanner as chairman of the Social Democratic Party in 1957 helped split the party and undermined the foundations of the coalition government led by the centrist social democrat, Karl-August Fagerholm. Efforts to keep the coalition in being came unstuck in May 1957. The minority agrarian government that succeeded it had to resort to frankly illegal methods to push through an emergency programme of measures to tackle a grave financial crisis, and was eventually forced to devalue the mark by 39 per cent. In August, five leading members of the Social Democratic Party opposition joined the government without official party approval. Kekkonen was accused of having precipitated the final split in the Social Democratic Party by encouraging the prime minister to sound out the opposition, though there is plentiful evidence to show that the leader of the rebels, Emil Skog, was more than capable of engineering such an outcome.

The patched-up government fell on a vote of no confidence in October. Attempts to form a new government lasted forty-two days. The prospect of a five-party coalition government headed by Tanner, and excluding the SKDL, raised a storm of protest on the left, and caused Moscow to break off planned trade talks. Kekkonen himself was confident that Tanner would not succeed in forming a government, but he let him try to avoid the accusation of partiality. In the end, rather than accept another minority agrarian government, the president appointed a purely non-party administration. Although composed of leading figures in the business and labour world, it failed to bring the economic crisis under control. The state had to suspend payments for a day in January 1958 on account of a lack of cover in the accounts. The inexperienced prime minister drew criticism from all sides and failed to provide firm direction; the government fell on a vote of no confidence in April and was replaced by yet another interim non-party administration until the elections.

The main winners in the 1958 elections were the communists, who picked up an additional seven seats to become the largest group in the *eduskunta*. As there was no likelihood of the communists being able to forge or join a coalition with other parties (and there appears to have been no real pressure from Moscow for communist participation in government), the onus for forming a new government rested with the agrarians and badly divided social democrats. The Agrarian Union leadership ignored the president's warnings, echoed by the Soviet ambassador, that the inclusion of right-wing social democrats and conservatives in government would be interpreted as an unfriendly act by Moscow. In theory able to command the support of almost three-quarters of the members of the *eduskunta*, the five-party coalition that Fagerholm finally managed to put together ran into stormy water from the outset. The Soviet ambassador was recalled with no mention of a replacement, trade talks were suspended, and there were veiled threats that the Soviet Union would activate the military consultation clause of the FCMA treaty in the light of German–Danish military collaboration in the western Baltic. Kekkonen's attempt to dissuade the Danes from further close military collaboration with a rearmed Germany received a dusty answer, and his efforts to alter the composition of the government were strongly resisted within his own agrarian party and by the prime minister, who, with previous experience of pressure from Moscow during his minority government of 1948–50, believed that the threats could be ridden out. Kekkonen had been especially irritated by the behaviour of his erstwhile protégé in the Agrarian Union, Johannes Virolainen, who had defied his warnings and entered government to ensure the passage of the farms income legislation. By December 1958, however, Virolainen appears to have been persuaded of the seriousness of the crisis, and succeeded in pushing his party to leave government.

The departure of the agrarians brought down the coalition, and ushered in a period of minority and centre-right governments. The agrarians and the parties of the left between them accounted for almost three-quarters of the seats in the *eduskunta*, but were unable to work together in government. The social democrats remained politically unacceptable to Moscow until the hated Tanner–Leskinen clique was replaced in the early 1960s by a new generation more willing to accommodate to Kekkonen's foreign policy line. They were also badly divided internally, with the minority eventually splitting off to form its own party, the Workers' and Small Farmers' Socialist Union (TPSL). The communists remained isolated, neglected by Moscow and shunned by the other Finnish political parties. The Agrarian Union itself was riven by personal rivalries, and as the government crisis of 1958 had shown, was far from subservient to the president's bidding. If there was to be no return to the past, as one observer of the fifties in Finland noted, there was still plenty of puffing and fretting to be done before the parties and the public at large aligned themselves with the foreign policy of the president.

The so-called 'night-frost crisis' of autumn 1958 was at the time seen by his opponents as inspired by Kekkonen himself, a view that has resurfaced in recent interpretations. It is beyond dispute that the president believed from the start that nothing good would come of the Fagerholm government, or that he did nothing to prevent its collapse. It is also fair to claim that one of the lessons drawn from the experience was that in future, the opinion of Moscow would in the end count for more than the need to have the backing of a parliamentary majority in the formation of a government. Kekkonen virtually ordered the agrarian leader V. J. Sukselainen to abandon any idea of a coalition to replace the fallen Fagerholm government, and to include in his minority administration men known to be loyal to the president, and he was deeply involved in the intrigues and plotting which were ultimately intended to weaken the still dominant position of opponents of his policy within the conservative and social democratic parties. His 'surprise' meeting with Khrushchev in Leningrad in the immediate aftermath of the crisis was in fact secretly prearranged, the first major initiative along the path of personal diplomacy that President Kekkonen was to use with great effect to boost his status and authority at home and abroad. Khrushchev made it clear that the Soviet government would not tolerate any government in which supporters of Tanner were present, and hinted that the exclusion of the communists from office might be construed as discrimination according to the terms of the FCMA treaty. The president's critics at home accused him of failing to repudiate Soviet attacks on the Finnish press and political system, and redoubled their efforts to mount a serious challenge in the forthcoming presidential election.

It is unlikely, however, that the crisis was simply conjured up by Kekkonen to enhance his own power, not least because it patently did not do this. It was as important for Khrushchev to ensure that a central element in his policy of peaceful coexistence stayed on track, especially in the light of German rearmament and admission to NATO. The Russians were also concerned about the increasing volume of Finnish trade with OEEC countries, and were well aware of the desire of the Finns to be associated with the process of postwar economic integration. Moscow had reacted sharply to news that Finland had decided to enter into confidential negotiations with a view to joining the OEEC, and Kekkonen had been obliged to put these talks on hold.

Trade was in reality the vital element in Kekkonen's foreign policy, and there is much to support the view that the protracted and wearisome arm-wrestling with Moscow that allowed Finland to sign agreements with EFTA in 1961 and the EEC in 1973 were the real tests of the Soviet–Finnish relationship. The Soviet Union was deeply suspicious of any coming together of western European nations, fearing that political motives lay behind such moves; but it was also jealous of its own rights as a trading nation, and this gave the Finns a slender opportunity to manoeuvre and thus keep in contact with western markets.

When the Finns announced at a meeting of Nordic government delegations in July 1959 that they were ready to accept the draft plan for a Nordic customs union, they learnt that the other governments now wanted to go ahead instead with a new European free trade association of seven states (EFTA), comprising non-members of the European Economic Community (EEC), including Britain. Since a quarter of Finland's exports went to Britain, in competition with Swedish and Norwegian goods, membership or at least favourable association with the planned organisation was essential, and the Finnish government was anxious to express its interest. The Russians were not slow however to remind Finland that by the terms of the 1948 treaty, it had promised not to join any association directed against the Soviet Union. The tactic adopted by Kekkonen was to try and soothe the Russians' fears whilst authorising his trusted lieutenant Ahti Karjalainen to explore the possibilities of association with EFTA. This option was acceptable to the EFTA partners and agreed upon with little difficulty in talks held in Paris in January 1960. Moscow, however, refused to countenance this, and the Finns were obliged to delay initialling of the agreement. Kekkonen seems to have thought that the heightening of international tension following the shooting-down of the U2 spy plane by the Russians could be used to Finland's advantage, since it offered Khrushchev an opportunity to show that the Soviet Union was able to get along with its neighbour in a spirit of co-operation and peaceful coexistence. The Russians refused to budge, however, and Finland missed the first tranche of customs reductions within EFTA.

The Finnish presidential elections were now looming, and they promised to be a hard and bitter fight between the beleaguered president and his opponents. Kekkonen linked the EFTA question to the prospects of his re-election in talks with Khrushchev in September 1960. Khrushchev once more chose to go against those in the Soviet hierarchy who adamantly opposed Finnish association with EFTA and he also turned down an alternative offered by

Kekkonen for a free trade agreement that would have associated Finland with the socialist countries, reasoning that this would have unfortunate consequences for the stability of northern Europe. The Soviet Union still regarded any blocs with suspicion, but agreed to recognise Finland's interests in associating with EFTA, provided that this did not harm the most favoured nation status accorded to the Soviet Union by the terms of the 1947 Paris peace treaty. In subsequent talks in Moscow, where the Finns were also able to secure a leasing agreement for use of the canal which connected the Saimaa lake system of eastern Finland to the sea through territory now part of the Soviet Union, the price that Finland paid for the tacit consent of the Russians was a secret appendix to a tariff agreement, signed by the trade and industry minister Ahti Karjalainen. This promised to allow the same benefits and tariff reductions to Soviet imports as to those from the EFTA countries. The signing of a bilateral customs agreement with the Soviet Union annoyed the British, who suspected that the Finns had had to do some sort of deal with Moscow (the secret letter signed by Karjalainen was fortunately not leaked). Worried that the Finns might fall completely under Moscow's control if left outside the EFTA arrangement, however, Britain and Sweden took it upon themselves to plead Finland's case. The protocols and final agreement were signed in March 1961. Finland also joined the OECD (formerly the OEEC) in 1968. The steady increase of Finnish trade with OECD countries during the 1960s, reaching 80 per cent of total value in 1970, is an indication of how important these markets were for Finland.

Hints dropped by Kekkonen about the forthcoming presidential election during Khrushchev's visit in September 1960 were quickly picked up; that same month, the Soviet ambassador to Helsinki was instructed to investigate the possibilities of assisting the re-election of the incumbent. His opponents were frantically searching for a suitable non-party candidate, and after several had been approached and declined the honour, they were able to announce in March 1961 that the chancellor of justice, Olavi Honka, would stand for election. Moscow immediately, and correctly, detected the hand of the Tannerites behind this; Honka was from the start a front man for the malcontents and this, together with his lack of political experience, set doubts against his candidature even amongst those who wished otherwise to be rid of Kekkonen. Pro-Kekkonen minorities soon surfaced in the two small people's parties, and the withdrawal of support by these two parties, at a time when opinion polls were beginning to suggest that Kekkonen had a clear lead, played a part in persuading Honka himself to pull out of the race. This he did, however, at the height of the so-called 'note crisis', which some have seen as deliberately manufactured by Kekkonen himself. The principal evidence for this seems to be the decision arrived at on 18 April 1961 by the president, in consultation with two of his closest allies and the prime minister, that there would be a dissolution of the *eduskunta* in November, with parliamentary elections to take place a week after the presidential election, but before the electoral college met to select the president. This was something the president was entitled to do, although in practice, parliaments had usually been allowed to run their course, and a premature dissolution in the run-up to a vital presidential election would certainly have been construed as manipulation. Kekkonen clearly wanted to split his opponents, but he was also hoping that new elections would bring about a realignment of political forces and lay the foundations for a more stable coalition government, which he consistently believed was essential to cope with the pressures of maintaining good relations with the Soviet Union whilst at the same time keeping in touch with vital western markets.

The plan hatched in mid-April may be criticised as a ruthless political manoeuvre, and it may also be construed as a clever attempt to tie the hands of the prime minister, Sukselainen, whose own political ambitions were suspected by the president, but it was constitutionally legitimate. What was far more dubious was the revelation of the plan by the president to the Soviet ambassador the very next day, and the incontrovertible evidence that Kekkonen and his supporters actively and regularly consorted with known agents of the KGB, and certainly hoped to use these connections to influence Finland's internal affairs. It may be that Kekkonen and his allies felt this was a necessary measure to counter the activities of the communists, who regularly received instructions from Moscow, but it was at best a dangerous game to play, and at worst opened them up to the charge of being instruments of Soviet policy.

The note in question was handed to the Finnish ambassador in Moscow on 30 October 1961. It detailed the threat of German militarism and revanchism in general and in particular in northern Europe and the Baltic, and concluded by proposing consultations on measures to secure the defences of both countries against the threat of an attack by West Germany and its allies, as provided for in Article Two of the FCMA treaty. Something of this sort had been predicted throughout the summer by the ambassador, and the army had also drawn up its own plans for possible consultations. The immediate reaction in Helsinki was that consultations could not be avoided: the army in particular seemed prepared to follow that route, though it may be that they saw this as a useful lever to force government to update equipment. The president and the foreign minister, Ahti Karjalainen, were in Hawaii when the note was delivered, relaxing after an official visit to the United States. Kekkonen's refusal to return immediately to Finland has been interpreted as further evidence that the note crisis had been somehow ordered in advance, though his biographer claims that rushing back to Helsinki would have undone his efforts to convince the Americans that Finland was independent and not bound to Moscow.

Although Kekkonen was at pains to show that the note was not directed against Finland as such, it did nonetheless contain a veiled criticism of his ability to control the Finnish press, which, the note claimed, acted as the mouthpiece of 'certain circles', actively supporting NATO warmongering and thereby violating the terms of the peace treaty of 1947 and the 1948 FCMA treaty. According to Finnish intelligence sources, this paragraph had been added to the note at the insistence of the Finnish communist leaders, who were shown the text in Moscow at the end of October, and it was certainly welcomed by the Finnish Communist Party's central committee as a useful weapon with which to destroy the Honka front. The Soviet ambassador to Helsinki made it clear to Foreign Minister Karjalainen on 3 November that Kekkonen's initial response to the note underestimated the threat of anti-Soviet forces within Finland. This may have provoked the president to express

Plate 35 President Kennedy welcoming President Kekkonen to the
United States, 1961. Urho Kekkonen began his first official visit to the
United States as the Berlin crisis was at its height, and his recent
encounter in Finland with Leonid Brezhnev aroused a great deal of
interest in the State Department. Kekkonen endeavoured to assure the
Americans that he was not merely a messenger-boy for the Russians. In
his speech to the National Press Club, he claimed that the better
Finland's relationship with Russia, the freer it was to pursue close
co-operation with the western countries. Although the communiqué
issued at the end of the discussions between the two heads of state spoke
of American understanding of the basis of Finnish neutrality, and promised
to respect Finnish policy, the reaction of the State Department to the
subsequent 'note crisis' would seem to indicate that the United States
continued to believe that Finnish independence was limited, if not
seriously undermined by Soviet pressure. The defection at this time of
the KGB agent Anatoly Golitsyn from his post in Helsinki and his
subsequent revelations also seem to have reinforced American suspicions
that the Soviet Union exercised considerable internal control through its
agents and fellow-travellers in Finland. The Finnish foreign minister,
Ahti Karjalainen, is on the left of the picture, flanked by Secretary of
State Dean Rusk. President Kekkonen is the other heavily bespectacled
gentleman.

his annoyance at the timing of the note, and to drop heavy hints that he would withdraw from the presidential race if he felt he was unable to succeed in achieving his life's work of maintaining Finland's neutrality, a threat that could be used to frighten the Soviet leadership as well as his opponents in Finland.

Karjalainen was dispatched to Moscow on 10 November to argue the Finnish case that the international situation did not warrant military consultations, and to press the Russians to engage in further political discussions to defuse the crisis. His counterpart, Andrey Gromyko, proved unwilling to drop the idea of consultations, which he claimed, rather disingenuously, had been demanded by the Soviet military. In spite of Karjalainen's heavy hints of impending political changes, and the actual announcement on 14 November of the dissolution of parliament, with elections to be held in February, the Soviet side obdurately insisted that consultations were urgently needed. Faced with a seeming impasse, the Finnish government seized upon the 'hint' that Kekkonen should travel to meet Khrushchev in the Siberian city of Novosibirsk and unanimously urged the president to take up this offer. As the talks were getting under way in Novosibirsk on 24 November, Honka withdrew from the presidential race, making Kekkonen's re-election a certainty. What was discussed or agreed in the private talks between Kekkonen and Khrushchev before lunch remains a subject of speculation, since no minutes of this meeting have emerged from the archives; but in his lunch-time speech, Khrushchev voiced his full confidence in the Finnish president's ability to maintain and strengthen the Paasikivi–Kekkonen foreign policy line, and announced that the Soviet government now felt it was possible to postpone military consultations. On behalf of the Soviet government, however, the first secretary of the CPSU expressed the hope that the government of Finland would in future closely follow developments in northern Europe and the Baltic region and, where necessary, present its thoughts on what measures should be taken to the Soviet government.

The unfolding of the note crisis in the autumn of 1961 undoubtedly reinforced Kekkonen's position. To suggest, however, that this was an elaborate plot to ensure the re-election of the president overlooks the background of international tension over issues relating to Germany, and ignores the political undercurrents in Moscow, and Khrushchev's own motives. The resolution of the crisis was not all to Kekkonen's advantage, either. He could claim personal credit for defusing a potentially dangerous situation, and was able to reassure the Finnish people that his meeting with Khrushchev had strengthened mutual trust and respect. In his radio and television address on 25 November, he even went so far as to interpret the communiqué issued by the two leaders as meaning 'that the initiation of possible military consultations would henceforth be in the first instance the duty of Finland'. Khrushchev's willingness to speak of Finnish neutrality was encouraging, reinforcing the acknowledgement of neutrality as the underlying basis of Finnish foreign policy made in the official communiqué issued after the talks between the American and Finnish presidents in October 1961. In western capitals, however, the talks in Novosibirsk reinforced the impression that Finland had become a watchdog for Soviet interests, and worries about Kekkonen's connections with the Russians continued to surface. The note crisis also affected Finland's relationship with the Nordic countries. One of the most powerful weapons in Kekkonen's arsenal, and he used this to good effect, was that anything that threatened to upset the status quo in northern Europe could drive Sweden into the arms of NATO and persuade Norway and Denmark to abandon the restrictions on NATO activities on their territory. But it was also a weapon that could blow up in his own face. His various initiatives for a neutralised northern Europe, stretching from 1952 to the 1970s, may have been meant to serve Finland's own interests by lessening perceived threats to Soviet security in the region, but they invariably provoked an angry reaction from Denmark and Norway. They were also seen, with some justification, as inspired by the Soviet Union.

The president's hopes for a significant realignment of the political parties after the elections was not realised, either. Moderates within the Social Democratic Party failed to mount an effective challenge to the leadership of Väinö Tanner. The party lost ten seats in the elections, which saw a shift to the right; the communists remained the largest party with forty-seven seats, but stayed outside government in spite of Moscow's efforts to have them included as a guarantee of continuity in foreign policy. The conservative *Kokoomus* party, which entered the coalition put together by Karjalainen after the elections, was at best ambivalent about Kekkonen's foreign policy, which the conservative press continued to attack. Continuing economic difficulties further weakened the chances of creating a stable, broad-based coalition. Karjalainen's government managed to struggle on after the withdrawal of trade unionist members of the social democratic opposition (TPSL) in protest at the agrarians' farm incomes policy, but finally collapsed when it ran into difficulties over the budget at the end of 1963. Karjalainen's main rival within the Agrarian Union, Johannes Virolainen, fared little better as head of another centre-right government between September 1964 and May 1966. In the elections of that spring, the pendulum swung back to the left. Changes in the leadership of the two main parties of the left enabled Kekkonen to realise his long-held ambition of reconstructing a coalition of the centre-left. The new government was headed by the social democrat Rafael Paasio, who had masterminded the removal of the Tannerites from the party leadership, and included the communists, then in the process of jettisoning the old guard leadership in favour of a younger generation of moderates. As a guarantee of the continuity of a friendly policy towards the Soviet Union, Ahti Karjalainen occupied the post of foreign minister.

The formation of the Paasio government returned the social democrats to the political fold, and ushered in a period of significant and often quite radical change in Finnish life, which will be considered in more detail later. It also marked the beginning of a new phase in which all the major parties were to subscribe to the Paasikivi–Kekkonen line, and sought to cultivate contacts with Moscow via the embassy on Factory Street (*Tehtaankatu*). But, as the Finnish politicians began to line up behind their president in support of his foreign policy – the most spectacular conversion being that of Väinö Leskinen, who managed to make his peace with Moscow and to become foreign minister in 1970 – there was a perceptible hardening of Soviet attitudes. After the invasion of Czechoslovakia and the enunciation of the Brezhnev doctrine, the Soviet press and leadership spoke far less of Finnish neutrality, laying emphasis instead on the FCMA treaty as the foundation of the relationship between the two countries. This has been seen in part as a reaction to attempts by senior officials of the Finnish foreign ministry to detach the concept of Finnish neutrality from the preamble of the FCMA treaty, but this does not take into account the mood of suspicion and hostility to change that prevailed in Moscow after the demise of Khrushchev. Kekkonen was still able to pursue his policy of personal diplomacy, but he never enjoyed the same degree of confidence with Brezhnev and Kosygin as he had with Khrushchev, a man who was also determined to break with the past, and who, like Kekkonen, was prepared to use ruthless means to break his opponents.

Kekkonen may have enjoyed close and friendly contacts with the Soviet leadership, but that did not mean he did not have to fight long and hard to obtain agreements and concessions vital to Finland's interests. He was never able to persuade Khrushchev even to consider returning a part of the Karelian isthmus, and he had to abandon the idea of anything more than a leasing agreement that would allow the Finns to use the Saimaa canal. During his third term of office, between 1968 and 1974, he was faced with a number of knotty issues that threatened to undo much of the work he had done to maintain a close and trusting relationship with the Soviet Union whilst at the same time allowing Finland to keep in touch with its European trading partners. Foremost amongst these was the question of Finland's relationship with an expanded Common Market (EEC). The reopening of discussions on EEC enlargement in 1969 threatened to throw off course negotiations for a Nordic economic agreement (Nordek). Initially keen on signing up to an agreement that seemed to offer prospects for increased inward flows of investment and technical know-how, Finland suddenly began to blow cold at the end of the year. In January 1970, the government made it clear that Finland would not proceed with Nordek if any of the proposed members entered into negotiations to join the EEC, and suspended all negotiations a couple of months later. Finland's withdrawal caused bad blood with her Nordic neighbours, who suspected Soviet pressure. Kekkonen, who had been much keener on pressing ahead with the Nordek project than his prime minister, the social democrat Mauno Koivisto, blamed the Danes for playing a double game, using Nordek as a springboard for joining the European Common Market. The fact that the Finnish government itself opened negotiations with the EEC in April 1970 would, however, give some weight to the argument that Finnish exporters, particularly the wood-processing industries, preferred a free trade agreement with their biggest customers to increased co-operation with their rivals in Nordek.

Whereas there had been strong support in Finland, apart from the communists, for association with EFTA, there were reservations about the EEC across the political spectrum. The Finnish negotiators made it clear from the outset that they were not looking for any institutional links with the EEC, but merely for trade advantages. The terms offered in Brussels were deemed unsatisfactory by the Finns, who were also unsettled by the pace at which the talks were conducted. By July 1972, however, a deal which managed to protect sensitive Finnish industries had been struck, though the period of transition was thought too long by leading exporters. The minority social democratic government was unwilling to take the responsibility for pushing through the agreement alone, and resigned in order to make way for a broader centre-left coalition. The increasingly powerful left-wing within the Social Democratic Party demanded in compensation for a free trade agreement greater regulation and control of the domestic economy. This in itself delayed the final outcome, with the industrial lobby at one stage arguing that it would be better not to sign the free trade agreement if such laws were passed. There was also the possibility that a 'no' vote in the Norwegian and Danish referenda on joining the Common Market might once more return the Nordek proposals to the political agenda, an option the prime minister Kalevi Sorsa and the president seem to have favoured. Norway voted 'no' at the end of September 1972, but the Danes voted 'yes' a week later. The Swedes were keen on Finland joining them in securing a free trade agreement with the Common Market, partly for political reasons, but also to safeguard the trade between the two countries that had accelerated under the EFTA arrangement.

Much depended on what attitude the Soviet Union might take. The Finns had prepared the ground carefully. As in 1960, Karjalainen once again made a secret agreement with the Russians that Finland would grant them the same trading rights and advantages as the members of the EEC. Kekkonen felt confident that the Soviet leadership, though having considerable reservations about the political motives of the EEC, trusted him to make a deal that would not jeopardise the Finnish–Soviet relationship.[1] Here, he probably overestimated his ability to win over the dour and inordinately suspicious Brezhnev. Other circumstances combined to make his task more difficult. Moscow was alarmed by what it believed to be a resurgence of the right in Finland, and was concerned about the growing split within the ranks of the Finnish Communist Party. Having crushed the reformist movement in Czechoslovakia, the Soviet leaders were determined to tighten their grip on other areas they regarded as under their control, and that included Finland. Recent research has suggested that a senior member of the international department of the CPSU, Aleksey Belyakov, was sent as ambassador to Finland to ensure that the communists stayed in government, and worked harder to bring about socialist hegemony in Finland.[2] It is difficult to say how far the upsurge of youthful radicalism, which by 1970 was beginning to channel off into the parties of the left, deceived the ideologues of the CPSU into believing that a revolutionary situation was at hand in Finland. If they did entertain this prospect, they were to be quickly disabused, for in neither of the two parties of the left did the young radicals manage to exert much influence. Belyakov, accused at the time of stirring up trouble, was quickly recalled on Kekkonen's insistence; as on earlier occasions, the president was able to use his KGB contacts to good effect to secure his own position.

As 1974 approached, the unresolved question of Finland's free trade agreement with the EEC became linked with the possible re-election of Kekkonen as president. Opinion polls showed that a large majority of the electorate wanted Kekkonen to remain head of state, though only a small percentage favoured the option being considered in political circles of facilitating this through exceptional legislation that would circumvent the electoral process. During these months of rumour and speculation, Kekkonen showed that he had lost none of his skills as a manipulator. Some idea of the way in which he proceeded can be gleaned from his own notes taken at a sauna session with a select group of his confidants in the business world, at which he remarked that 'I'll never own up to saying it, but wouldn't it be best to tie a presidential election in the *eduskunta* to the EEC agreement and the package of bills [regulating the Finnish economy]. The boys were enthusiastic. I said, you won't succeed. We bet a bottle of whisky per man on it. They – that they would succeed – me – that they wouldn't.'

These plans were nearly upset by the revelation shortly afterwards in a Swedish newspaper of details of confidential discussions between the president, Leonid Brezhnev, and Aleksey Kosygin. Suspicion fell on a group of young socialists, who were opposed to the EEC agreement, and the political fallout of the subsequent investigation has lasted until the present day; but if the leak was intended to blow the free trade agreement out of the water, it failed in its intention. Claiming that it had seriously damaged the Soviet leadership's trust in him, Kekkonen threatened not to allow his name to be put forward for re-election. This was enough to persuade the most ardent supporters of the free trade agreement in the business world and the conservative party to rally behind the president, and to abandon their reservations about the method being proposed to ensure his continuance in office. All the major parties agreed to support the re-election of the president, who received the blessing of Brezhnev in Moscow at the end of the year, and finally consented in January 1973 to remain in office for a further four years. The necessary legislation to extend the term of office was passed in short order by the *eduskunta*.

Kekkonen's fourth term of office began on 1 March 1974. Within months, he was being urged by Moscow to consider staying on beyond 1978. He was also pressed by the social democrats to remain in office, mainly in order to spike the guns of the ambitious Ahti Karjalainen. Karjalainen had cultivated close relations with Moscow, and had long been regarded as Kekkonen's most likely successor. There was, however, a marked deterioration in his relationship with the president during Kekkonen's third term of office, in part brought about by Karjalainen's often erratic behaviour under the influence of alcohol. Although approaching his eighties, Kekkonen was in good physical condition, and had lost little of his appetite for power and politicking. He still retained the confidence of the Soviet leaders, who were the most anxious for him to stay in office. There appeared to be no one other than Karjalainen anxious to step forward to claim the crown; the circumstances were such, as Kekkonen himself observed to one of his intermediaries in the Soviet embassy in January 1974, 'that it is difficult to see the way ahead unless I agree [to remain in office]'. By April 1975, Kekkonen had made up his mind to continue, and, with the support of the major parties, was re-elected president once more in 1978. Increasing ill health obliged the president to resign in 1981.

The final decade of Kekkonen's long tenure of presidential office brought some well-publicised triumphs, most notably the hosting of the Helsinki conference on European security and the strategic arms limitation talks, but also many disappointments. Soviet insistence on the FCMA treaty as the basis not only for the Soviet–Finnish relationship, but increasingly as the only acceptable guideline for Finnish foreign and security policy was a blow to the efforts to advance the doctrine of active neutrality.[3] The 'finlandisation' debate in western Europe did little for Finland's reputation, either, in spite of Kekkonen's attempts to give the term a positive gloss. The revelations of a couple of Swedish journalists in 1973 concerning the activities of their country's military intelligence (IB), including evidence of operations on Finnish soil which Finnish intelligence sources were able to confirm, caused a furore. The allegations were vigorously denied by the former defence minister of Sweden, Sven Andersson, in spite of strong evidence to the contrary being produced in open court. A discreet Finnish protest leaked to the press prompted a flurry of angry exchanges in spring 1974, further eroding an already distinctly edgy relationship between the Finnish president and the Swedish premier, Olof Palme.

The Finns also had to fend off attempts by the Soviet high command to encourage closer military co-operation. The activities and pseudo-revolutionary posturing of the Stalinist minority of the Finnish Communist Party were in themselves no great threat; what was more worrying was that they were being encouraged by the chief ideologue of the CPSU, Mikhail Suslov. Kekkonen's threat to resign if the Finnish economy continued to slip out of control as a result of labour unrest and the breakdown of prices-and-incomes policy, made on the occasion of President Nikolay Podgorny's visit in October 1974, was clearly meant to put a stop to communist agitation. When Podgorny insisted that he continue in office, Kekkonen made entry into government of the communists the condition for restoring order, and hinted that the two wings of the party had to be brought under control by the CPSU.

The oil crisis of 1973 hit Finland hard, and had a big impact on its commercial relations with the Soviet Union. The Finns suspected that the Russians were using the crisis to push up their own oil prices. For their part, the Russians argued that they could not be seen to accept lower prices than they themselves were paying to their Arab allies for oil, though, as Suslov told the Finnish communists, the crisis did offer an excellent opportunity to bind Finland more closely economically and politically to the USSR, and for the communists to play an active part in this process. In February 1974, Kosygin proposed the initiation of negotiations that would lead to the Soviet Union supplying Finland's entire energy needs for the next fifteen years. Although the Finns were willing to increase co-operation, they did not wish to go that far. In the tough round of negotiations over oil that followed, Kekkonen did not hesitate to use the threat of possible unrest and political instability should Finland be forced to accept a price higher than that on the spot markets to beat down the asking price. The president – and it is significant that he was increasingly called upon by Finnish business circles as well as the Russians to become actively involved in trade talks – faced an even more uphill struggle over the question of Finnish exports to the USSR. A series of planned major construction projects began to run into difficulties as inflation obliged Finnish firms to revise their costs sharply upwards. The Finnish president, who pursued the construction projects resolutely, fearing that the consequences of delay or cancellation would be disastrous for the trade balance and for employment in the north-east, had to admit openly that inflation meant Finnish construction firms could no longer compete at the price levels demanded by the Soviet side. His only defence was that failure to agree would gravely threaten trade between the two countries and that this would have political consequences. The Russians agreed to work with the Finnish side to resolve the problem, but were not willing to give way much on price. Moscow finally and reluctantly gave its tacit consent in the autumn of 1973 to Finland signing the free trade agreement with the EEC. The agreement on co-ordinating economic, scientific, and technical co-operation with Comecon, the socialist equivalent of the EEC, concluded in 1973, was part of the delicate balancing act that Finland had to play. The bilateral clearing trade with the Soviet Union and other countries in the socialist bloc did offer benefits to Finland, securing vital energy supplies during a very uncertain period, and sustaining labour-intensive industries that supplied the Soviet market with consumer goods such as footwear and clothing. It was, however, a cumbersome method of conducting business, creating a top-heavy and rigid apparatus that did not survive the collapse of the Soviet Union, with serious consequences for the many Finnish firms that had grown reliant on a virtually captive market for their goods.

A faltering economy and continuing political instability made the 1970s a difficult decade for Finland. The social welfare programmes embarked upon in the 1960s began to come under strain as successive governments battled with inflationary costs. The price and incomes package, to which was also tied a range of social policy measures and benefits, which employers and a reinvigorated (and reunited) trades union movement reached in 1969 under the auspices of the national arbitrator Keijo Liinamaa, was remarkably successful in the short term, but set a benchmark which negotiators in the far more choppy waters of the recession of the late 1970s found impossible to reach. Parliament's frankly irresponsible action in voting for an extravagantly expensive financial package to fund the pensions scheme helped bring down the minority Paasio government in 1972, and posed severe problems for its successor. President Kekkonen intervened actively behind the scenes, even personally attending a committee meeting of his old party, the Agrarian Union (since 1965, the Centre Party), where he made it plain that if the party continued to support the inflationary pensions package it would serious weaken its chances of being a party of government for some time to come. Throughout his political career, Kekkonen developed to a fine art the writing of pseudonymous articles, a tactic he used to good effect to criticise parliament for its extravagance and government for its inability to deal firmly with the growing economic crisis. In 1974, inflation was running at around 2 per cent a month, whilst the trade deficit grew to threatening proportions (around 10 per cent share of GNP). As in previous decades, the standard response of government was devaluation, which a growing number of Finnish economists claimed merely reinforced a cyclical pattern which in the long term was harmful to development.

Economic problems were the root cause of disagreement, which saw a return in the 1970s to the formation of non-party governments, the classic sign of political impasse that had characterised Kekkonen's first term of office. The foreign policy of the Paasikivi–Kekkonen line now commanded the full support of all the major parties. The most tenacious of the dissidents had been pushed to the political margins. Veikko Vennamo, the one long-term opponent of Kekkonen who did manage to keep the president awake at night, owed his success more to his astute creation of a personal following and his ability to appeal to sections of the populace who truly believed they were 'the forgotten people' than to his views of Finnish foreign policy.[4] The 'protest politics' of the seventies arose from the processes of social and economic transformation in Finland, and the world at large. They proved to be less damaging to the established party political structure in Finland than they were in other Scandinavian countries, most notably, Denmark; the eighteen seats won by Vennamo's Rural Party in the elections of 1970 and 1972 was a high-water mark from which the tide of discontent rapidly ebbed.

The established parties have, however, been themselves a source of political instability, largely as a result of personal rivalries and a frequent lack of party discipline, which has led to occasions when the parliamentary party has taken a completely contrary line to that of the party's members in government. The left-wing People's Democratic Union (SKDL), of which the Communist Party constituted the core, was the most notorious, but not the only culprit in this respect. Government coalitions were often badly divided over key issues, such as the free trade agreement with the EEC, which the communists consistently opposed, or regional policy, which caused many bitter disputes between the Centre Party and the social democrats. The tendency towards centre-left coalitions, which included representatives of the reformist wing of the SKDL for twelve of the sixteen years between 1966 and 1982, facilitated the realisation of social policies of the kind adumbrated by the social democrat Pekka Kuusi in his important blueprint study, *60-luvun sosiaalipolitiikka* (*Social Policy for the Sixties*, 1961), but it can hardly be said to have generated the kind of socialist thinking or activity that was taking place in contemporary Sweden or France, for example.

Finland's experience of the wave of new-left thinking that affected much of western Europe in the sixties and seventies was rather unusual. The significant shift to the left amongst students in higher education has been seen as a belated encounter between intellectuals and the working-class movement, a final reconciliation some half-century after a bitterly divisive civil war, even a tacit acknowledgement that Finland was no longer an agrarian land, but one dependent on industry for national prosperity.[5] Reconciliation, an acceptance of communists as members of the national community by the intelligentsia, was, however, far more important than any revolution of ideas, or indeed any serious willingness to imbibe new currents of thought (that only occurred in the 1990s, as the radical left began to shrivel as a political force). The inward-looking and obsessive concern with Finland and Finnishness was shaken, but in all its essentials, remained untouched by the radicalism of the sixties and seventies. It can be argued that it was actually reinforced by the frequently reiterated call to preserve good relations with the Soviet Union, a mantra that the young generation, even within the conservative *Kokoomus* party, made their own. Loyalty to the Paasikivi–Kekkonen line became, in other words, a kind of patriotic duty. Obedience to higher authority, preached for centuries from the pulpit by Lutheran clergymen who functioned as the vital link between central government and the people, a system of government developed during the nineteenth century which established a practice in which laws and decrees were handed down from on high and administered by officialdom, meant that contesting the power and authority of the state and its agents was not undertaken lightly. Acceptance of the authority of the state was the unspoken assumption that lay behind demands for national solidarity after the tragedy of the civil war, as was the vesting of strong executive powers in the presidency in the constitution of 1919. It was the message under-pinning the foreign policy of presidents Paasikivi and Kekkonen. It was the relentless and at times ruthless pursuit of good relations with the Soviet Union, in a country with little tradition of dissent, that allowed a systemic authoritarianism to flourish, and made open criticism of that policy tantamount to an unpatriotic act.

Since the Soviet Union and the FCMA treaty were swept into the rubbish-bin of history in the early nineties, there has been a great deal of agonised self-examination in Finnish intellectual cir-cles of the degree to which the elite, or even the Finnish people as a whole might have been complicit in the censorship of free expres-sion. The fact that, with few exceptions, the intellectuals were unwilling to discuss such questions before 1990 adds a whiff of uneasy conscience to the whole debate, which may be construed as a public act of penance or an attempt to seek forgiveness *ex post facto* so that Finland may be fully accepted into the European club, as one participator in the discussion has observed.

The recent past is certainly littered with examples of fatuous and embarrassing statements. One of the most notorious was the pro-posal made by the chairman of the Centre Party parliamentary group in November 1974 that the ending of the war between Finland and the Soviet Union on 19 September 1944 be recognised alongside Independence Day as 'our second national day of com-memoration, as the independence day of the second republic'.[6] Self-censorship did not lack its defenders, either: it was held to reflect a proper understanding of the wisdom of Finnish foreign policy.

The degree to which self-censorship was exercised or imposed remains a matter of debate. State control of or interference with freedom of expression has a long history in Finland, stretching back to the establishment of a national censor's office in the late seven-teenth century. The 1919 constitution guaranteed freedom of assembly, association, and expression, but an amendment to the criminal law code making it a crime to publish and disseminate material derogatory of the government and the established legal order gave the authorities powers to control the left-wing press. The law was tightened still further in 1930, and for a brief period,

Plate 36 Finnish communism, old-style, new-style. The traditional May
Day demonstrations of the Finnish Communist Party acquired a more
colourful and youthful tone during the late 1960s, as radicalised students
began to join the party. There is a striking contrast in this photograph,
taken in Helsinki in 1969, between the grim-faced, drably dressed party
veterans with their time-worn banners and slogans, and the lively, rather
disorderly students with their distinctly different slogans. Unlike their
counterparts elsewhere in Europe, who were drawn to libertarian or
Trotskyite movements, Finnish students with leftist inclinations tended to
align themselves with the Stalinist minority of the Communist Party. This
has been seen rather as an alliance of necessity than a coming together of
like-minded people; but it can also be argued that a desire for security and a
need for authority may have impelled these youthful, mostly middle-class
radicals towards a rigidly orthodox hard-line communism.

was also directed against articles that belittled or mocked national institutions and monuments. In 1948, publishing comment that might damage Finland's relations with foreign powers was made a criminal offence, something described by a British foreign office official as 'deplorable. . . an interference with the freedom of the press [that] has been placed on the statute book solely to protect the Soviet Union against criticism. . . the government will no doubt only act if criticism is directed against more sensitive states than the western democracies daily subjected to abuse by the communist press'. To this might be added an evident willingness of officialdom to show compliance with, or even to anticipate, the wishes of Finland's great eastern neighbour. The sending of a circular to the country's university libraries by the ministry of justice in the autumn of 1944, asking that all works deemed to be anti-Soviet be removed from open access to the public, was an early example of this. Publishing houses also came under pressure not to publish works that might cause offence in Moscow. The socialist-controlled firm of Tammi pulped the potentially damaging memoirs of Yrjö Leino, the communist minister of the interior in the late 1940s, after the government made it be known that this might jeopardise Finland's relations with the Soviet Union, and was persuaded not to publish Solzhenitsyn's *Gulag Archipelago* in 1974.

Against all this must be set the fact that the Soviet press found plenty to complain about, even during the 1970s, a period now generally regarded by Finns as the nadir of self-abasement. On one famous occasion in the early 1970s, the president himself threatened the editor of a weekly magazine with prosecution under the 1948 legislation after the Soviet ambassador had complained about articles that spilled the beans on Suslov's role in inciting the Finnish communists to stage strikes. The media was perhaps not as 'silenced' as Esko Salminen's book of that title would suggest (and indeed as he implicitly recognises in the many examples he gives of writers critical of self-censorship). What is perhaps more worrying is the point made in 1975 by the artist Carl-Gustaf Lilius. Writing in a Finnish journal, Lilius argued that self-censorship was a way of hiding from reality, of forgetting the existence of the Soviet Union. In other words, it could become a cosy blanket, cocooning the Finnish people from the nastiness of the big bad world outside.

There was an unwillingness or inability to ask awkward questions during the last months of Kekkonen's presidency, when the failing mental health of the octogenarian head of state became increasingly and embarrassingly obvious. Politicians and the media studiously refrained from comment, thereby allowing a rich crop of sometimes cruel jokes to flourish: where the media is silent, the people have other means of expressing opinion, as any study of the political jokes of the Soviet era shows. Kekkonen's withdrawal from public life did not bring to a close the Soviet–Finnish relationship. His successor may have been perceived as the antithesis to a politically compromised manipulator, but he continued to operate the system of working through trusted agents to influence Moscow, and to adhere to the principles of the Paasikivi–Kekkonen line.

In spite of his faults, Urho Kekkonen was closely attuned to his times. Unlike his irascible predecessor, he was less given to administering public dressings-down and more willing to encourage his fellow-citizens to engage in open debate about their past. He was also a man of the people, approachable and affable, in sharp contrast to the stiff figures of the Soviet leadership, distant and remote in the Kremlin fortress or in their speeding limousines. During his long term of office, Finland became an affluent country, with an extensive social welfare system, and a greatly expanded range of activities in which its citizens could freely engage, from mass tourism to becoming a Jehovah's Witness (activities which their Soviet counterparts could not enjoy). Urho Kekkonen, the son of a small farmer, ardent pure Finnish nationalist in his youth, the embodiment of 'cold reason' in post-war foreign policy, presided over a period of unprecedented change that was to lead Finland into a radically different world of urban, even cosmopolitan values.

8

From nation state to Eurostate

Urho Kekkonen's successor as president was the social democrat Mauno Koivisto. A war veteran, Koivisto had made a name for himself in the early 1950s as a determined and active opponent of communist influence in the trade union movement in his home town of Turku, before moving to the capital in 1958 to become director of the Helsinki workers' savings bank. Minister of finance in the centre-left Paasio government (1966–68) and prime minister from 1968 to 1970, Koivisto managed to preserve his reputation during the next decade, when many other aspiring candidates for the presidency were coming to grief, by staying out of active politics as head of the bank of Finland. Appointed prime minister for a second time in May 1979, and riding high in the public opinion polls as the man favoured by the electorate to become the next president, Koivisto further strengthened his position and prestige in the country by countering Kekkonen's veiled ultimatum in April 1981 that he sort out delays and confusion in government business or resign with the argument that he still commanded majority support in parliament. Kekkonen's resignation at the end of October on the grounds of ill health gave Koivisto the added advantage of being able to enter the presidential campaign as acting president. Of the eight candidates, Koivisto was the clear favourite of the voters, who turned out in record numbers (an astonishing 87 per cent of the electorate). With 43 per cent of the popular vote, and the support of the reformist communists, he was elected president on the first ballot in the electoral college.

Koivisto's election can be seen as a public rejection of the old political order, though in truth, that order was already showing signs of wear and tear. Ahti Karjalainen, for so long the president-in-waiting (and still favoured by Moscow), failed to gain the endorsement of the Centre Party, whose members preferred his long-time rival Johannes Virolainen as their candidate. The reformist communist leadership had already privately agreed to back Koivisto in the decisive ballot, thus breaking the agrarian/centre–communist/SKDL axis that had operated since the 1950s. A further sign of shifting winds was the ditching of the communists from government at the end of 1982, after a majority of the SKDL parliamentary group opposed a defence item in the budget unanimously approved by government. Hitherto, such dissent had been tolerated in order not to cause trouble with Moscow. Now, it was deemed no longer necessary. The loss of seven seats in the 1983 elections marked the end of the communists as a major political force in Finland. From the high point of the immediate post-war years, when it had regularly commanded the support of between a fifth and a quarter of the electorate, the SKDL dwindled to the status of a minor party, winning only nineteen seats in its reincarnated form as the Union of the Left in the 1991 elections. Another indication of how times had changed was the inclusion of representatives of the Finnish Rural Party (*Suomen maaseudunpuolue*) in government after that party's electoral success in 1983. Veikko Vennamo, the leader of the Rural Party, had been one of Kekkonen's most vociferous opponents, and his claim to speak for the 'forgotten people' of Finland had long rankled with his former colleagues of the Agrarian Union, now anxiously seeking to establish a solid urban following as the Centre Party. The loosening of the political framework of the Kekkonen era was also evident in the return of the conservatives to office in 1987, after two decades in opposition, and the formation of a coalition with the social democrats.

This rearranging of the political furniture was made easier by the lessening of pressure from Moscow, where the wind of change was also blowing. In his dealings with the Soviet Union, however, Koivisto maintained continuity, even in the use of the channels of communication that his predecessor had built up. The FCMA treaty was extended for a further twenty years in 1983, and the careful phraseology of firm and friendly relations remained in place. In difficult situations, such as the accidental landing of a Soviet missile on Finnish territory close to the Norwegian border at the end of 1984, or the Chernobyl nuclear power station disaster of 1986, the Finnish government refrained from issuing statements that might upset or annoy their eastern neighbour. Koivisto's support for Kekkonen's old proposal of a Nordic nuclear-free zone was largely rhetorical; in practice, he did nothing to push the idea. Intensive discussions of this proposal, however, may have helped dispel much of the mistrust of Finnish intentions in the Scandinavian countries.[1] Finland becoming a full member of EFTA in 1985 also helped bring the northern countries closer together.

President Koivisto established a good working relationship with Mikhail Gorbachev and George Bush, and played a useful role as mediator in the final stages of the cold war. Finland's official policy in the face of the impending breakup of the Soviet Union remained cautious, though considerable assistance and support was given unofficially to leading figures in the movement for independence in neighbouring Estonia. The seemingly passive and non-committal stance of the Finnish government towards the aspirations of the Baltic states contrasted sharply with the more enthusiastic support offered by the Scandinavians, and gave rise to criticism. Koivisto, whose tolerance of the media was at best limited, was angered by reports carried by Yleisradio, the Finnish broadcasting corporation, that seemed to cast doubt on the viability of the Soviet Union and even challenged the Finnish government to adopt a bolder policy towards the Baltic states. Prime Minister Harri Holkeri and Foreign Minister Pertti Paasio were sternly, if somewhat obliquely enjoined (Koivisto was renowned for his convoluted prose) to stay out of any Nordic Council commitment to the Baltic cause, and the Baltic leaders themselves were publicly advised to moderate their impetuous dash for freedom and to take a leaf out of the Finnish book in their future dealings with the men in the Kremlin.

The Finnish government remained faithful to the policy of saying nothing that might be construed as detrimental or hostile to the Soviet Union right up until the final moment. Paavo Väyrynen, the foreign minister in the centre-right Aho government that took office in spring 1991, was unable to join his Nordic colleagues in issuing a strong denunciation of the coup that took place in Moscow in August 1991, and the Danish foreign minister, Uffe Elleman-Jensen, made sure that the press knew that the Finns were responsible for the final cautiously worded statement issued by the Nordic foreign ministers' meeting. Once the coup had failed, and the breakup of the Soviet Union became inevitable, however, the Finnish government was swift to act. The government's foreign affairs committee took up the idea advanced by the foreign ministry of a simple resumption of relations with the three Baltic states, whose loss of independence the Finns had never formally recognised, and as early as 3 September 1991, the prime minister himself publicly announced that his government had begun to weigh up the pros and cons of applying for membership of the European Community.

The Finnish government had already declared in September 1990 that German reunification now weakened the relevance of many of the military provisions of the Paris peace treaty. The dismantling of the Soviet Union a year later also made the 1948 FCMA treaty redundant, and it was replaced in January 1992 with a series of simple political and economic agreements between Finland and Russia. The disappearance of the FCMA treaty, upon which much of Kekkonen's presidential powers has rested, and the prominent part played by the government during the final days of the Soviet Union, were significant stages in the process which has brought about a decisive shift in the balance of power between president and government, as we shall see.

These momentous events on Finland's borders unfolded against the background of a particularly severe economic recession. Output declined sharply, firms began to fold as trade slumped, and the banking system had to be rescued by massive state intervention. Unemployment rose to unprecedented levels, reaching a peak figure of 17 per cent in 1993. Curiously, the state of the Finnish economy did not dominate discussion over Finland's possible membership of the European Community; that debate centred largely upon questions of national identity, brought to the fore with the demise of the Soviet Union. The uncertainties and anxieties attendant upon that collapse, fuelled by daily press stories about the flow of refugees, drugs, prostitutes, and organised crime across Finland's borders, made security an issue, though Finnish political opinion has preferred to look to European union and regional co-operation rather than NATO as the means of resolving it. More importantly, the disappearance of the Soviet Union brought to an abrupt end an era in which the necessity of good relations with the powerful eastern neighbour had become a virtual mantra for much of the Finnish elite. What had been projected as a policy based on the recognition of harsh reality could in fact be traced back to the nineteenth century, when the Finnish nationalist leaders denounced those who still hankered after the old connections. A profound sense of historical determinism, drawn from the teachings of Hegel, underpinned the nationalist doctrine expounded by Snellman and Yrjö Koskinen. Small nations could expect no favours from history, and flying in the face of the harsh realities of power politics would bring only disaster. The nation could only survive if it was internally strong and united, with one language and culture; there was no place for cosmopolitan liberalism or individualism. The advancement of an internal unity based upon the hegemony of the Finnish language and culture was also closely linked to Finland's relationship with Russia; maintaining good lines of communication to those with power and influence in St Petersburg became an integral element in the process of nation-building. It was the neglect of these precepts that was at the root of all Finland's troubles in the crisis months of 1939, in Paasikivi's view, and his post-war policy, continued and developed by his successor, was meant to restore a sense of cold realism as the guideline for the nation's destiny.

The sudden dissolution of the web of constraints that had held Finland at a distance from the process of European integration, and the subsequent heated debate on finlandisation, offered powerful emotive arguments to the supporters of Finnish membership of the European Community. As an earlier opponent of closer Finnish involvement with the process of economic integration, the social democrat Paavo Lipponen, declared in 1994, Finland 'would finally achieve an equal status in western Europe after all the talk of finlandisation', and as a nation, it would acquire a western European 'maturity' by joining the European Community. For the conservative Pertti Salolainen, who played a key role as minister for foreign trade in negotiations in Brussels, membership of the Community would make a European identity a fundamental part of Finnish foreign policy. Supporters of membership also argued that any delay would be highly damaging to Finland's image, for if Finland failed to join Sweden and Austria in applying, it would have to join the queue with the former socialist countries of eastern Europe at a later stage. For so long left outside the great debates on European unity, partly because of its peculiar wartime trajectory, but also because of the overriding need to make terms with the USSR, Finland came late to integration, and with all the wild enthusiasm of the neophyte, the political and intellectual elite hailed Europe as the new focus for the nation's identity.

One of the ironies of the situation in March 1992, when a majority of the members of the *eduskunta* voted in favour of applying to join the Community, was that opposition to membership was strongest in the Centre Party, which was the cornerstone of the coalition government. In trying to win over his party, the prime minister, Esko Aho, adopted a cautious step-at-a-time approach, though his veiled threat of resignation during the debate in parliament on the membership application was enough to crush opposition and secure a comfortable majority. The foreign minister, Paavo Väyrynen, was lukewarm at best, and eventually resigned from government, ostensibly to pursue his presidential ambitions. Väyrynen was one of a number of politicians who had grown up and become closely identified with the foreign policy line of the Kekkonen years and who were unwilling to abandon the principles underlying that policy. They condemned the 'westernisers' for their obsession with catching the train without any real regard for where it might lead the country, they were critical of the attempts to equate membership of an association of twelve states with becoming European, and worried that, in trying to escape from what in many eyes was seen as a tainted recent past, the 'westernisers' would diminish or even destroy Finland's independence. Membership of the Community would rule out neutrality, which, its defenders claimed, had served Finland well in its relationship with the Soviet Union and the rest of the world.

The debate had a number of twists and turns, not least the belated attempt of Väyrynen to develop the idea of an alternative Nordic community. Agreement on a transition package which the Aho government felt able to recommend to parliament helped strengthen the economic arguments for entry, though it did little to assuage the fears of the dwindling numbers of small farmers, who were amongst the fiercest opponents of Finnish accession. Finland, along with Sweden and Austria (but not Norway, whose citizens once more rejected membership), voted 'yes' by a clear majority in the referendum held on 16 October 1994 (56.9 per cent for, 43.1 per cent against membership, on a turnout of 74 per cent). The under-forties, and the urban middle classes of southern Finland were strongly represented in the 'yes' camp; the older age groups and the rural population, especially in the northern and eastern regions, tended to vote 'no'.

Finland joined the European Union in January 1995, under the presidency of Martti Ahtisaari. An experienced diplomat who made his name as UN commissioner and special representative in Namibia, Ahtisaari had never held elected office, and his choice as the candidate of the Social Democratic Party reflects an awareness of how deeply the public distrusted politicians in the post-Kekkonen years and in the immediate aftermath of the banking crisis (the popular perception being that the politicians had rescued the banks at the public's expense). Ahtisaari was the first person to be elected president by direct ballot, defeating another relatively 'new face', the Swedish People's Party candidate Elisabeth Rehn, in the second round.

Finland's accession to the European Union highlighted the tricky question of the exact relationship between president and government. Ahtisaari made it clear that he intended to maintain presidential control over security and foreign affairs, and would represent Finland at major EU meetings. This brought him into conflict with the prime minister, Esko Aho: a clash of wills that reached crisis point over the question of who should represent Finland at the dinner table. Ahtisaari insisted on being the sole representative of Finland at the Corfu meeting, but later agreed to the 'two plates' principle at future EU summit dinners. Aho and his justice minister, Anneli Jäätteenmäki, then worked through parliament and its constitutional committee to bring about change, by transferring to the government the right to decide who represented Finland at EU meetings. Ahtisaari complained of a coup without legislation, thereby calling the bluff of his opponents. The situation remained unclear until the introduction of a new constitution in 2000, which removed matters relating to the EU from the presidential area of competence.

The constitution of 1919 had placed executive powers very firmly in the hands of the president, and much of the constitutional reform that had been first seriously aired in the 1970s and effected during Koivisto's presidency was intended to redress the balance in favour of the Council of State (the official title of the Finnish government). Constitutional amendments in 1987 and 1991 decreed that members of the Council of State had to enjoy the confidence of parliament, and although the president retained the right to appoint the government, he was to have due regard to the views of the party groupings in parliament. Governments or individual ministers could only be dismissed if they no longer enjoyed the confidence of parliament, or at the specific request of the prime minister. Parliament could only be prematurely dissolved on the recommendation of the prime minister, and after consultations with the speaker and the parliamentary parties. The 1991 reforms also limited the period of office for the president to two terms, and instituted direct elections on the French model.

Foreign affairs remained, however, the presidential prerogative, and the president also retained considerable powers of initiative and control over the legislative process. The new constitutional act, however, has shifted the balance quite strongly towards parliament and government. Legislative powers now reside firmly in parliament. The presidential veto on legislation, which until 1987 could only be overturned by a new parliament, has virtually disappeared: any bill returned to parliament by the president for further consideration can be readopted and passed without delay. The constitution stipulates that discussions about the composition and programme of the government are conducted by the parties in parliament. On the basis of these negotiations, and having consulted with the speaker of the house, the president announces the nominee for the post of prime minister, whom the *eduskunta* has to elect. The president appoints the person elected to office, and also appoints the ministers recommended by the prime minister. The president retains powers of appointment to most of the high offices of the land, and is still the acting supreme commander of the armed forces. The direction of foreign affairs is still exercised by the president, now in co-operation with the Council of State, a division of responsibilities that has posed problems of protocol and practice.

The constitution which the newly elected parliament approved by the requisite two-thirds majority in March 1999 came into force a year later on the day that Tarja Halonen, the eleventh president of the republic, took office. Much of the impetus for constitutional change was undoubtedly occasioned by Kekkonen's excessive use of presidential power, though it can also be argued that the shift towards a parliamentary regime was a long-term goal of the Social Democratic Party which established itself as a major player in Finnish politics during the post-Kekkonen years. Koivisto, Ahtisaari, and Halonen, who had served as foreign minister in the Lipponen government during the 1990s, were all successful presidential candidates of the Social Democratic Party, which was also a major component of government for all but four years between 1982 and 2003.

Halonen's victory in the presidential elections of 2000 also marked a significant shift in the political gender balance. The presidential elections of 2000 were in fact something of a breakthrough in that four of the seven candidates were women. Finnish women were the first in Europe to be granted full and equal suffrage rights, and nineteen were elected to the first *eduskunta* in 1907. That number did not significantly increase during the next fifty-odd years, and only began to grow during the last quarter of the twentieth century. Since 1987, women have become slightly more active in voting in parliamentary elections than men, the margin of difference rising to almost 4 per cent in the 2003 election. Few women actually got to serve in government until the 1990s, and the premiership of Anneli Jäätteenmäki after the Centre Party victory in the 2003 elections proved to be of short duration as she was forced to resign because of allegations of leaking information intended to discredit her opponents. In politics, as in many other echelons of public life, women continue to be disproportionately under-represented at the highest levels.

The Finnish administrative system has also undergone a radical overhaul in the past few decades. The shift towards a ministerial system since the war tended to undermine the position of the

Map 5 Finland at the beginning of the twenty-first century.

central administrative boards, even though the number of these boards increased, especially between 1965 and 1973. There was also an upsurge in the number of offices alongside the national boards, covering everything from film classification to film archives, and embracing a wide range of research institutes, from peace to wild game. Spending on public services rose from under 30 per cent of GDP in the early 1960s to 40 per cent in 1985. The conservative–social democratic coalition government led by Harri Holkeri set in train measures to reduce expenditure, mostly through streamlining and rationalisation to overcome overlapping between ministries and boards. Many boards have been made responsible for their own budgeting, or have been turned into state-owned joint stock companies, such as post and telecommunications and the railways. The old boards have however re-emerged under different guises, and a plethora of new offices have also been created. The one-tier system has, in effect, replaced overlapping with a vast number of offices which now occupy space between the ministries and regional administrative authorities.

In 1996, the eleven mainland counties were reduced to five: Oulu, Lapland, south, west, and east Finland. This was a top-down rationalisation intended to save money, criticised at the time for destroying regional identity and subordinating the regions to central administration. Central administration does in fact exercise strong control over the counties. County governors are appointed by the president, and are subordinated administratively to the ministry of the interior, and each relevant ministry sets targets and monitors their implementation through the provincial state offices.

These reforms, in many respects similar in pattern and intention to those being carried out elsewhere in Europe, took place against a background of rapid social transformation. Only a small fraction of the population now earns a living from farming and forestry, which for decades was the lifeblood of the Finnish economy and still employed a fifth of the working population in 1970. Fewer than one in three Finns lived in a town fifty years ago; now, fewer than one in three live in the countryside. There has been a marked drift of population away from the northern and eastern peripheries to the southern towns, especially the capital, which has mushroomed from the medium-sized city surrounded by forests, as portrayed by the

Plate 37 A new settler farmstead in the early 1950s. Finland lost slightly more than one-tenth of its cultivated land area to the Soviet Union by the terms of the armistice in 1944. It also had to settle over four hundred thousand refugees from the lost territories. To this end, some 2,781,366 hectares of land, half of it state-owned, was requisitioned (around a quarter of the total through compulsory purchase) and used to provide land for housing and farming. A proportion of this land went to those who had fought in the war and their families, but most was for the resettlement of refugees, such as the family portrayed here, originally from Koivisto in the Karelian isthmus, and relocated at Askola in southern Finland. The house is typical of those erected across Finland during the 1950s, a compact family home built to a standard design. The way that the children are playing at ploughing indicates that the horse was still the principal means of traction for most small farmers. For a good ten years after the war, the number of horses on the land averaged around 350,000: by 1976, that number had dwindled to 33,000. The decline in the numbers of those earning a living from the land has been almost as dramatic. There are now only around a hundred thousand Finns who make a living from the land; fifty years ago, it was over a million.

Plate 38 Log-cabin consumerism: the Helsinki trade fair, 1958. The summer cottage by the shore has become a 'must-have' for most Finns, and increasingly, foreign visitors. In proportion as those farming the land have dwindled, so has the number of summer cottages mushroomed, from around forty thousand in 1950 to ten times that number in 2000.

A purpose-built log cabin of the kind displayed here would probably have been beyond the reach of most Finns in 1958; the industry only began to take off in the late sixties or early seventies. Most Finns in the late 1950s would, however, have had ready access to accommodation in the countryside; there would have been few town-dwellers without relatives down on the farm, and very many (especially women) were in any event only recently departed from the land.

poet Pentti Saarikoski in the 1960s, to a metropolis of over a million people. In common with other advanced economies, Finland is facing the problems of an ageing population, though it has so far relied far less on immigrant labour to plug gaps in the labour market.

The transformation of a largely rural, agrarian country whose citizens lived a frugal and often isolated existence on the northern periphery of a divided Europe into an affluent post-industrial land of instant communication (the Nokia mobile telephone has become almost a symbol of national identity) and active European inter-change owes much to resourcefulness and resilience, and above all, to enlightened education policies and the careful nurturing of Finland's most valuable asset, human capital. This is not to say that the

trajectory of economic growth has been without hitches and difficulties. Fiscal and economic policies have at times been downright
detrimental to progress. Although Finland benefited from the general post-war boom, the economy throughout the fifties and well
into the sixties was constricted by tight regulation and government
controls. The gradual freeing of trade from restrictions in the sixties
brought greater diversity, lessening Finland's heavy dependence in
foreign trade on the products of the forest, but this was not accompanied by any significant change in monetary policy. The main
instrument of control at the bank of Finland's disposal was ration-
ing, in the form of tight credit controls and restrictions in the
money supply. The favoured method of keeping Finnish exports
competitive was devaluation; the mark was devalued twelve times
between 1947 and 1987. This, if anything, tended to reinforce the
rather jerky nature of economic growth in Finland, where severe
recessions, for instance, in 1957, 1975, and the early 1990s, have
been followed by equally rapid upsurges thereafter.

The state has traditionally played a central role in the economy,
and in spite of the general shift in favour of privatisation, is still a
major shareholder or even outright owner of a number of big
Finnish enterprises. It was closely involved in the hammering out
of incomes policy, which from the late sixties onwards, was linked
to social welfare provisions. The resettlement of the refugees from
Karelia during the war years was perhaps the single most important
act of state intervention, increasing the number of farms, and
actually diminishing the average size of the farmholding in Finland.
In general, it is well-organised interest groups – business, banking,
the unions, and the farmers' central organisation, MTK – which
have largely determined the direction of the economy. Parliament
was not a forum for serious debate and decision-making on matters
of economic policy during the post-war decades, and the representatives of the people were for the most part left outside this process.

The essentially corporatist structure that directed the Finnish
economy (and with it, provided the guidelines for social policy as
well) creaked and groaned on numerous occasions, but in general,
it encountered little in the way of sustained criticism. This may be
partly attributed to the undeniable fact that it was seen to be
delivering not only economic growth, but also benefits, whether

in the form of social welfare payments, the growth in job opportunities in the services sector, or subsidies and guaranteed incomes to
farmers. In coming together each year to hammer out a stabilisation
policy, the business leaders, trade union bosses, and spokesmen for
the agricultural lobby were seen to represent more than mere sec-
tional interest, even if their claims and grievances made settlement a
contentious and difficult matter. They could legitimately claim to
be acting alongside the state, in the person of its chief arbitrator, on
behalf of the nation. For the trade unions, which had been badly
divided by internal strife in the 1940s and 1950s, participation in
the formation of a national and comprehensive incomes policy
afforded an opportunity for consolidation and growth. The new
central organisation of the Finnish trade unions that reunited the
two rival groupings at the end of the 1960s, grew from around
600,000 members to over a million at the end of the century. The
two other confederations for white-collar and professional workers
experienced even more spectacular growth, and together now
represent a further million workers, giving Finland one of the highest rates of trade union membership in Europe. The unions have
rarely agreed wholeheartedly to the decisions arrived at, which
have often become badly eroded by new wage demands and inflationary pressures, but their involvement has been an important step
along the road towards complete integration of a significant element of society that had been stigmatised by the civil war, and has
further strengthened the strong consensual tendencies that flow
through the Finnish body politic.

A more cynical view would be that the union bosses, in the
seventies and eighties, joined the elite that runs the country and
makes the really important decisions at sauna sessions or in the
private rooms of certain restaurants. A survey of the appointments
to the management boards of key institutions such as the bank of
Finland would indeed tend to give some credence to this notion. As
long as Finland continued to experience economic growth, affluence and security, however, the Finnish public at large seemed
disposed to accept the consensual management of their affairs,
and to trust those in power. What happened in the early 1990s,
however, severely shook that confidence, and the reverberations
continued to echo throughout the decade.

The 1980s was a decade of unprecedented growth, especially in productivity. The big rise in domestic demand sucked in imports, and threatened to create a net indebtedness as large as in the mid-1970s, when the trade deficit had grown to almost 10 per cent of GDP. The eighties also saw a general dismantling of restrictions on the money markets. In Finland, this was managed rather poorly, with the result that cheap money helped push up prices of stocks and shares and property. Caught up in a frenetic competition for business, the banks lent beyond their resources, and were badly burnt when recession began to bite. Recession coincided with the collapse of the Soviet Union. The sudden ending of bilateral trade, which had helped sustain labour-intensive industries producing consumer goods for the Soviet market, made the recession far worse, ruining many businesses and forcing up levels of unemployment to unprecedented levels. Total output fell by over 6 per cent between 1900 and 1991, trade with Britain and Sweden fell by over 10 per cent, and with the former Soviet Union, by over 70 per cent.

The crisis was made far worse by the ill-considered decision to tie the Finnish mark to the European currency unit, or ecu, in 1991. This rather hasty response to Sweden's decision to join the ecu was meant to protect the mark against speculation, but it failed to do so. Devaluation had long been the favoured weapon of the big exporters, but was now opposed by the leading economists of the bank, and by those who had borrowed heavily abroad. As the crisis deepened, the inexperienced new prime minister of the centre–right coalition, Esko Aho, tried the old trusted tactic of consensual agreement, but soon discovered that it no longer worked. Negotiations on Aho's proposed social contract were torpedoed by growing demands for devaluation, and irreconcilable differences between unions and industry. By the autumn, a flight of capital had begun and the bank of Finland had been forced to intervene by raising short-term rates of interest, and finally by moving the exchange rate band up 14 per cent against the ecu, in effect, devaluing the mark by 12 per cent. In the meantime, the government had proceeded with its plans for an across-the-board package of cuts that might diminish the need for an even fiercer devaluation. The threat of the imminent collapse of the mark was enough to persuade the union leaders to go along with such a programme, the drafting of which was entrusted to the veteran social democrat leader, Kalevi Sorsa. Sorsa's proposals would have cut 7 per cent off labour costs, largely by shifting pensions payments from employers to wage-earners. The unions initially seemed prepared to swallow this; but in the end, neither of the two main unions, representing workers in key export sectors, engineering and paper, were willing to go along with a deal, fearing that a swingeing devaluation would still follow. Faced with stiff resistance and the threat of a general strike, the government was obliged to retreat.

The state of public finances on the eve of the crash was good; the budget was in surplus, and national debt low by international comparison. By 1992, however, the budget deficit was seventy-two billion marks, nearly 15 per cent of GDP, because of falling revenues and rapidly increasing expenditure. Forcing through the necessary savings cuts was made easier by replacing the two-thirds majority principle by a simple majority vote in parliament for fiscal measures. Politicians also took refuge behind their officials, who laid out unpopular proposals in their memoranda and reports, and in general, tried to apply the principle of equal misery for all. A series of savings packages, at roughly six-month intervals, were implemented right up to 1994. Estimated in total at between thirty-five and fifty billion marks, these were mostly in the form of cuts in grants to local authorities, reductions in allowances, an upward revision of the tax bands, and increased social security contributions from employers and employees alike. Efforts to make unemployment benefits no longer earnings-related had to be abandoned, however, in the face of union opposition and the threat of a general strike.

These measures severely tested the limits of solidarity and consensus, but what really incensed the public was the way in which the banking system was rescued from disaster. A large number of savings banks had been drawn into what the public termed the 'casino economy' of the late 1980s, when the stock exchange index tripled and housing prices doubled, and were to find themselves in deep trouble when the share index started to fall and interest rates began to rise in 1989. One of the biggest of the savings banks, SKOP, began to flounder in 1990, but not until it finally had to be rescued by the bank of Finland in autumn 1991 did the extent of the crisis become known. Dozens more small local or regional savings banks declared their inability to meet their liabilities. The initial proposal of an eight-billion mark rescue package made by the working group set up to mount a salvage operation turned out to be a gross underestimate; over forty billion marks were eventually needed to rescue the banks. This costly rescue operation may have helped restore international confidence in Finnish financial institutions, but it caused deep resentment in the public at large, forced to bear the burden of cuts in services and real earnings, and faced with mounting unemployment. A number of claims for compensation came before the courts, but many of the much-vilified *rötösherrat* (a highly expressive epithet, which combines elements of the bounder and the rogue) got off lightly or escaped altogether. In one famous case, a former chairman of the Social Democratic Party who had been made chief executive of the workers' savings bank was found liable to pay twenty-five million marks in compensation, but managed not only to have the sum reduced on appeal, but also to make a deal to pay just over a million. This deal was approved by a junior finance minister from the Social Democratic Party, who was subsequently forced to resign when questions were asked in parliament.

The Finnish economy emerged remarkably well from the crisis. Exports doubled in volume within seven years, total output grew with a far smaller labour force, and there were quite profound structural changes. The growth of the electronic equipment industry has been nothing less than spectacular, with a surge in exports throughout the second half of the nineties that challenged the long dominance of the wood and paper industries. Big business and industry have become fully integrated into the global market; over 60 per cent of the production of the leading Finnish companies is now carried out abroad. A 2003 OECD report singled out for praise the high level of investment in research and development, a healthy financial sector, and an economic growth in the second half of the 1990s double the rate of the OECD as a whole. It also applauded the measures taken to open up the economy through deregulation, whilst pressing the case for further reform, not only in the large and cost-inefficient public sector but also in parts of the private sector as well.

There is also a downside to this successful recovery. Domestic demand took a good deal longer to recover than did the export trade. Unemployment levels remain high; over 400,000 jobs disappeared during the recession. The electronics industry, which has in large measure led the recovery, looks to young people with the requisite skills in its drive for productivity. There is a growing disparity between the areas of dynamic economic growth, located in the southern cities, and the rest of the country. The costs of supporting those out of work, aged, or infirm are disproportionately higher in the rural regions from which the young and able-bodied have migrated in droves during the last three decades. There is also the overhanging threat of a rapidly ageing population: Finland is expected to have the biggest increase of all OECD countries in the number of people over the age of sixty-five in the next two decades; this, coupled with the fact that almost half of those in their fifties are at present officially retired from active employment, presents major problems for public finances. A report published in 2001 by the ministry of finance admitted that current policies would make it difficult for Finland to cope with this burden without further raising the already high tax rate or allowing the national debt to soar once more. Reducing government debt and grappling with the disparities between labour supply and demand were identified as the principal challenges, with a focus on education as 'the backbone for long-term growth' as the best response.

The report also recognised the need for increased labour immigration, though acknowledged the difficulties of attracting labour. In comparison with Sweden, Finland has a very small immigrant workforce, and was indeed a net exporter of labour, largely to Sweden, until the 1980s. In the peak years of 1969 and 1970, some eighty thousand Finns moved to Sweden in search of work, and it has been estimated that up to three-quarters of a million made the short passage across the sea looking for work between 1945 and 1994. Finns make up the largest of Sweden's immigrant communities, although a large number of migrants and their families have subsequently returned to Finland, bringing new skills and making a welcome addition to the labour pool.

The vast majority of these migrants were from rural areas. The abandonment of the land has been one of the most striking and

Plate 39 'A nursery for every block'. This demonstration on the steps of the parliament building in the late sixties highlights one of the many problems caused by the rapidly increasing urban population, the lack of day care for the children of working women. The welfare state in Finland was constructed essentially during the 1970s and 1980s, and many of its provisions have been made in response to social pressures; day care for poignant aspects of the transformation of Finland during the second half of the twentieth century. In 1950, some 1,670,000 people in a population of four million were engaged in farming and forestry; by 2003, that number had dwindled to 120,000 out of a population of five million. The decline is even more dramatic when set against the background of the immediate post-war years. The resettlement policy adopted as a consequence of the war and loss of territory set Finland on a course that was sharply at odds with trends elsewhere in western Europe. By 1969, Finland had reclaimed an extra 14 per cent of cultivated land, more than had been lost to the Soviet Union. It was the only country in western Europe in which the average size of the farmholding diminished after the war, and the number of farms actually continued to increase until the 1960s. The resettlement policy was to a large extent driven by a desire to ensure a regular supply of labour for the forests to replace the floating workforce of lumberjacks and loggers. It was, as the Westermarck committee appointed in 1958 to consider the future options for Finnish agriculture observed, a temporary solution which paid little heed to the long-term consequences. The committee recommended a wholesale rationalisation of agricultural policy, with measures to combat over-production. Its recommendations were supported by the socialists and conservatives, but not the farmers' representatives or the communists, many of whose supporters were small farmers. The agrarian minority government led by Ahti Karjalainen refused to accept the recommendations, insisting instead on strengthening settlement policy;

Caption for Plate 39 (*cont.*)
children, for example, is now an entitlement, with parents paying according to their income and family size. The presence in parliament and government of parties who have traditionally represented certain occupational and/or regional interests has also ensured that people who otherwise have little opportunity to make their needs known, such as farmers' wives, have been able to obtain entitlements. Cutbacks in welfare provision during the 1990s spawned several organisations, including a couple of political parties, to fight for pensioners' interests, and the problem of an ageing population is likely to be one of the most contentious issues facing the generation who has arguably benefited most from the welfare reforms of the 1970s and 1980s.

Plate 40 'Once we got paid for clearing rocks. . .'. On the back of this undated and untitled photograph, someone has scrawled what might be roughly translated as 'Once we got paid for clearing rocks, now fields are put into set-aside'. Sizeable subsidies and premiums were paid in the immediate post-war years to those who brought new land into cultivation. Even when machines can be put to use to uproot stumps, drain bogs, and move rocks, this is back-breaking work; and although yields increased substantially (average wheat yields rose from 1,565 kilogrammes per hectare in 1950 to 2,330 kg/ha. twenty years later, average milk yields/cow rose over the same period from 3,175 kg to 4,400 kg), agricultural output as a percentage of the gross domestic product declined significantly. Set-aside, known in Finland as putting fields into a package, was begun in the early 1970s. Since the peak years of the early 1960s, there has been something like a 20 per cent reduction in the total area of land under cultivation.

Karjalainen even set 600,000 hectares of new land as the target. This would have meant Finland would have almost a million hectares of unnecessary land, according to the Westermarck committee's estimates.

Many of the committee's recommendations were, however, quietly adopted in subsequent years. The resettlement policy gave way during the sixties to a regional development strategy. Less successful in attempts to attract new sources of employment to the peripheral northern and eastern regions, regional development policy has nevertheless built up the infrastructure of communication and services that has helped integrate even the remotest village – and made it easier to leave. Mechanisation greatly reduced the need for labour in the forest and on the land, but there is something to be said also for the view that changes in agriculture were brought about less by chain-saws and tractors than by the farmers' daughters, who chose in their thousands to leave the land rather than become a farmer's wife.

From the late 1960s until Finland's entry into the EU, which imposed new parameters for policy-making, a variety of strategies have been followed in order to modernise and rationalise farming in Finland. Not all have been successful, and most have aroused fierce opposition. In 1968, the basis for taxation was shifted from the land held to real incomes. This increased revenue, but also bore more heavily on the small dairy farm than the big arable farm. The contemporaneous dismantling of the land settlement board that had looked after the interests of the small farmers, and the replacement of income for production with a salary for withdrawing land from cultivation or for sending unwanted dairy cattle to the abattoir were additional blows. The massive migration to Sweden in 1969 and 1970, and the electoral success in the early 1970s of Veikko Vennamo's Rural Party, which claimed to speak for 'the forgotten people', are indicators of how deep was the impact of these changes. The social democratic leader Kalevi Sorsa later admitted that his party in government had failed to understand the mood of desperation in the villages already affected by out-migration. 'A generation of country folk, still in harness, had given their all to clearing and cultivating the fields, something which up to now had always been accorded full honour and glory in Finland. . . Now the value of this labour had been literally reduced to nothing.'

Farming as such has rarely been a full-time occupation for most of those who live on farms in Finland, and it remains for very many a way of life, rather than a way of making a living, even at the beginning of the twenty-first century. Between 1950 and 1990, the number of farms shrank from 465, 655 to 199, 385, whilst the average size rose from 5.2 ha. to 12.7 ha. There has been an even greater decline in the number of farms since Finland joined the EU, and the average size is now around thirty hectares. Around half of these farms are owned by full-time farmers, of whom a third are over fifty-five years of age. Even these full-time farmers rely heavily on income from other sources. Farming and forestry in fact generate only about one-third of the income for the family farm in Finland; pensions, salaried part- or full-time employment for one or both partners, and income from tourism and other activities make up the other two-thirds. Farming families have had to be adaptable in order to survive, but they have also shown a remarkable degree of resilience, as a moral community as well as a workforce, to borrow Ray Abrahams' apposite conclusion.

Much of the distinctiveness of rural life has been lost in the process of modernisation and rationalisation. Methods and patterns of work, the names of different tools and implements, even the dishes prepared and served, all very different from region to region, even fifty years ago, often survive only in memory, village histories, or folk museums. The depopulation of the land has gravely weakened the bonds of sociability and community activity, although the village committee movement, started in the 1970s, has proved very effective in voicing the concerns of the countryside and in stimulating new social or productive activities. The car and electronic communications have replaced the bus service and neighbourhood gossip, and the farming family now lives in the same global village of satellite entertainment as the urban dweller – and expects the same standard of living. The countryside has, of course, attracted incomers, but only during the brief summer months. The number of summer cottages more than quadrupled during the last forty years of the twentieth century, and is now approaching the half-million mark. For many Finns, the summer cottage provides a valuable link to the countryside, and is usually located in an area where there are strong family connections. The lakes and forests are still very much part of the Finnish identity, although like so much else in what was until relatively recently a distinctive, homogenous, and rather closed part of Europe, they have been opened up to a wider world – in the case of the Finnish countryside, to tourism and the tender care of the heritage industry.

The main story of the past fifty years, however, has been of the countryside coming to town, or centres of population. Forty per cent of the total workforce in 1980 were children of farmers, and three-quarters of this number worked in occupations other than farming. A respectable number obtained higher academic qualifications and were employed in high-status jobs, or ran their own businesses; but the majority ended up in the lower echelons of the salariat or as blue-collar workers – the Finnish working class has always recruited heavily from the ranks of those leaving the land. The movement of population to the south has also seriously altered the balance between the two language groups in the immediate environs of the capital and of Turku. Finnish has become the majority language in districts which had been for centuries inhabited mainly by Swedish speakers. This can cause strain and tension across the whole stratum of everyday life, from shopping to the playground. Swedish-speakers in the Helsinki area interviewed in 1977 revealed that there were clear discrepancies between situations in which they might *wish* to use Swedish, for example, whilst in hospital, but in practice refrained from doing so. The interviews also brought to light a complex web of loyalties. Few felt any closeness to Sweden, in spite of the fact that many had relatives there. Language was important, and the great majority made education in a Swedish-language school a priority; but in most other respects, the interviewees shared the same preferences and concerns, and showed the same level of patriotic commitment to being Finnish as their Finnish-speaking fellow-citizens. There is indeed little that marks out most Swedish-speaking Finns from the rest of society, which has made assimilation through the erosion of the linguistic boundary much easier, especially in the cities, where Finnish is the ubiquitous language of everyday discourse, and mixed marriages are common. If anything, there is a greater divergence in attitudes between the bilingual urban majority and the monolingual minority living in rural communities in Ostrobothnia or on the Åland islands (which in any case have their own administrative autonomy) than there is between those who share the same public space in the cities, though recent surveys have detected an increased awareness and willingness to protect the status of Swedish.

Swedish and Finnish remain the two official languages of Finland, and in spite of its relative decline from being the mother-tongue of 10 per cent of the population in 1930 to less than 6 per cent today, Swedish is extremely well represented at all levels of public life. There is provision for education in the language from primary to postgraduate level, Swedish-language radio and television channels, newspapers and journals, theatre, and a wide range of cultural and philanthropic associations. The constitution of 2000 also recognises the right of the autochthonous Sami people, the Roma, and 'other groups' to maintain and develop their language and culture, and the language act of 1991 gives the Sami the right to request a translation or interpretation of official documents or proceedings. The teaching of and in Sami has also been augmented, and there has been a significant revival of interest in the language and culture of the Sami people. In Finland, the Sami minority is largely confined to the far north. Estimates of their number vary between four and six thousand, of whom around a third speak one of the three sub-branches of the language. There are much larger communities in Norway and Sweden, and the general shift towards a more positive and supportive attitude amongst the Nordic governments since the 1970s has encouraged the growth of activities across frontiers, the most notable being the creation in 1956 of the Sami council, which now has fifteen members from Norway, Sweden, Finland, and Russia.

The Roma, whose numbers approximate to those of the Sami minority, have been far less fortunate. Both communities have found their ways of life and traditional livelihoods threatened. The Chernobyl disaster of 1986, for example, affected the grazing lands of the reindeer-herders, though these lands have been far more seriously eroded by the inexorable advance of farming settlements, mining, and quarrying; but whereas the Sami have been able to adapt and even turn their traditions to their advantage in the tourist trade, the Roma, with their migratory way of life on the margins of settled society already threatened by social and economic change and the well-meaning efforts of officialdom, have found themselves increasingly drawn into a kind of social welfare limbo. Finland has since the 1970s acquired other distinctive minorities, mostly refugees from Chile, Vietnam, and more recently, Somalia. In comparison with other western European countries, however, it remains remarkably homogenous in terms of ethnic composition. One of the largest minority groups is that of the Ingrians, over ten thousand of whom moved to Finland in the early 1990s. Welcomed as returnees with the same rights as the Finns and their descendants returning from Sweden, but in reality coming from a vastly different culture, they have experienced problems of adaption. Finnish policy has now shifted towards support for the Ingrians who remain in Russia and Estonia.

Much has been made in recent years of the shifting contours of boundaries and borders, and Finnish writers have emphasised that, even at the height of the cold war, there was still considerable cross-border contact between Finland and Soviet Karelia (mostly on construction projects), whilst Nordic co-operation played a pioneering role in breaking down rigid notions of territoriality. There has been a huge upsurge in inter-Baltic and Nordic–Baltic collaboration since 1989, and considerable time and energy has been devoted to imaginative reworkings of the spatial dimensions of the northern European region. New interregional assemblies, committees, and consultative groups have sprung up, and a number of initiatives designed to foster and promote the exchange of people and ideas have been launched. It has also been claimed by Christopher Browning that 'post-modern narratives of the Finnish self delink the nation from the state and in so doing open up new possibilities for our understanding of national security, sovereignty, the role of the state and the character of region-building that this facilitates'. Others, however, have been more cautious about writing off the influence of the state (and even Browning concedes the continuing importance of *realpolitik* and state interests). The northern European initiative, launched by Finland, and adopted as policy by the EU in 1997, may be cited as one example of a proposal ostensibly designed to foster interregional co-operation by linking member states with partner states in northern Europe, from Iceland to Russia, but in reality designed to further Finnish objectives.

The partial dismantling of the apparatus of rather authoritarian and top-down control of public affairs that has taken place in the past twenty-five years has allowed Finns to speak and act more freely about topics hitherto deemed taboo, such as Karelia. There has also been a rapid shift away from the somewhat introverted nationalism that still prevailed in the 1960s and 1970s into a globalised world where the largest Finnish companies employ more workers abroad than at home, and in which the young and educated travel and work. In this transformation, many everyday symbols of Finnishness have been relegated to the dusty shelves of nostalgia – or, in the case of Nokia, have undergone complete metamorphosis from rubber boots and car tyres to cellphones. The patina of age and fond remembrance is perhaps an essential, integral part of identity. The loss of immediate resonance can however be painful and disorienting. Much of what for decades reaffirmed a sense of place and belonging to Finns no longer has the same importance or meaning to a younger urbanised generation. The at times vehement reaction to the political inheritance of the recent past has only served to highlight the distinction between a peasant-rural past and a 'European' future. A study of the attitudes of young people to history and historical identity at the end of the 1990s, carried out as part of a European 'Youth and History' project, concluded that, because the older generation found it hard to make sense of the rapid social changes of the middle decades of the twentieth century, they left their stories untold, leaving the younger generation to construct their own history as consumers of the past.

As has been pointed out in many studies, Finnish entry into the European Union had more to do with identity than with any other single issue. Having for decades existed in a curious kind of political no-man's-land between the two great power blocs, to all intents and purposes a 'western' country and yet prevented from fully proclaiming that in word or action by virtue of an association dictated by necessity, an association that in over four decades enervated rather than invigorated or deepened the relationship, the prospect of belonging was undeniably appealing to a great many Finns. 'Europeanisation' as a project is, however, more the concern of the elite than of the ordinary voter. Few Finns identify themselves simply as Europeans; far more than the EU average placed nationality first, and rejected 'Finnish-European' as a descriptor of their identity in a Eurobarometer poll in late 2001. The 'Youth and History' project also found much stronger attachment to and identification with episodes of the national past, such as Finland's fight to survive during the war, than to more abstract values such as democracy or Nordic society.

There are, in truth, a very wide range of often overlapping identities. Not all of these have fared well in modern Finland. The rural and the regional have suffered from the flight from the land; the collection and publication of past memories, dialects, local customs or dishes, and the activities of various pressure groups can never hope to replace the on-the-spot vigour of a working community that generated by everyday activity its own culture. For those of the generation that devoted their working lives to settlement and cultivation of a rather hard and unforgiving land, now entering or already in retirement, the sight of so many abandoned fields and buildings must be especially painful. Religious identity is never easy to evaluate, though it is fairly certain that religious beliefs and practices have far less impact on Finnish life than was the case even fifty years ago. Immigration has provided a welcome addition to the membership of certain churches and religions (the Filipino wives of Finnish farmers have helped give the Catholic church a base in central Finland, for example), but Finland remains an overwhelmingly Lutheran country, even though few Lutherans are regular churchgoers.

It is also hard to say how much remains of the identity for Finland that was built up during the long years of the Kekkonen presidency, since rather few of those who were closely involved with the forging of that construct have come forward subsequently to speak in its defence. The most evident feature of that identity, the Finnish foreign policy that was once indelibly associated with the name and personality of President Kekkonen, no longer exists. The shift from individuality to corporate solidarity in political life which prominent supporters of the so-called 'K-line' during the sixties and seventies believed had occurred during the post-war era has arguably now begun to reverse itself once more. A rather more substantial achievement of that period does, however, still remain, and that is the basic infrastructure of a modern, fully functioning society. It is unlikely that many Finns would think of KELA, the social insurance institution, as an integral part of their national identity, or would see the suburbs that radiate out from the sea-girt peninsula upon which Helsinki sits as symbols of the change from a rural to a neomodern country.[2] If identity means anything, however, it surely must touch intimately upon people's everyday lives, and this the pensions and social security system, the blocks of flats, schools, shopping and health centres built since the sixties most emphatically do. This concrete modernity may compare poorly with the idyllic log-cabin by the lake in the image-projection business, but it is, nevertheless, the real legacy of Finland's immediate past, and the foundation of its foreseeable future as well.

KEY DATES

1155–60	Purported 'first crusade' in Finland, culminating in the murder of the Englishman Henry by a peasant, Lalli. Henry subsequently is elevated to the status of a saint.
1229	*Finlandia* and its people placed under papal protection.
1323	Delineation of the frontier in the Karelian isthmus between Sweden and Novgorod at the treaty of Oreshek (Pähkinäsaari, Nöteborg).
1397	Union of the three northern kingdoms of Denmark, Norway, and Sweden established; finally dismantled in 1523.
1527	King Gustav Vasa declared head of the church in Sweden, and measures to confiscate church property approved by the Diet of Västerås.
1548	Publication of Mikael Agricola's Finnish translation of the New Testament.
1617	Sweden acquires further territories around lake Ladoga and the river Neva at the treaty of Stolbovo, excluding Muscovy from the Baltic.
1640	Foundation of the university in Turku.
1700–21	Great Northern War fought by Sweden against Russia, Denmark, and Saxony-Poland. Much of Finland occupied by Russian forces from 1714.
1721	Sweden cedes to Russia the Baltic provinces of Estonia and Livonia, the territories acquired in 1617, and the Karelian isthmus, including the fortress and city of Viipuri, at the peace of Uusikaupunki (Nystad).
1742–43	Second Russian occupation of Finland; further territory in south-eastern Finland ceded at the peace of Turku.
1788	Gustav III launches an unsuccessful attack on Russia, which precipitates a mutiny of army officers in the camp at Anjala.

	A handful of Finnish officers unsuccessfully seek Russian support for some sort of independent Finnish state.
1808	*February*: Alexander I launches Russian invasion of Finland. June: the province of Finland declared united with the Russian empire by imperial edict.
1809	*February*: Alexander I orders the convocation of the Finnish estates as a *lantdag*, a provincial assembly or diet, in the town of Porvoo.

1808 **February**: Alexander I launches Russian invasion of Finland.
June: the province of Finland declared united with the Russian empire by imperial edict.

1809 **February**: Alexander I orders the convocation of the Finnish estates as a *lantdag*, a provincial assembly or diet, in the town of Porvoo.

March: announcing that he has entered into possession of the Grand Duchy of Finland, Alexander I confirms and ratifies the religion and fundamental laws of the country, as well as the rights and privileges of each estate, in a charter issued to the estates assembled in Porvoo.

July: in his concluding speech to the estates, Alexander speaks of a 'loyal people. . . placed from this time on amongst the rank of nations'.

September: Sweden cedes to Russia certain named provinces in the peace concluded in the town of Hamina.

1812 The territories acquired by Russia in 1721 and 1743 (Russian, or 'Old' Finland) are merged with the newly acquired provinces of Swedish Finland. Helsinki is declared to be the new capital of the Grand Duchy.

1828 The university is moved from Turku to Helsinki, and renamed the Imperial Alexander University.

1831 Foundation of the Finnish Literature Society.

1835 Publication of the first edition of the *Kalevala*, compiled on the basis of folk-poems collected in eastern Finland and Karelia by Elias Lönnrot.

1838 Israel Hwasser's *Om allianstractaten emellan Sverige och Ryssland år 1812* (*On the Treaty of Alliance between Sweden and Russia of 1812*) prompts debate over Finland's status within the Russian empire.

1843 Zachris Topelius raised the question of whether the Finnish people possessed a history, and concluded that it had not until 1809, when it acquired a political existence.

1851 Mattias Castrén appointed to the new chair of Finnish language at the Imperial Alexander University in Helsinki.

1854–56 Britain and France, at war with Russia, send fleets to the Baltic. Fortified positions off Helsinki and on the Åland islands are attacked, and some destruction caused in Finnish coastal towns.

1858 First Finnish-language secondary school opened.

1862 Opening of the railway line from Helsinki to Hämeenlinna; the line to St Petersburg completed eight years later.

1863   Convocation of the Diet by Alexander II. Finnish is declared of equal status with Swedish in all matters which directly concern the Finnish-speaking population; this status to be enforced by the end of 1883.

1867   The Bank of Finland, founded in 1811, and authorised to issue its own currency, the mark, from 1860, placed under parliamentary scrutiny.

1869   Diet Act establishes the principle of regular parliaments. The Lutheran church separated in principle from the state; the church also ceased to have control over education and local administration.

1870   Publication of Alexis Kivi's novel, *Seitsemän veljestä* (*The Seven Brothers*).

1878   Diet passes a conscription act which allows for the creation of a force of five thousand men, to be trained and stationed in Finland.

1890   The postal service in Finland placed under Imperial Russian control by imperial decree.

1898   Appointment of Nikolay Ivanovich Bobrikov as governor-general of Finland, with a brief to bring the Grand Duchy into line with the empire.

1899   Nicholas II's 'February manifesto' outlines a programme of measures designed to curb Finnish autonomy and bind the Grand Duchy more closely to the empire. Foundation of the Finnish Labour Party. First performance of Sibelius' patriotic symphonic poem *Finlandia*.

1900   Measures to implement the full use of Russian as a language of administration in Finland are outlined in an imperial edict; further measures to improve the status of Finnish are also announced.

1901   The military service law abolishes the Finnish armed forces and institutes conscription into the Imperial Russian army, provoking widespread resistance; passive resistance is organised nationally.

1903   Governor-General Bobrikov given dictatorial powers to deal with opponents of his policy. The Finnish Labour Party becomes the Social Democratic Party and adopts a Marxist-inspired programme.

1904   Assassination of Bobrikov by a student, Eugen Schauman, who immediately commits suicide. The military service law suspended, with the Diet agreeing to an annual payment towards the costs of defence.

1905   *October–November*: revolution in Russia, patriotic national strike in Finland, ending, however, in discord, with the workers' red guards nearly coming to blows with the bourgeois white

guards. An imperial decree rescinds much of the legislation of
the Bobrikov era.

1906 The Parliament Act replaces the four-estate Diet with a unicameral legislature, elected on the basis of proportional representation by all citizens, male and female, over the age of twenty-four.

1907 In the first elections to the new parliament (*eduskunta*), the
social democrats are the big winners, taking eighty of the two
hundred seats.

1908 Nicholas II dissolves parliament prematurely, setting a pattern
for the remainder of his reign; he also nominates a new government without reference to parliament. Within two years, the
government is entirely in the hands of men wholly sympathetic
to imperial policy.

1915 Military training initiated in Germany of Finnish volunteers,
who were to form the 27th Royal Prussian *Jägerbattalion*.

1917 *February–March*: outbreak of revolution in Russia; officials
and agents of the old regime disappear or are replaced; the
provisional government in Russia authorises the renewal of
the Finnish government and the convening of the *eduskunta*.
The social democrats, holding an absolute majority of the seats
in the *eduskunta*, also enter a coalition government.

June–July: the social democrats press for complete internal
independence for Finland, winning the conditional support of
the All-Russian Congress of Soviets, and pushing through an
enabling law in the *eduskunta* on 18 July. The provisional
government calls their bluff, ordering the dissolution of
parliament and new elections.

October: the elections reduce the socialists to ninety-three seats;
the initiative passes to the bourgeois bloc, determined to put a
stop to lawlessness.

November: the labour movement calls a general strike and its
revolutionary council assumes virtual control, but fails to agree
upon a complete seizure of power. The *eduskunta* once more
affirms the enabling act and passes a number of reforms, which
persuades the majority of the labour leaders to abandon the
strike and to strive to form a socialist government. Instead, a
bourgeois government led by P. E. Svinhufvud and committed to
independence and restoration of law and order wins the backing
of the *eduskunta* majority.

6 December: independence declared, and finally conceded at the
end of the month by the new Soviet regime.

1918 *January*: the socialists seize power in Helsinki and set up a
Council of People's Commissars; members of the Svinhufvud
government establish a base in Vaasa.

February–March: the white army, commanded by ex-imperial Russian army officer C. G. E. Mannerheim and reinforced with volunteers from Sweden and returning *Jägerbattalion* officers, thwarts red advances.

March: German–Finnish treaty binds Finland closely to German war aims.

April: the capture of the city of Tampere by the white forces is a decisive defeat for the reds. German troops land on the southern coast of Finland and take Helsinki. First Finnish military expedition to eastern Karelia.

May: the last remnants of the red forces surrender; red leaders flee to Russia.

August: foundation of the Finnish Communist Party in Moscow.

October: Prince Friedrich Karl of Hesse chosen as king of Finland; he declined the honour in December, after the German defeat in the world war.

1919   *March*: new elections to parliament see the return of eighty social democrats.

July: adoption of the new constitution, and election by parliament of K. J. Ståhlberg as first president of the republic.

1920   Signing of the peace treaty between Finland and Soviet Russia at Tartu in Estonia.

1921   Autonomy granted to the Åland islands.

1923   Activities of the Finnish Socialist Workers' Party declared illegal.

1924   The 'flying Finn' Paavo Nurmi wins four gold medals in the Paris Olympics, establishing Finland's dominance of middle-distance running during the inter-war years.

1926   Väinö Tanner forms a minority social democratic government.

1929   *November*: Young communists beaten up in the town of Lapua, sparking off a wave of anti-communism, the so-called Lapua movement.

1930   *June*: communist members of parliament arrested for plotting treason.

October: seizure of ex-president Ståhlberg by Lapua activists widely condemned.

November: anti-communist legislation passed by requisite two-thirds majority of newly elected parliament.

1931   Election of Svinhufvud as president.

1932   *February–March*: defying police orders to disperse, Lapua activists in the town of Mäntsälä provoke a national crisis, only resolved by Svinhufvud's direct intervention and the refusal of the army high command to back the rebels.

July: non-aggression treaty between Finland and Soviet Russia ratified.

1937   Formation of a centre-left government of agrarians, progressives, and social democrats.

1938   Talks over remilitarisation of the Åland islands initiated by the Soviet Union.

1939   *August*: the secret protocol of the Nazi–Soviet pact assigns Finland to the Soviet sphere of influence.

October–November: talks over frontier adjustments in Moscow break down.

30 November: the Red Army attacks Finland.

1 December: a Finnish people's government headed by the exiled communist leader O. V. Kuusinen established at Terijoki.

December–January: Soviet advance halted and severe defeats inflicted in battles fought in sub-zero temperatures.

1940   *February*: French and British promises of intervention to aid Finland cause the Finnish government to hesitate about seeking peace with the Soviet Union.

13 March: peace signed in Moscow; Finland cedes the Karelian isthmus, and leases a naval base to the Soviet Union.

August: transit agreement with Germany, allowing troops to pass through Finland to northern Norway.

December: plans to invade the Soviet Union ('Operation Barbarossa') set in motion in Berlin. Election of Risto Ryti as president of Finland.

1941   *June 25*: Finland re-enters the war after Soviet air attacks, but seeks to claim it is fighting a separate war to that of its German co-belligerent. By the end of the year, Finnish troops have occupied much of Soviet Karelia.

6 December: Britain declares war on Finland.

1943   American efforts to mediate a peace between Finland and the Soviet Union fail.

1944   Resumption of peace talks in Stockholm.

June: Red Army breakthrough on the Karelian isthmus. Ryti signs an agreement with the German foreign minister von Ribbentrop not to conclude a separate peace. His subsequent resignation releases his successor as president, Marshal Mannerheim, from that agreement.

September: armistice agreement signed; allied control commission established in Helsinki to oversee implementation of its terms, which include not only the restoration of the 1940 frontiers and a new naval base west of Helsinki, but the proscription of organisations deemed anti-Soviet, and a massive reparations payment; Finland also obliged to clear the country of German troops.

November: J. K. Paasikivi forms coalition government, including a member of the Communist Party, now legalised.

1945   *March*: in the first post-war elections, the communist-led People's Democratic Union secures a quarter of the seats, and becomes one of the 'big three' parties in government (agrarians, social democrats, people's democrats).

November: eight wartime leaders tried by a Finnish court on charges under article 13 of the armistice of having criminally led Finland into war in 1941. Their sentences (in 1946) increased after pressure from the allied control commission, though all are eventually released early.

1946   Paasikivi elected president in succession to Mannerheim.

1947   Signing of the Paris peace treaty. Finland decides not to accept Marshall Aid.

1948   *April*: Finland and the Soviet Union sign a treaty of friendship, co-operation, and mutual assistance; this becomes the foundation of the Soviet–Finnish relationship during the Cold War years.

July: 'big three' coalition replaced by a social democratic minority government.

1950   Urho Kekkonen forms the first of his five governments.

1952   Olympic games, originally scheduled to be held in Finland in 1940, staged in Helsinki. Last reparations payment delivered to the Soviet Union.

1955   Porkkala naval base returned to Finland. Finland joins the Nordic Council and United Nations.

1956   *February–March*: Kekkonen elected president by a narrow margin, and begins his first presidency with the country in the grip of a general strike.

1958   Worsening relations with the Soviet Union leads to the so-called 'night-frost crisis'; the social democrats, already internally divided, are identified as the prime opponents of Kekkonen's policy of improving relations with the USSR.

1961   *March*: Finland becomes an associate member of the European Free Trade Association (EFTA).

November: in the light of international tension, the Soviet Union asks for consultations under the terms of the 1948 mutual assistance treaty; Kekkonen succeeds in persuading the Soviet leader, Nikita Khrushchev, to abandon consultations, enhancing his own position and authority in Finland. The anti-Kekkonen candidate in the presidential election campaign withdraws as Kekkonen meets Khrushchev in Novosibirsk.

1962   *February*: Kekkonen secures a comfortable victory in the presidential election.

1966   *May*: Rafael Paasio forms a centre-left coalition including agrarians, social democrats, and people's democrats.

1968   *February*: Kekkonen re-elected for a third term as president.

1973   Finland signs agreements on trade with the European Economic Community (EEC) and the eastern bloc trading association, Comecon.

1974   *March*: special legislation passed by parliament in January 1973 allows the septuagenarian Kekkonen to extend his term of office by four years.

1975   Conference on security and co-operation in Europe hosted in Helsinki.

1981   *October*: Kekkonen resigns the presidency on grounds of ill health; Prime Minister Mauno Koivisto exercises the functions of head of state until the elections.

1982   *February*: Koivisto wins support across party lines, and is elected president.

1985   Finland becomes a full member of EFTA.

1987   *April*: the conservatives enter government after an absence of two decades, in coalition with the social democrats.

1991   *August*: initially cautious in its response to the attempt of the old guard to stage a coup in Moscow, the Finnish government moves quickly to recognise the independence of the Baltic states.

      September: the government announces it is considering the pros and cons of Finnish membership of the European Community (EC).

      November: the Bank of Finland forced to devalue to restore confidence in the mark as Finland slides into financial crisis and economic recession.

1992   *January*: the 1948 mutual assistance treaty is replaced by a series of political and economic agreements between Finland and Russia.

      March: a majority in the *eduskunta* votes for membership of the EC.

1994   *January–February*: Martti Ahtisaari emerges as the second-round winner in the first direct elections for the presidency of the republic. Unemployment figures reach record levels.

      October: Finland votes 56.9 per cent to 43.1 per cent for joining the EC in a national referendum.

1995   *January*: Finland becomes a member of the European Union.

1999   *March*: parliament approves the new constitution, which comes into force a year later.

2000   *January–February*: Tarja Halonen is the first woman to be elected president.

PRESIDENTS OF FINLAND

Kaarlo Ståhlberg (Progressive)	1919–25
Lauri Relander (Agrarian)	1925–31
Pehr Evind Svinhufvud (Conservative)	1931–37
Kyösti Kallio (Agrarian)	1937–40
Risto Ryti (Progressive)	1940–44
Carl Gustaf Emil Mannerheim (Non-party)	1944–46
Juho Paasikivi (Conservative)	1946–56
Urho Kekkonen (Agrarian)	1956–81
Mauno Koivisto (Social Democrat)	1982–94
Martti Ahtisaari (Social Democrat)	1994–2000
Tarja Halonen (Social Democrat)	2000–

ELECTIONS AND GOVERNMENTS

The Parliament Act of 1906 (see Chapter 4) laid the foundations of the modern party political system in Finland. The left has always been strong in Finland, in spite of the absence of a significant urban industrial proletariat. The share of seats won by the two main parties of the left has rarely slipped below 40 per cent since the first elections for the new single-chamber legislature, the *eduskunta*, in 1907.

The Finnish Social Democratic Party (*Suomen sosiaalidemokraattinen puolue*) entered the 1907 election with an effective national organisation and several years' experience of agitation and propaganda, and this undoubtedly gave it a clear advantage over the other parties, which had suffered internal splits and quarrels during the years of turmoil immediately preceding the revolution of 1905. In 1916, it succeeded in winning an absolute majority of 103 seats, a feat which no other avowedly Marxist party has ever been able to emulate in a fully democratic parliamentary election. Weakened by the internal scission of 1920, it was nevertheless able to regain ground after the elimination of the communists from parliament in 1930, and managed to survive a far stronger challenge from a resurgent (and legalised) communist party after 1944. From 1944 until 1990, the main challenge from the left came from the Finnish People's Democratic Union, *Suomen kansan demokraattinen liitto*, basically an electoral front organisation of dissident left-wing socialists and communists, with the Finnish Communist Party (*Suomen kommunistinen puolue*), founded in Moscow in 1918 by exiles from the civil war, playing the leading role. As Figure 2 indicates, there has been a long-term gradual decline in support for the parties of the left since the 1980s, although the social democrats have fared better at the polls than their rivals, who have reconstituted themselves since 1990 as the Union of the Left (*vasemmistoliitto*).

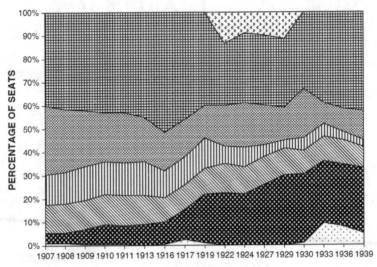

Figure 1 Elections in Finland, 1907–39.

Of the four non-socialist parties contesting the 1907 election, the Swedish People's Party (*Svenska folkpartiet*) was very successful in mobilising support from its constituency, the Swedish-speaking minority, and it has managed to retain the loyalty of the majority of Swedish-speaking voters to the present time. The liberal-constitutionalist Young Finn party lost support in northern and eastern Finland to a new party, the Agrarian Union (*maalaisliitto*), and trailed behind the conservative Old Finn party in the contest for the Finnish nationalist vote. There was a clearer realignment of the Finnish national camp in 1918, when the monarchist conservatives formed the National Coalition (*kansallinen kokoomus*) and republican liberals the National Progressive Party (*kannen edistyspuolue*). Support for the progressives dwindled to a handful of seats by the 1940s. The party experienced a brief revival of its fortunes

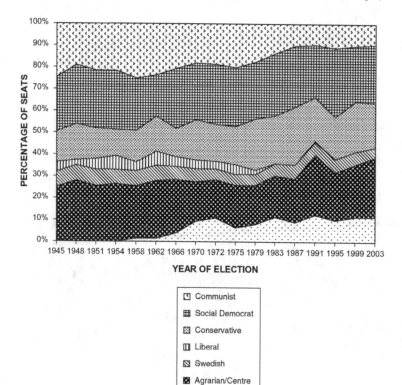

PERCENTAGE OF SEATS

YEAR OF ELECTION

☑ Communist
⊞ Social Democrat
☒ Conservative
⊞ Liberal
◩ Swedish
◪ Agrarian/Centre
☐ Other

Figure 2 Elections in Finland, 1945–2003.

after it was reformed and renamed the Finnish People's Party (*Suomen kansanpuolue*) in 1951, but as the Liberal People's Party (*liberaalinen kansanpuolue*) from 1965, its fortunes continued to diminish: the party lost its only seat in parliament in 1995.

The Agrarian Union drew its support mostly from the farming population, and was the largest non-socialist party from 1919 until 1970. Renamed the Centre Party (*keskustapuolue*) in 1965, it suffered losses to the Finnish Rural Party (*Suomen maaseudunpuolue*) and lost ground to the conservatives in the battle for the urban middle-class vote during the 1970s and 1980s. Since the 1990s, however, the Centre Party has returned to the level of support it enjoyed during the 1940s and 1950s, and is one of the 'big three' parties (social democrat, conservative, and centre) competing for what has become a largely urban, or urbanised vote.

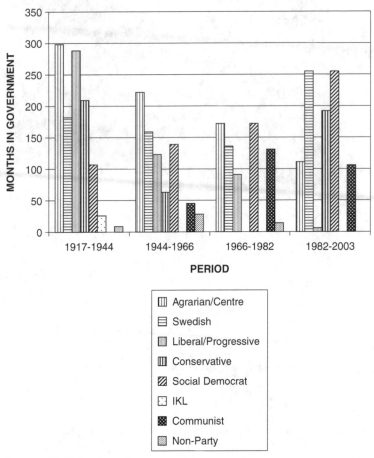

Figure 3 Participation in government, 1917–2003.

As support for the far left (and the liberal inheritors of the Young Finn tradition) has dwindled, a number of new parties have emerged, of which three have now become established players, even participating in government. The fortunes of the Finnish Rural Party have fluctuated, from a high point in the early 1970s, when the party won 10 per cent of the vote in two elections, followed by collapse, a brief resurgence in 1983, and decline in the 1990s. The Christian People's Party, now known as the Christian

Democrats, entered parliament in 1970, and has managed on a couple of occasions (1979 and 1999) to secure over 4 per cent of the vote. The Greens entered parliament in 1983, and have steadily built up support, coming within striking distance of the left alliance in the 2003 elections (fourteen seats to the greens, nineteen for the left).

Governments in Finland are invariably coalitions. Minority or non-party governments are infrequent, and have usually indicated impasse or stalemate in the process of government formation. Figure 3 divides up the decades of independence into four distinct periods; the vertical bars represent the number of months in total in which each named party has participated in government.

The average length of time the governments of the period 1919–44 was less than a year (11.57 months), and only slightly more than a year between 1944–66 (12.9 months). Between 1966 and 1982, the average duration of governments increased to 15.21 months, but there was a remarkable leap to an average of 31.75 months over the next two decades, with the majority of governments remaining in office for the full four-year parliamentary term.

A striking feature of the pattern of governments in Finland is the high level of participation by the two smaller parties. Despite dwindling support at the polls (see Figures 1 and 2), the Progressive Party continued to be a regular member of government throughout the first decades of the republic. Nine governments were headed by a member of the Progressive Party, including the first centre-left government of A. K. Cajander in 1937–39, and the wartime Ryti governments (1939–41). Although maintaining a higher level of support, the Swedish People's Party has only once provided a prime minister, and then for less than half a year, but it has been an integral part of government throughout the entire period of Finland's independence. Although not indicated in the bar chart, the newer small parties that have succeeded in building up a presence in the *eduskunta* since the 1980s have also been actively involved in government.

NOTES

1. Although various groups such as army officers claimed the right of representation as an estate of the realm, by the mid-seventeenth century there were four recognised estates (*stånder*): the clergy, nobility, burghers, and peasants.
2. The image of the Russians as cruel barbarians was amply exploited in print during the sixteenth century, as the Teutonic Order in Livonia came under attack.
3. The frontier town of Viipuri, grouped around its strong fortress, was the exception. The Franciscans and Dominicans both had houses here.

THE SWEDISH LEGACY

1. The French dramatist Regnard did, however, manage to lay his hands on a magic drum in the 1690s, in spite of the campaign of destruction mounted some twenty years earlier by Gabriel Tuderus, priest in charge of the Kemi district.
2. Elizabeth had already determined on the duke as her successor and was in consequence backing another member of the Holstein family as heir to the Swedish throne.
3. The notorious Ostrobothnian knife-fighters (*puukkojunkkarit*) of the early nineteenth century used knives to terrorise and inspire fear, and as a lethal means of exacting vengeance.

FROM STOCKHOLM TO ST PETERSBURG, 1780–1860

1. G. M. Armfelt was the nephew of General Carl Gustav Armfelt, commander of the Finnish army and a member of the Anjala confederation in 1788.

2. *valtiopäivät*: in Swedish, however, the older term *lantdag* – a regional or provincial diet, as distinct from the Diet of the realm, or *riksdag* – was retained.

3. The writer Santeri Alkio, who was very influential in the development of a populist-agrarian ideology in the early twentieth century, claimed that it was Paavo Ruotsalainen, rather than the great men of the national pantheon such as Lönnrot, who was dear to the hearts of the peasants, for whom religious revivalism was their own national movement.

THE EMBRYONIC STATE, 1860–1907

1. 'Culture' is an inadequate term to convey the full meaning of the Finnish word *sivistys*, which is really an all-embracing process of national identity-building.

2. The 1904 congress of the socialist Second International had condemned 'minister-socialism', and urged socialists not to participate in government as long as the bourgeois order prevailed.

THE INDEPENDENT STATE, 1907–37

1. Many of these units had sprung up in the summer of 1917 in response to a wave of sometimes violent strikes in the countryside; they were known as 'butchers' (*lahtarit*) by their red guard opponents.

2. Svinhufvud himself went into hiding, eventually escaping across the Gulf of Finland on board a minesweeper.

3. These prerogatives included the right to order where necessary the premature dissolution of parliament and the calling of new elections; the presentation of legislative proposals to parliament and the approval of acts passed by parliament; and acting in peacetime as commander-in-chief of the armed forces. Members of the government and senior officials were also appointed by the president.

4. The communists had to wait until the 1960s, however, for some sort of official recognition of their patriotic credentials by a president anxious to create a centre-left coalition that would be broadly supportive of his peaceful coexistence initiatives towards the Soviet Union.

5. One of the most interesting fringe characters was the *demi-mondaine* Minna Craucher, who was murdered in mysterious circumstances just as she was threatening to reveal all about the movement. Craucher seems to have created her own fantasy world, but sucked in a number of men attracted by her charms, including the fastidious cosmopolitan Olavi Paavolainen as well as the rougher types from up north.

6. The traveller arriving today at Finland's main airport may be forgiven for thinking English is the country's second language.

7. There had, for example, been a lack of understanding and even hostility towards the pioneering poetry of Edith Södergran, now widely acclaimed as the leading poet of her generation.
8. Levels of Finnish emigration to the New World were, however, lower than from Sweden or Norway; the peak period for migration to the USA was also later, in 1900–10.

THE KEKKONEN ERA, 1956–81

1. Kekkonen had taken up in 1969 the idea of a European Security Conference that had been periodically on the Soviet agenda since 1954, and clearly hoped this would allow him more room to manoeuvre over the EEC issue.
2. Belyakov's backers in Moscow even seem to have toyed with the idea of Väinö Leskinen as the candidate of the left in the forthcoming presidential elections. Earlier vilified as a Tannerite, Leskinen had made his peace with Moscow in the 1960s, and was now making appropriately radical noises, even courting the young revolutionaries.
3. This doctrine has been ascribed more to Finnish diplomats such as Risto Hyvärinen and Max Jakobson, both of whom fell out of favour in the 1970s, than to the president himself.
4. Kekkonen's biographer claims however that the president insisted on his term of office being extended by extraordinary legislation in order to avoid a contest with Vennamo that might have damaged Finnish relations with Russia.
5. Some of the groundwork that made reconciliation possible had been laid down by writers such as Väinö Linna and Veijo Meri, whose novels helped reshape attitudes towards Finland's divided past, and by historians who were bold enough to present interpretations of that past in the face of establishment hostility.
6. The idea that a 'second republic' had come into existence in 1944 was much favoured by leading proponents of the Paasikivi–Kekkonen line.

FROM NATION STATE TO EUROSTATE

1. The idea of a nuclear-free northern Europe had hitherto been rejected in Scandinavia but was taken up by the socialist governments of Norway and Sweden in the early eighties, partly as a response to the deployment in western Europe of Pershing II and cruise missiles to counter the Soviet SS-20s.
2. 'Neomodern' is the term used by Pesonen and Riihinen in their comprehensive survey of politics and society in Finland at the beginning of the twenty-first century.

GUIDE TO FURTHER READING

BIBLIOGRAPHIES

Elemer Bako, *Finland and the Finns. A Selective Bibliography* (Washington, DC: Library of Congress, 1993)
John Screen, *Finland*, World Bibliographical Series, vol. 31, rev. edn (Oxford: Clio Press, 1997)

GENERAL

Max Engman and David Kirby (eds.), *Finland. People – Nation – State* (London: Hurst, 1989)
Osmo Jussila, Seppo Hentilä, and Jukka Nevakivi, *From Grand Duchy to Modern State. A Political History of Finland since 1809* (London: Hurst, 1999)
D. G. Kirby, *Finland in the Twentieth Century* (London: Hurst, 1979)
Matti Klinge, *A Brief History of Finland* (Helsinki: Otava Publishing Co., 1980)
Let Us Be Finns. Essays on History (Helsinki: Otava Publishing Co., 1990)
The Finnish Tradition. Essays on Structures and Identities in the North of Europe (Helsinki: SHS, 1993)
Lars-Folke Landgren and Maunu Häyrynen (eds.), *The Dividing Line. Borders and National Peripheries*, Renvall Institute Publications 9 (Helsinki: University Printing House, 1997)
Tuomas M. S. Lehtonen (ed.), *Europe's Northern Frontier. Perspectives on Finland's Western Identity* (Jyväskylä: PS-Kustannus, 1999)
Anssi Paasi, *Territories, Boundaries and Consciousness. The Changing Geographies of the Finnish-Russian Border*, Belhaven Studies in Political Geography (Chichester: Wiley, 1996)

Pertti Pesonen and Olavi Riihinen, *Dynamic Finland. The Political System and the Welfare State* (Helsinki: Finnish Literature Society, 2002)

Jorma Selovuori (ed.), *Power and Bureaucracy in Finland 1809–1998* (Helsinki: Edita, 1999)

Hugh Shearman, *Finland - the Adventures of a Small Power* (London: Stevens & Sons, 1950)

Fred Singleton, *A Short History of Finland* (Cambridge: Cambridge University Press, 1989; 2nd edn revised and updated by A. F. Upton, 1998)

Sven Tägil (ed.), *Ethnicity and Nation-Building in the Nordic World* (London: Hurst, 1995) (contains chapters on the Sami, Finns in northern Sweden and Norway, Finnish- and Swedish-speakers in Finland, and on the Karelians in Finland and Russia)

FINLAND FROM THE MIDDLE AGES TO 1809

Robert Bartlett, *The Making of Europe. Conquest, Colonization and Cultural Change 950–1350* (Harmondsworth: Allen Lane, 1993)

Eric Christiansen, *The Northern Crusades. The Baltic and the Catholic Frontier, 1100–1525* (London and Basingstoke: Macmillan, 1980)

Matts Dreijer, *The History of the Åland People. From the Stone Age to Gustavus Vasa* (Stockholm: Almqvist & Wiksell International, 1986)

Robert Frost, *The Northern Wars. War, State and Society in North-Eastern Europe, 1558–1721* (Harlow: Pearson Education, 2000)

Maija Kallinen, *Change and Stability. Natural Philosophy at the Academy of Turku 1640–1713*, Studia Historica 51 (Helsinki: Suomen Historiallinen Seura, 1995)

Martti Kerkkonen, *Peter Kalm's North American Journey. Its Ideological Background and Results*, Studia Historica 1 (Helsinki: The Finnish Historical Society, 1959)

Heikki Kirkinen, 'Finland in Russian Sources up to the Year 1323', *Scandinavian Journal of History*, 7 (1982), pp. 255–75

Anu Koskivirta, *The Enemy Within. Homicide and Control in Eastern Finland in the Final Years of Swedish Rule 1748–1808* (Helsinki: Finnish Literature Society, 2003)

Erkki Lehtinen, 'Notions of a Finnish National Identity during the Period of Swedish Rule', *Scandinavian Journal of History*, 6 (1981), pp. 277–95

Olaus Magnus, *A Description of the Northern Peoples 1555*, ed. Peter Foote, trans. Peter Fisher and Humphrey Higgens, Hakluyt Society, Second Series, Nos. 182, 187, 188 (Hakluyt Society: London, 1996, 1997, 1998)

Heikki Ylikangas, *The Knife Fighters. Violent Crime in Southern Ostrobothnia 1790–1825* (Helsinki: Annales Academiæ Scientarum Fennicæ, 1998)

FINLAND UNDER RUSSIAN RULE, 1809–1917

Steven Huxley, *Constitutional Insurgency in Finland: Finnish 'Passive Resistance' Against Russification*, Studia Historica 38 (Helsinki: The Historical Society of Finland, 1990)

Osmo Jussila, 'The Historical Background to the February Manifesto of 1899', *Journal of Baltic Studies*, 15 (1984), pp. 141–47

Aira Kemiläinen, 'Nationalism in Nineteenth-Century Finland', *Societas Historica Finlandiae, Studia Historica*, 33 (1989), pp. 93–127

D. G. Kirby (ed.), *Finland and Russia 1808–1920. From Autonomy to Independence* (London and Basingstoke: Macmillan, 1975)

Keijo Korhonen, *Autonomous Finland in the Political Thought of 19th Century Russia* (Turku: Annales Universitatis Turkuensis, B. 105, 1967)

C. Leonard Lundin, 'Finland', in Edward Thaden (ed.), *Russification in the Baltic Provinces and Finland, 1855–1914* (Princeton: Princeton University Press, 1981)

Juhani Paasivirta, *Finland and Europe. The Period of Autonomy and the International Crises 1808–1914* (London: Hurst, 1981)

Kari Pitkänen, 'The Road to Survival or Death? Temporary Migration During the Great Finnish Famine in the 1860s', in Antti Häkkinen (ed.), *Just a Sack of Potatoes? Crisis Experiences in European Societies, Past and Present*, Studia Historica 44 (Helsinki: The Historical Society of Finland, 1992), pp. 87–118

Tuomo Polvinen, *Imperial Borderland: Bobrikov and the Attempted Russification of Finland, 1898–1904* (London: Hurst, 1995)

George Schoolfield, *Helsinki of the Czars. Finland's Capital: 1808–1918* (Columbia: Camden House, 1996)

Robert Schweitzer, 'The "Baltic Parallel" – Reality or Historiographical Myth: the Influence of the Tsarist Government's Experience in the Baltic Provinces on its Finnish Policy', *Journal of Baltic Studies*, 15 (1984), pp. 195–215

The Rise and Fall of the Russo-Finnish Consensus. The History of the 'Second' Committee on Finnish Affairs in St Petersburg (1857–1891) (Helsinki: Hallintohistoriakomitea & Edita, 1996)

Edward Thaden, *Russia's Western Borderlands, 1710–1870* (Princeton: Princeton University Press, 1984)

Päiviö Tommila, *La Finlande dans la politique européenne en 1809– 1815*, Studia Historica 3 (Helsinki: la Société historique de Finlande, 1962)

William Wilson, *Folklore and Nationalism in Modern Finland* (Bloomington: Indiana University Press, 1976)

THE FIRST DECADES OF INDEPENDENCE, 1917–47

Risto Alapuro, *State and Revolution in Finland* (Berkeley: University of California Press, 1988)

James Barros, *The Aland Islands Question. Its Settlement by the League of Nations* (New Haven: Yale University Press, 1968)

Michael Berry, *American Foreign Policy and the Finnish Exception: Ideological Preferences and Wartime Realities* (Helsinki: Suomen Historiallinen Seura, 1987)

John Hodgson, *Communism in Finland* (New Brunswick: Princeton University Press, 1967)

Max Jakobson, *The Diplomacy of the Winter War, 1939–1940* (Cambridge, MA: Harvard University Press, 1961)

Markku Kangaspuro, 'Nationalities Policy and Power in Soviet Karelia in the 1920s and 1930s', in T. Saarela and K. Rentola (eds.), *Communism National and International* (Helsinki: Suomen Historiallinen Seura, 1998), pp. 119–38

Jukka Nevakivi, *The Appeal that was Never Made. The Allies, Scandinavia and the Finnish Winter War 1939–1940* (London: Hurst, 1976)

Jukka Nevakivi (ed.), *Finnish-Soviet Relations, 1944–1948* (Helsinki: University of Helsinki, 1994)

Juhani Paasivirta, *Finland and Europe. The Early Years of Independence, 1917–1939*, Studia Historica 29 (Helsinki: Suomen Historiallinen Seura, 1988)

Tuomo Polvinen, *Between East and West. Finland in International Politics, 1944–1947* (Minneapolis: University of Minnesota Press, 1986)

Kimmo Rentola, 'Finnish Communism, O. W. Kuusinen, and Their Two Native Countries', in T. Saarela and K. Rentola (eds.), *Communism National and International* (Helsinki: Suomen Historiallinen Seura, 1998), pp.159–81

J. E. O. Screen, *Mannerheim. The Finnish Years* (London: Hurst, 2000)

A. F. Upton, *Finland in Crisis 1940–1941* (London: Faber, 1964)

Anthony Upton, 'Finland', in Martin McCauley (ed.), *Communist Power in Europe, 1944–1949* (London: Macmillan, 1977)

The Finnish Revolution, 1917–1918 (Minneapolis: University of Minnesota Press, 1980)

Carl Van Dyke, *The Soviet Invasion of Finland, 1939–40* (London: Frank Cass, 1997)

Olli Vehviläinen, *Finland in the Second World War Between Germany and Russia* (Basingstoke: Palgrave, 2002)

FINLAND SINCE THE SECOND WORLD WAR

Ray Abrahams, *A Place of Their Own. Family Farming in Eastern Finland* (Cambridge: Cambridge University Press, 1991)

Sirkka Ahonen, 'The End of the Common School – Change in the Ethos and Politics of Education in Finland Towards the End of the 1900s', in Sirkka Ahonen and Jukka Rantala (eds.), *Nordic Lights. Education for Nation and Civic Society in the Nordic Countries, 1850–2000* (Helsinki: Finnish Literature Society, 2001), pp. 175–203

Pirkkoliisa Ahponen and Pirjo Jukarainen (eds.), *Tearing Down the Curtain, Opening the Gates* (Jyväskylä: SoPhi Academic Press, 2000)

David Arter, 'The EU Referendum in Finland on 16 October 1994: A Vote for the West, not for Maastricht', *Journal of Common Market Studies*, 33 (1995), pp. 361–87

Christopher Browning, 'From Modern to Post-Modern Region-Building: Emancipating the Finnish Nation from the State', in M. Lehti, and D. Smith (eds.), *Post-Cold War Identity Politics. Northern and Baltic Experiences* (London: Frank Cass, 2003), pp. 101–27

Jussi Hanhimäki, *Containing Coexistence. America, Russia and the "Finnish Solution", 1945–1956* (Kent, OH: The Kent State University Press, 1997)

Keijo Immonen (ed.), *Pitkä linja - The Long Perspective. Mauno Koivisto, valtiomies ja vaikuttaja - statesman* (Helsinki: Kirjayhtymä, 1993)

Tim Ingold (ed.), *The Social Implications of Agrarian Change in Northern and Eastern Finland* (Helsinki: The Finnish Anthropological Society, 1988)

Max Jakobson, *Finland: Myth and Reality* (Helsinki: Otava, 1987)

Finland in the New Europe (Westport, CT: Praeger, 1998)

Pertti Joenniemi, 'Finland in the New Europe. A Herderian or Hegelian Project?', in O. Wæver, and L. Hansen (eds.), *European Integration and National Identity. The Challenge of the Nordic States* (London: Routledge, 2002)

Urho Kekkonen, *A President's View*, trans. Gregory Coogan (London: Heinemann, 1982)

Walter Laqueur, 'Europe: the Specter of Finlandization', *Commentary*, 64 (1977), pp. 37–41

Tuomas Martikainen, *Immigrant Religions in Local Society. Historical and Contemporary Perspectives in the City of Turku* (Åbo: Åbo University Press, 2004)

George Maude, *The Finnish Dilemma. Neutrality in the Shadow of Power* (London: OUP for the Royal Institute of International Affairs, 1976)

Juha Pentikäinen and Marja Hiltunen (eds.), *Cultural Minorities in Finland. An Overview Towards Cultural Policy* (Helsinki: Finnish National Commission for Unesco, 1995)

Tuomo Polvinen, *Between East and West. Finland in International Politics 1944–1947* (Minneapolis: University of Minnesota Press, 1986)
Teija Tiilikainen, *Europe and Finland. Defining the Political Identity of Finland in Western Europe* (Aldershot: Ashgate, 1998)

THE ECONOMY

Jorma Ahvenainen, 'The Competitive Position of the Finnish Paper Industry in the Inter-War Years', *Scandinavian Economic History Review*, 22 (1974), pp. 1–21
Finland (Paris: OECD Reviews of Rural Policy, 1995)
Finland. A New Consensus for Change (Paris: OECD Reviews of Regulatory Reform, 2003)
Riitta Hjerppe, *The Finnish Economy 1860–1985. Growth and Structural Change* (Helsinki: Government Printing Centre, 1989)
Yrjö Kaukiainen, *A History of Finnish Shipping* (London: Routledge, 1993)
Kimmo Kiljunen, *Finland and the New International Division of Labour* (Basingstoke, London: Macmillan, 1992)
Timo Myllyntaus, *The Gatecrashing Apprentice. Industrialising Finland as an Adopter of New Technology*, Communications of the Institute of Economic and Social History 24 (Helsinki, 1990)
Matti Peltonen, 'Agrarian World Market and Finnish Farm Economy: the Agrarian Transition in Finland in the Late Nineteenth and Early Twentieth Centuries', *Scandinavian Economic History Review*, 36 (1988), pp. 26–45
Fred Singleton, *The Economy of Finland in the Twentieth Century* (Bradford: University of Bradford, 1986)

LITERATURE AND THE ARTS

Olli Alho (ed.), *Finland. A Cultural Encyclopedia* (Helsinki: Finnish Literature Society, 1997)
Books from Finland, published quarterly by the University of Helsinki Library since 1967, offers a comprehensive guide to translations of Finnish works into other languages, with articles and translated extracts from recent publications; particularly good on poetry.
Keith Bosley (ed. and trans.), *Skating on the Sea: Poetry from Finland* (Newcastle: Bloodaxe Books/Helsinki: Finnish Literature Society, 1997)
Matti Kuusi, Keith Bosley, and Michael Branch (ed. and trans.) *Finnish Folk Poetry-Epic. An Anthology in Finnish and English* (Helsinki: Finnish Literature Society, 1977)

Kai Laitinen, *Literature of Finland. An Outline* (Helsinki: Otava, 1985)

James Richards, *800 Years of Finnish Architecture* (Newton Abbot: David and Charles, 1978)

Sixten Ringbom, *Stone, Style and Truth. The Vogue for Natural Stone in Nordic Architecture, 1880–1910* (Helsinki: Suomen muinaismuistoyhdistys, 1987)

John Boulton Smith, *The Golden Age of Finnish Art. Art Nouveau and the National Spirit* (Helsinki: Otava, 1975)

Renja Suominen-Kokkonen, *The Fringe of a Profession. Women as Architects in Finland from the 1890s to the 1950s* (Helsinki: Suomen muinaismuistoyhdistys, 1992)

Markku Valkonen, *The Golden Age: Finnish Art, 1850–1907* (Helsinki: Werner Söderström, 1992)

INDEX

CAMBRIDGE CONCISE HISTORIES

Titles in the series:

A Concise History of Portugal 2nd edition
DAVID BIRMINGHAM

A Concise History of South Africa
ROBERT ROSS

Other titles are in preparation